Leslie
Marmon Silko

BLOOMSBURY STUDIES IN CONTEMPORARY NORTH AMERICAN FICTION

Series Editor: Sarah Graham, Lecturer in American Literature, University of Leicester, UK

This series offers up-to-date guides to the recent work of major contemporary North American authors. Written by leading scholars in the field, each book presents a range of original interpretations of three key texts published since 1970, showing how the same novel may be interpreted in a number of different ways. These informative, accessible volumes will appeal to advanced undergraduate and postgraduate students, facilitating discussion and supporting close analysis of the most important contemporary American and Canadian fiction.

TITLES IN THE SERIES INCLUDE:

Leslie Marmon Silko

Ceremony, Almanac of the Dead, Gardens in the Dunes

Edited by
David L. Moore

Bloomsbury Academic
An imprint of Bloomsbury Publishing Plc

B L O O M S B U R Y
LONDON • OXFORD • NEW YORK • NEW DELHI • SYDNEY

Bloomsbury Academic

An imprint of Bloomsbury Publishing Plc

50 Bedford Square
London
WC1B 3DP
UK

1385 Broadway
New York
NY 10018
USA

www.bloomsbury.com

**BLOOMSBURY and the Diana logo are trademarks of
Bloomsbury Publishing Plc**

First published 2016

British Library Cataloguing-in-Publication Data
A catalogue record for this book is available from the British Library.

ISBN: HB: 978-1-4725-2451-5
PB: 978-1-4725-2366-2
ePDF: 978-1-4725-3060-8
ePub: 978-1-4725-2312-9

Library of Congress Cataloging-in-Publication Data
A catalog record for this book is available from the Library of Congress.

Series: Bloomsbury Studies in Contemporary North American Fiction

Cover design: Eleanor Rose
Cover image © Getty Images

Typeset by Integra Software Services Pvt. Ltd.

CONTENTS

"Linked to the Land": An Introduction to Reading Leslie Marmon Silko

David L. Moore

A major American writer at the turn of this millennium, Leslie Marmon Silko is one of the primary figures in the flowering of Native American literature in the last generation. Amid thousands of generations of storytelling, Indigenous literary voices have been publishing in colonial languages for centuries, and the end of the twentieth century saw a blossoming of traditional and contemporary stories in print and new media. Silko's role in that new level of expression cannot be overstated. She writes both within a long-arcing momentum of those ancient traditions and with a modern pulse of the postcolonial turn toward diversity in globalism. Countless readers and critics have been drawn to her unique voice, as she brings a lyrical force to epic themes.

This collection of chapters provides an overview and close analysis of her major fiction as a lens into the full body of her work that also includes poetry, essays, short fiction, film, photography, and other visual arts. Amid the vast array of critical articles and monographs on Silko, who for decades has shared the popular and critical spotlight on Native American literature with only a handful of other canonized Indigenous writers (N. Scott Momaday, James Welch, and Louise Erdrich being the most comparably prominent), here are new and summary readings of her three novels. In addition to placing her in the broad context of modern American and global literary history, this book works to contextualize her pivotal role in unleashing the vast flood of other Native American, Aboriginal, First Nation, Indigenous, and non-Indigenous writers who have entered the conversations she helped to launch. Following the pattern of Bloomsbury's series on Contemporary North American Fiction, this book focuses on Silko's three central novels thus far in her oeuvre: *Ceremony* (1977), *Almanac of the Dead* (1991), and *Gardens in the Dunes* (2000), studying her historical themes of land, gender, ethnicity, race, trauma, and healing, as well as her narrative forms and her mythic lyricism. The chapters map intertextual links to her other works and to other writers as they clarify Silko's Indigenous perspectives on modern America and beyond. In this introduction, I will offer some biographical, cultural, and literary lenses for reading Silko. From the ground of her Laguna Pueblo culture, she revises both the history and the future of this nation still shaped by the land. Thus, this book reads Silko's remarkable contribution both to a broader American literature and to Native American literary history—while interrogating those very categories.

Life and land: "The center of a spider's web"

Born in 1948 in Albuquerque, New Mexico, Silko grew up in the high desert pinyon hills and sandy arroyos of Laguna Pueblo in New Mexico—directly beside a major highway of the "outsiders" (Silko, 1996, p. 17). She continues to express her connections to the ancient land and to modern times across her years of walking the dry Sonoran ridges of her home in the Tucson Mountains of Arizona.[1] She explains in her work, "The People and the Land ARE Inseparable," that in Tucson, as much as at Laguna, she is *at home* where "long ago the people had ranged far and wide all over the desert plateau region"—before "exact boundaries" were imposed on their homelands by "the European slave hunters" (1996, pp. 85–86). Across the years she taught as a professor of English and fiction writing at both the University of New Mexico and the University of Arizona. She has traveled, yet the Southwest remains the center and source of her work. As Silko announced early on, "This place I am from is everything I am as a writer and human being" (Rosen, 1974, p. 176).

Her childhood at Old Laguna village included not only "the Rio San José that arcs below the village," but also, as Robert Nelson points out, America's most famous highway just across the river, U.S. Route 66, which is now Interstate 40. Nelson grounds Silko's perspective in this geography:

> Silko's own affinity for this place reflects, perhaps, her own felt "position," occupying as she does a marginal site with respect to both Laguna "within" and the dominant Anglo mainstream "out there"—and as she depicts it, it's not a bad place to be. (1999, p. 16)

Many, like Nelson, have made much of Silko's "liminal" position as a mixed-blood writer between worlds, where "living in two worlds" has long been an issue in Native American experience. Such a critique repeats across a generation of postcolonial theory about marginalized voices.

Nelson in his definitive and deeply insightful biographical work on Silko goes further to explain her aesthetic in terms of this literal position of family of origin in relation to Keresan pueblo culture and language on the land: "This same sense of contact zone becoming meeting ground also characterizes the position of the family household with respect to its Keresan and non-Keresan surroundings" (1999, p. 16). Indeed, Louis Owens has asserted, along with many others, that such a liminal position of "mixed-blood identity" is the key to understanding the modern American Indian novel (*Other Destinies*, 1994). Owens locates Silko within such an aesthetic tradition of major authors who voice such racial marginalization, including nineteenth-century Cherokee writer John Rollin Ridge, and several prominent Native American authors of the twentieth and twenty-first centuries: John Joseph Matthews, D'Arcy McNickle, N. Scott Momaday, James Welch, Louise Erdrich, Michael Dorris, and Gerald Vizenor. Such voices certainly do address issues along the boundaries of culture and from both sides of the so-called frontier.

However, scholarly controversies abound as to whether issues of mixed-blood identity are the driving force of Native American novels or whether these voices primarily express a dynamic commitment to community in the text, rather than an anxiety over identity.[2] Certainly, both dynamics are at work in Silko, where, for instance, Tayo's mixed blood and other mixed-up confusions set up the sickness that must be healed by kinship and the land in the communal narrative of *Ceremony*. In the autobiographical introduction to her collection of essays, *Yellow Woman and a Beauty of the Spirit* (1996), Silko herself explains this very dichotomy:

> The mesas and hills loved me, the Bible meant punishment. Life at Laguna for me was a daily balancing act of Laguna beliefs and Laguna ways and the ways of the outsiders. No wonder I preferred to wander in the hills by myself, on my horse, Joey, with Bulls-eye, my dog. (1996, p. 17)

Clearly, she dealt intimately with the mixed-blood issues that Owens and so many others identify. Yet I'd suggest that such conflict and resolution are more than Silko's "liminal" position being healed by "community"—even more than Nelson's map, where "The story of Laguna, like the biography of Silko and the fictional lives of her novels' protagonists, has always been a story of contact, departure, and recovery" (p. 15).

Such a map certainly traces a narrative arc in *Ceremony*, *Almanac of the Dead*, and *Gardens in the Dunes*, where enforced alienation from the land requires a return to the land, where "homing in" remains the narrative structure.[3] Yet it is not splitting hairs to point out that Silko's actual authorial position and the narrative substructure are not liminal, but central—in that decentering move that is the healing itself. "The mesas and hills loved me" indicates that Laguna ground remains the center of her identity, especially where "the Bible meant punishment." Her identity and community are clear. Her position precedes that borderland.

For the drama of narrative, for the excitement of storytelling, her fictional characters may seem mixed up and torn away, torn apart, but the author's journey—like the journey of the reader-witness—begins and ends at the center. As she writes:

> It begins with the land; think of the land, the earth, as the center of a spider's web. Human identity, imagination and storytelling were inextricably linked to the land, to Mother Earth, just as the strands of the spider's web radiate from the center of the web. From the spoken word, or storytelling, comes the written word, as well as the visual image. (1996, p. 21)

Silko the writer is indeed like *Ceremony*'s protagonist Tayo, who never was mixed up after all: "He was not crazy; he had never been crazy. He had only seen and heard the world as it always was: no boundaries, only transitions through all distances and time" (1977, p. 246). This beautiful, classic passage remains one of the most resonant lines in twentieth-century literature—not because it is a voice in the margin, but because it decenters or recenters the map of margins; not because it speaks from across the border of otherness, but because it erases those very borders into "no boundaries."

Further, because it does not merely reverse the center and margin, but remaps it entirely by blurring those boundaries, the strength made visible by this new articulation is practical and political, rather than sentimental. Its cosmic insight is nonromantic in the context of such oppressive forces. Silko fundamentally affirms a recentering of Tayo's, of her own, of Laguna's, and indeed of America's identity, as an infinite center of change, "no boundaries, only transitions." This is not a liminal position, but a central one. It is a heartbeat.

A hunter's eye: "Searching for motion"

Silko seems to have always felt that rhythm. Call it a drum. It beats in the stories and in the voices she heard as a child. Fundamentally, it is a rhythm of the seasons, of life and death. It means Indigenous, that is, living close to the land. For example, Silko's *Storyteller* includes family photographs of the author's preschool-age sisters smiling beside a freshly shot deer carcass in the bed of their father's pickup truck, its eyes facing the camera, and their small hands on the mule deer buck's antlers (1981, p. 176). Another photo shows Leslie and her Uncle Polly with five bucks lying on a cabin porch after a hunt. Leslie had "walked with my father on hunts since I was eight" (p. 77). At age thirteen, she carried a family friend's. 30–30 Winchester, "so happy to be hunting for the first time" (p. 77). The photographic images accompany her formative experiences of "hours of searching for motion, for the outline of a deer, for the color of a deer's hide" (p. 77) among the junipers and tall

yellow grass. She recalls guidance from her elders both to trust her
childhood skills with a gun and to respect and thus eat whatever she
shoots, never to shoot anything she won't eat:

> In the old days there had been no boundaries between the people
> and the land; there had been mutual respect for the land that
> others were actively using. This respect extended to all living
> beings, especially to the plants and the animals. We watched our
> elders behave with respect when they butchered a sheep ... When
> the hunter brought home a mule deer buck, the deer occupied
> the place of honor in the house; it lay on the best Navajo blanket
> with strings of silver and turquoise beads hanging from its neck;
> turquoise and silver rings and bracelets decorated the antlers.
> (1996, pp. 85–86)

This ethic of literally living off the land permeates her storytelling
from the start, and I'd suggest that the practicality and respect in
this ethos of subsistence hunting deeply informs her work. It is an
ethos where hand, heart, and head are familiar with blood, with
unsentimental understanding of the cycles of life and death, and
with compassionate and unflinching recognition of such balance.
It is almost surgical in its healing perspective, willing to penetrate
incisively the normal boundaries of flesh and spirit.

A crucial aspect of this biographical background on the land
applies directly to Silko's fiction. Fundamental to her experiences
of hunting as a child and a young woman is that certain form
of "respect," an Indigenous quality so pervasive in an animist
universe that some may overlook it as a given. Clearly, when her
elders trained her to eat whatever she killed, they were inculcating
respect in her for her prey; but in their confidence in her own
emerging will, in their trust that she would handle a gun not only
skillfully but also wisely, they also were expressing their respect for
her. Numerous ethnographic studies have focused on Indigenous
parental respect for children, spanning a spectrum from adoration
to noninterference.

As a key example of this cultural and biographical link to her
fiction, I'd suggest that this fundamental quality of respect for
children is part of the motivating power of *Gardens in the Dunes*.
To many readers, the tone in that novel is so strikingly different
from *Ceremony* or *Almanac of the Dead*, which of course are also

different from each other in tone, that they are tempted to consider *Gardens* as a novel geared to the young adult market. The point here is not to accept such hierarchies of markets, young adult or adult. Certainly, a primary narrative point of view in *Gardens*, balanced with other narrative voices, is through the eyes of the Indigenous girl, Indigo, and her innocence and optimism tend to simplify some of the actions and themes set at the turn of the twentieth century. Further, linking to Silko's biography, Indigo's self-chosen role emerges from her hunter-gatherer-gardener culture: to gather seeds in her global travels. When that structural choice in point of view on the novelist's part is understood through this Indigenous quality of special respect for children—and when that particular respect is understood through a larger quality of respect for life, including plants, seeds, and the living land—then this novel's point of view is no longer a reduction or a simplification. Some of it may be child-like, but it is not childish. That youthful voice crafted by the novelist is worthy of respect, and it grows out of Silko's own experience of being respected as a girl.[4]

As an ethic and an aesthetic without romantic baggage, this respectful practicality in Silko's aesthetic gaze of the hunter links further to John Keats' landmark concept of "negative capability," a poet's certain fearless courage to move outside of oneself into the experience of the other, a receptiveness to the world and a sense of comfort with "uncertainties, mysteries, doubts" (1899, p. 277), ultimately with mysteries of meaning, of life and death. *Almanac* certainly expresses such courage, and perhaps Silko's mythopoesis of the witchery in *Ceremony*, in *Storyteller*, and elsewhere requires such negative capability. Rather than analytical distance, such an aesthetic expresses engaged feeling, even as it remains objective. We see this complex identification, this negative capability, as both objective and subjective voice in the sacred *Yaqui Deer Songs* of the Sonora Desert, which narrate the hunt from many perspectives, via the hunter, the buzzard, and the deer itself. The dancer and singers become the deer: "Killed and taken, killed and taken, there in the wilderness, I am killed and taken" (Evers and Molina, 1986, p. 168). Even as the master singer explains, "Guts, deer guts, it is the guts the song talks about here," the voice of the song speaks as the deer itself: "I am just glistening, sitting out there, here I am scattered, I become enchanted. My enchanted flower body is glistening, sitting out there" (p. 172). Such scenes and their songs, multiplied many times across many seasons, and sanctified in ceremonies, generate a rhythm on the land. In Silko, that eye of the hunter translates into both the intimacy of courageous witness and the testimonial language of concision and compassion.

The writer's calling:
"The power of the stories"

This negative capability at the heart of storytelling is an element in Silko's choice early on to leave law school at the University of New Mexico and to pursue writing instead. She carried this poet's gift, and she chose to be true to that. In an interview, Silko clarifies the principle: "The way you change human beings and human behavior is through a change in consciousness and that can be effected only through literature, music, poetry—the arts" (Mellas, 2006, p. 14). As Silko explains in the introduction to her essay collection, the example of her elders had sent her toward a career in law:

> I was only five or six years old when my father was elected tribal treasurer. During his term, the Pueblo of Laguna filed a big lawsuit against the state of New Mexico for six million acres of land the state wrongfully took...What made the strongest impression on me, though, were the old folks who also were expert witnesses. For months the old folks and Aunt Susie met twice a week after supper at our house to go over the testimony. (1996, p. 18)

It was not until she was in law school some twenty years later that this case was unjustly concluded, with most of the pittance paid for the stolen land going to the lawyers. Silko discovered that, although the court "found in favor of the Pueblo of Laguna...the Indian Claims Court never gives back land wrongfully taken; the court only pays tribes for the land" (1996, p. 19). She writes, "The Anglo-American legal system was designed by and for the feudal lords; to this day, money and power deliver 'justice' only to the rich and powerful; it cannot do otherwise" (1996, pp. 19–20). With this informed perspective, with "invaluable insights into the power structure of mainstream society" (1996, p. 20), Silko left law school to pursue her calling: "I decided the only way to seek justice was through the power of the stories." While "justice" remains the end, she became clear about a different means.

Further, she immediately conceived "the power of the stories" in a combination, as she put it, of "text and photographs so that on the page there is a coherent whole" (1996, p. 20). As we shall see, this double aesthetic of text and image, of sound and silence, of language and presence, that moved her from the start, has moved throughout her work as testimony and witness. Indeed, this self-positioning functions as a crucial link between her aesthetics and ethics in an ethos of activism at the heart of her work. The hunter and her storytelling become the witness and her testimony.

The stories: "The only way to seek justice"

It is important to point out in this overview that Silko's first novel, *Ceremony*, because of the strength of its popular and critical reception, is among the most widely taught novels at colleges and universities, and it remains a standard in the field of Native American literature. It has sold more than a million copies. While Silko has continued her publishing career as a major American writer and primary figure in Native American literature across six decades so far, each of her publications has taken a unique approach to *Ceremony*'s complex themes of identity, community, and sovereignty on the land. Throughout Silko's work, she sets herself—and the reader—in the role of witness to history, as we shall see, with the power to retell "the story" in new ways. *Ceremony* deconstructs the racial rift at the heart of American identity in a mixed-blood protagonist, and offers an originary presence of the American land itself, the ground, as a healing power. *Almanac of the Dead* transcribes the brutal chaos of modern culture untethered from the ethos of that land, and prophesizes the reemergence of Indigenous values along the inexorable arc of history. *Gardens in the Dunes*, building on the themes of groundedness in *Ceremony* and of global interconnectedness in *Almanac*, narrates parallel and intimate processes of reconstructing postcolonial identities for both colonized and colonizer. This set of emergent themes is consistent across Silko's career, though built on significantly different forms of narrative representation among the three texts. Consistently, Silko pushes against monologist tendencies in the novel form, toward dialogism; or perhaps she affirms the dialogism available to that form. We may map a sequence in her dialogic approach throughout the three novels. *Ceremony* is the most focused on one character; *Almanac* sets up a cacophonous dialogue without a protagonist; and *Gardens* is focused cross-culturally on two women in dialogue, indeed an historicized distillation of *Almanac*'s dialogues. Thus, there is resonance but not repetition among the novels, as among these essays and between the sections devoted to individual novels.

Across her writing career, Silko's representations of Native American experience have also revised definitions of what it means to be American. Her imaginative narratives break down especially the classic categories of race, as well as gender and class, institutionalized in mainstream accounts of American history. Indeed her work has been key in the generational process of revising that history and of affirming American pluralism in literary terms. Because of her family's commitment to justice, she possesses or is possessed by a radical perspective, expressed with poetic strength, which cuts through historical boundaries and hierarchies. This commitment is one of the reasons for an immediacy, a topical and political force to her prose and poetry, even as she moves in mythic dimensions that invoke global Indigenous traditions and contemporary world news.

Because her work is grounded in her Laguna Pueblo land and culture, Silko's writing exposes dominant ideologies and practices as not "naturally" American, but as contingent, built on exploitative economic structures. She does this political work through an articulate voice, sometimes plainly eloquent, steeped in an animistic and communal world view. By this dynamic, she has helped to drive cross-cultural conversations in the late twentieth and early twenty-first centuries about not only American identity, but also posthuman ecology, epistemology, tribal sovereignty, cultural appropriation, intergenerational trauma, communities of difference (*e pluribus unum*), and, indeed, the meanings of freedom itself. Broadly, the contributors to this book investigate such themes in her novels, touching not only topical issues of ethnicity, gender, race, and trauma in the American materialist mythos at the millennial turn, but also alternative approaches to such issues from Indigenous perspectives.

Indeed, we pick up on half a century of scholarship and criticism addressing Silko's fiction, concurrent with her lifelong career in published storytelling. We find the following issues and questions that have come into focus among thousands of published studies on Silko: landscape/ecology; place-centered epistemology; cyclic versus linear time; mythopoetic versus realist aesthetics; oral and literary expression; narrative as ritual or ceremony; genre bending; mixed-blood identity; imperialism and dispossession; political, social, cultural critique; cross-cultural contrasts; ethnography; psychology; reciprocity; spirituality; religion; mythology; history; Indigenous rights; revolutionary pluralism; racial imbalance; gender representations; masculinity; sexuality; feminism; Marxism; cultural authenticity; war and peace in EuroAmerican versus Indigenous patterns; nonviolence; animism; the body; community; healing; kinship; witchcraft; death; ghosts; spirits and spirit messengers; borders (national, ethnic divisions figured geographically or otherwise); globalism; recognition; seeing/visual practices; water; capitalism; colonialism; resistance; and survivance. Never pretending to cover all of these topics, this book addresses many of these issues without presuming to give the last word. The texts themselves are too alive for definition, and each generation will find new conversations with and within them.

Craft as well as content is another focus of this book, as Silko's individual and cross-cultural aesthetics speak to her concerns with postcolonial and transnational ethics. Each of Silko's three major works discussed in this book not only generates dialogue for readers on vital American, Native American, and global themes, but her diverse narrative structures also prompt readers to reconsider Indigenous transformations of EuroAmerican narrative representation. Since Silko publishes and performs in various genres, these scholars draw on the rich context of her career for detailed treatments of the novels. Readers both new to and familiar with Silko thus may see how her novels emerge from the writer's complex patterns of artistic development and engagement with the world.

The essays employ a variety of critical methodologies. Theories of theory in Native American literary studies have evolved and revolved as the field emerged in the last generations. While there was discussion at the start, in the early 1970s, of the value of applying Indigenous theories and methodologies to Indigenous representations, the articulation of those theories took some decades to develop. Now such scholarly apparatus is in full flower, having emerged from Indigenous traditions, from structures of Indigenous texts, and from dialogue with and contention with EuroAmerican theoretical models as well. Thus, this book is designed to emphasize and to critique Indigenous perspectives in Silko, as well as to offer metalanguage on Indigenous methodologies in critiquing her work.

Each of the literary scholars in this book brings personal and professional experience of Indigenous community issues to the discussion. Silko's various topics of history and identity require an explicit theoretical framework, derived from evolving conversations in, for example, tribally specific ethnolinguistics; Indigenous historicism; literary ethnography; communitism; cosmopolitan gleanings from deconstruction; feminism; gender studies; queer studies; ethnic theory; race theory; critical legal studies; postcolonial theory; transnational theory; diasporic studies; trauma studies; historiography; and narratology. As such, some of the individual chapters extend through Silko's fiction to concerns of broader literary and theoretical interest.

Within those broad critical contexts, each section on one of the three novels strives for coverage of four standard approaches, four patterns that reflect current methodologies in the field of Native American literary studies: (a) tribally specific literary ethnography and history; (b) pan-Indian and global Indigenous analysis; (c) comparative analysis with other canonical and postcolonial literatures; and (d) political and legal perspectives in a (post)colonial moment. Such structures are not rigid, as each contributor's unique scholarship and criticism inevitably blurs these approaches. With fruitful cross-pollinations, there are variations according to each contributor's insights and choices. However, the book strives for coverage of such methodologies and of the issues each different approach makes visible.

For decades, the field of literary studies has been flooded with examinations of Silko from many perspectives, cross-culturally informed and not. Yet there has not been a collection of original scholarly and critical essays that summarizes and discusses her place in literary history, nor that analyzes her three major novels together, nor that sets them all in dialogue with each other, with the rest of her oeuvre, or with other Native and non-Native masters of the form. This book opens a door to those larger conversations, the next necessary step in critical study of Silko's emerging life work.

Two rocks: Witness and testimony

Indigenous texts in colonial contexts not only tend to promote agendas of resistance against dominant historical trajectories, but they also reaffirm the cultural and political existence and resilience of their own communities—in their own Indigenous contexts.[5] In a politics of text and context, these two projects of survivance and self-representation complement each other and interweave among various voices and various audiences. Artists balance these various acts of expression in unique and always changing ways. With her roots in Laguna, Silko tends toward survivance in the larger context of colonial, indeed global history, while her affirmations of self-representation and resilience form the local content of those survivance stories.

Silko's project—to reveal the mythic dimensions of modern history and the historical momentum of ancient myth—is structured by two pillars as it cycles through salient themes or spiritual emphases. (I use the term "spiritual" to recapture it in academic discourse as the ethics of ecosocial relationships, a focus of much Indigenous expression.) For the purposes of this book, we may consider two dynamics that overlap in her work and that quite neatly match survivance and self-representation: witness and testimony. These two larger structures, which I am referring to here as marker stones, as a single gateway, are foundational to her work. For the sake of space, I will concentrate my comments on this fundamental dual structure, this geologic substratum of witness and testimonial language use. This structure marks an opening to the field where issues of gender, class, and race (in that order) intersect. Some of the chapters in this book address the three latter intersecting issues, so here I will map that gateway by way of introduction to the fascination of focused conversations in the chapters that follow.

A certain logic might claim to reverse my categorical structures, as so many have suggested that race, class, and gender are the fundamental taxonomy, and that these would underlie any aesthetics of witness and testimony (or equally underlie Silko's key themes of animism and the land that I will address briefly below). I do not mean to be arbitrary here, but must recognize that such a theoretical reversal would indeed make sense, where the *a priori* thinking of binary structures in gender, class, and race prevails. Undeniably, the gendered epistemology of hierarchical, patriarchal binaries, or *kyriarchy* in the useful neologism by Elisabeth Schüssler Fiorenza, do tend to structure the modern mind, shaped by centuries of colonial capital and its hierarchical economies.[6] And I myself have long clarified such a fundamental politics of competing epistemologies.[7] However, I choose my categories here of witness and testimony in a methodological reversal for its focus on specific, grounded, active, pragmatic elements of Silko's storytelling as they may provide the analytical apparatus for understanding her prose. Thus, the requirements of silent witness and the resonant consciousness of uniquely crafted language for clearest testimony play out and interplay across her novels. Eventually, this analysis brings us back to origins, where the land itself is witness, rich with animist language as well as with silence, and the writer echoes these voices and silences.

To deal with these two structural elements, I will draw on some other Silko texts that are not a focus of this book, emphasizing the interactions of these two formations in Silko's work, two structures as fundamental and as eloquent as the stone snake in *Almanac of the Dead*. For the element of active witness, I will draw especially on her memoir *The Turquoise Ledge*; for testimonial and animist language, I will cite her novella *Oceanstory*. Witness and testimony interact like that eloquently silent messenger between the lines, as Silko explains, "...I realized that the giant snake had been a catalyst for the novel [*Almanac*] from the start" (1996, p. 144). "Even ordinary snakes are spirit messengers to the spirit beings and Mother Earth" (1996, p. 147). As we move through this dual structure, I also will gesture toward two rivers that flow through her work, two fundamental themes of animism and land. Again these structures and themes each intersect as form and content, as any text offers a macrocosm in the microcosm, Silko's universe in a grain of sand.

Standing on the ledge:
"Expert witnesses"

I focus on witness because it so implicates the reader. Such an effect is the whole point. It completes the circle at the start. It enacts the responsibility that each of us bears in our various ways to the lives and communities in these stories. The context of the text is flesh and blood, rock and river. As we saw, Silko is self-reflexive about her family's influence: "What made the strongest impression on me, though, were the old folks who also were expert witnesses," and she recounts the discipline of "the old folks and Aunt Susie" in meeting twice a week "to go over the testimony." Silko herself thus assumes the role of witness— that is, her legacy and her work—and she invites her readers to join her.

Not only is this role not passive, but indeed in an animist sense of pervasive consciousness, the attention given to a story, the witnessing act itself, expresses agency and alters reality. We are not looking at a two-dimensional screen. These stories are not scenes; they are acts; they are alive and thus responsive to us, in communication. In witnessing, we enter that realm where modern physics encounters ancient teachings: "a theory of consciousness should take experience as a primary entity alongside mass, charge, and space time" (Rosenblum and Kuttner, Loc 3768). The stories are the universe knowing itself, and we alter what we see because it is part of us and we are part of it.

As Rosenblum and Kuttner explain in *Quantum Enigma: Physics Encounters Consciousness*, physicists are turning their attention to subjectivity itself, where the elusive notion of "experience" is subject to mathematical formulation: "…physics has encountered consciousness in the quantum enigma, which physicists call the 'measurement problem'. Here, aspects of physical observation come close to those of conscious experience" (2013, Loc 3787). The witness steadily measures what she observes, bringing awareness and consciousness to what was hidden and secret. When this Heisenbergian dynamic is applied to understanding how storytelling works, drawing on traditional Keres narratives while applying modern sensibilities to the act of witness, the storyteller—and her readers—are reshaping the world. "Something is wrong," [the witchman] said. "Ck'o'yo magic won't work/if someone is watching us" (*Ceremony*, 1977, p. 259). In Silko's world—which is the world of Laguna myth as well as the world of nuclear weapons and corporate industrial domination—what could be more important than reshaping through witnessing?

The title of her 2010 memoir, *The Turquoise Ledge*, which she describes as more of a self-portrait than an autobiography (Olivo, 2010), draws from the central Keres pueblo oral tradition of Estoy-e-muut, or Arrowboy, the archetypal witness, a central theme explicit in *Ceremony* and *Storyteller*. When the witches seduce his wife into their ritual, Arrowboy follows her and climbs up to the ledge to peer into the witches' cave. It is there—because of his act of witness on that ledge—that the "magic won't work" because "someone is watching." Silko has been standing on that ledge her whole life. Of her ranch house where she has lived near Tucson for many years, she writes, "So the house I live in sits on top of a chalky turquoise ledge of brightest blue" (2010, p. 225). Thus, she alludes in the title for her major memoir to the Arrowboy myth that animates her entire life of expression.

Again, this dynamic works because the gaze of witness exposes and defuses evil through triangulation, through a public, communal eye that deflects and distracts the secretive, dualistic power of the violent gaze. A number of scholars have explained this defusing dynamic of witness.[8] Several have compared Silko's usage of the witness dynamic with other voices such as Chicana authors Gloria Anzaldúa and Cherrie Moraga, or feminist and antiwar authors Carolyn Forché and Tillie Olsen, all of whom are explicit about a literary voice of witness. Robert Nelson explains that the act of witness in Silko transforms witchery's secret energy into a public story of communal understanding (2004); while Rebecca Tillett explains, "The gaze of the witness therefore directly meets, recognizes, and subverts the gaze of the oppressors, and witnessing becomes a moral and ethical practice…" (2013, p. 76). Keepers of the almanac are indeed witnesses by vocation, and the almanac of the dead thus becomes an almanac of living witness. As Silko writes in "Notes on *Almanac of the Dead*," "I saw the United States of America that no one wants to talk about" (1996, p. 141). If the witchery won't work when someone is watching, Silko's text, her ethics and aesthetics here become an epic test in a cycle of death and life, a delicate balance between sunset and sunrise.

Indeed, among ruminations on geology, history, and mystery, *The Turquoise Ledge* documents a silent saga of Silko's own active witness where she protects a natural arroyo from a neighbor illegally quarrying rock with his backhoe for landscaping. With rain-washable tempura paint, she inscribes the glyph of the Star Beings, "the white cross figure of the star, on all sides of the boulders, and especially on the scars left by the metal claw of the machine" (p. 308). Silko understands that these small white crosses "worked a kind of magic," and it is precisely that magic of witness. "All human beings were put on notice that the boulders were under the protection of the Star Beings and must not be disturbed or damaged; all violators would pay terrible consequences" (p. 308). Silko as active witness is heartened by this image, as she identifies with the land itself: "The white crosses...made a pictograph of a constellation fallen to Earth" (p. 317). "Now instead of dread filling my heart when I walked up the arroyo past the gravel pit, I'll see the constellation of white crosses, the sign, the warning from the Star Beings, and my heart will be filled with happiness and hope" (p. 309). In fact, later, "...I got the feeling the man didn't want those rocks for his yard, so maybe the painting worked after all" (p. 317).

Not surprisingly, Silko's active witness, her activism, taking responsibility where she knew "the local authorities didn't bother to enforce the laws intended to protect the land from damage," is tied, as in *Almanac of the Dead*, with a deep faith in the spirit of the land. She writes lyrically toward the very end of the memoir:

The big arroyo itself is space, open space, empty space, carved for eons through the rocks by floodwater as it descends toward the sea. Slowly but relentlessly the erosion will work so the bank of the arroyo will be undermined and in a flood it will collapse, and the wall around the [neighbor's] house will topple into floodwaters with it. The boulders and rocks taken to landscape the yard will roll into the floodwater plop! plop! They always were travelers; the detour the man and machine took them on mattered less than a molecule. They will be on their way once more to the Santa Cruz River on its way to join the Salt River then on to the Colorado at Yuma and finally to the sea.

Again to the sea. The boulders and rocks of limestone and quartzite originated in the Great Sea. As the stones from millions of years reckon it, man and machine are no more than a shadow of a mote of dust. (2010, p. 315)

The confidence of "millions of years" reckons the story in terms beyond human history. Her language is spare yet poetic—embodying the silence of the land even as she invokes it.

Within that vast perspective, looking further than the five-hundred-year cycles that she describes in *Almanac of the Dead*, Silko's chosen role as witness has required her to return to the politics of race and the damage to the earth which, as she explains halfway through the memoir, she had wanted to avoid:

> I didn't want to write about it; I didn't want it to be in the *Turquoise Ledge* manuscript. I had decided before I started the memoir that I wanted as much as possible to avoid unpleasantness and strife and politics as much as possible. But the beautiful gray basalt and pale orange quartzite boulders had been torn loose from the sides of the arroyo and dragged out of the wash and skidded up the old road to "landscape" the yard of the preposterous house with its prison tower and prison wall. (p. 170)

The irony in "preposterous" is not personal, but pitiful and comical in the cosmic reckoning that she summons where "man and machine" are merely "a shadow of a mote of dust" across "millions of years." So toward the memoir's finale, the responsibility of witness returns her to a discussion of the neighbors' racial fears. They guess that her white crosses of the Star Beings were painted by gangs: "In Tucson 'gang' and 'gang graffiti' are code words white people use to indicate young brown or black men who they consider to be 'aliens' even if they were born in Arizona" (p. 317). In addition to misreading the Star Beings, the invaders continue to miss and to misrepresent the presence of Indigenous bodies on the land.

Yet she witnesses a further step. In a precise formulation of the witness dynamic, Silko follows with this affirmation: "Apparently the emblem of the Star Beings penetrated the psyches of the newcomers who got the message: indigenous forces are present to oppose you" (p. 317). Thus, at the very end of the memoir, Silko allows herself to relax into a sweet comfort of that Indigenous role, so linked to the forces of nature: "Gentle warm rains from the south have already graced us…This is a good place to end. Gratitude to all you beings of the stars" (p. 319).

If witness is her epic role shared with the reader on the ground and with the Star Beings, animism is the air she breathes—again shared with the reader and with all of creation, the earth. The scale moves from the epic to the cosmic, from historical to geological to metaphysical. This is what she does. She invokes the spirit in the stories, the text, and thereby triggers the spirit in the reader and the context. Again, my use of terms such as "animism" and "spirit," like hers, learning from her, is not romanticized or sentimental. In Chapter 3 of *The Turquoise Ledge*, Silko catalogs a number of stories of spirit visits in the clouds, in the rain, in birds, in animals. She writes matter-of-factly:

> So it seems that after the passing of a friend or loved one, a few days or a week after they go, they manifest their loving energy: the wind chimes tinkle in the twilight though there is no breeze; the chimney of the oil lantern rattles by itself; the electric fan blades make an unusual sound—the realm of the spirit beings and the ancestors contact us from time to time. (p. 15)

As old El Feo muses in *Almanac*, "The days, years, and centuries were spirit beings who traveled the universe, returning endlessly. The Spirits of the Night and the Spirits of the Day would take care of the people" (1991, p. 523) This is a sort of spirituality, as I suggested above, that tracks ethical responsibility, an energy of relationship invoked and embodied by the expression of stories about those relationships. It is not "otherworldly." Such a reflexive circle of representation and relationship, where the story conveys the relations and the relations are the story, may be like the biochemical loops of the brain–mind continuum that scientists recently invoke to explain "consciousness." The witness both sees and knows. The language of awareness becomes the awareness of language, and literary use of language adds another dimension of recursive attention, of witness, as well.

Articulating the silence: "To go over the testimony"

As I have written elsewhere, "…witnessing is a double power circulating in the silent power of sight, a necessary event that precedes the power of telling" (1999, p. 152). The second pillar of

Silko's structural gateway is the telling, the testimony, that articulates the images seen by the witness. These two are strands in the double helix that builds Silko's prose. Witness sees and testimony tells. We may approach this microscopic and macroscopic structure through the language of animism and what I will call earthen language.

Animism stands alert to the life in things, and its sense of attention can lead to a spare style that respects that life by not imposing the authorial blur of self-indulgent rhetoric on the page. The author remains on the ledge, seemingly off the page, so that the act of witness may directly testify. Thus, a spare style tries to speak the truth as in legal testimony: just the truth, the whole truth, and nothing but the truth. In a prose of testimony, there is no room for subjective distractions, though there is plenty of room for lyrical and poetic language. It cannot be flowery, but concise and compressed, focused on the reality at hand. We shall see how Silko's passages fit this requirement.

With such a minimum of subjectivity, her fiction does not project a personal voice, but a public, sometimes mythic one. She is relating the impressions of Thought Woman, not her own, as in the layered opening to *Ceremony*: "I am telling you the story/ she is thinking" (1977, p. 1). The point of view remains detached, like James Joyce's anonymous, objective narrator, frequently also employing stream of consciousness.[9] Indeed, like Momaday, Silko shares such aesthetics with the Modernists. (Questions about how their Indigenous voices carry Modernist tendencies have been the subject of much scholarly debate.) Silko may be a personal witness, but the forum for justice is the court of community, indeed on a global scale, and she enlists the reader in this public testimony.

As we look at her language, we listen for that stark honesty, an earthen integrity that focuses and amplifies both the seeing and the seen. We find such earthen language at the surprisingly nondestructive climax of *Ceremony*. She begins with concrete detail, before she moves into the relentless social critique: "...Tayo had almost jammed the screwdriver into Emo's skull the way the witchery had wanted, savoring the yielding bone and membrane as the steel ruptured the brain." The vivid, sensory, even sensationalist imagery here is ironized both by the witchery's flaunted will and by the hypothetical frame of the paragraph, where "It had been a close call. The witchery had almost ended the story according to its plan..." (p. 253).

Weaving together in this scene the many strands of the novel's spider web, she continues the hypothetical in "would," further ironizing the truth of what she witnesses and speaks so plainly:

The white people would shake their heads, more proud than sad that it took a white man to survive in their world and that these Indians couldn't seem to make it. At home the people would blame liquor, the Army, and the war, but the blame on the whites would never match the vehemence the people would keep in their own bellies, reserving the greatest bitterness and blame for themselves, for one of themselves they could not save. (1977, p. 253)

Silko's lyrical rhythms move like a drumbeat through this poetic yet diagnostic passage, largely via the iambs of a heartbeat, but punctuated with trochees and other longer, emphatic variations. Yet the actual diction is particularly revealing. As stylistic tools, adjectives and adverbs would provide a filter for nouns and verbs by articulating descriptive judgments—ultimately the author's judgments—of items and actions. Without such modifiers, unadorned nouns and verbs project more directly off the page. The writer remains on the ledge. In this passage of seventy-eight words, with seventeen nouns and nine verbs, there are only one adverb and four adjectives, one of which is repeated. ("White" repeats; "more" modifies "proud"; and "sad" provides contrast on the topic of "white people." Only one adjective, a superlative, applies to "the people," and that is "greatest" to emphasize "bitterness.") Such bare language is thus appropriate to testimony. Via direct diction, the witness does not filter the truth.

Similarly, the complexity of vocabulary remains spare and unswerving. Sixty-two words are actually one-syllable; twelve are two-syllable; and only four are three-syllable—and these rare four, slightly longer words are focused on the point of the passage: "Indians," "vehemence," "reserving," and "bitterness." Not only is the language straightforward and noncomplex in terms of parts of speech and vocabulary, but also the form of the very few contrasting tri-syllable words works to focus the specific drama of the content and theme: that Indians reserve their vehemence and bitterness for themselves, that they take responsibility, and, ultimately, agency. This is a lucid example of testimonial language where the witness stands aside to let the language "speak for itself"; that is, it bridges the abyss; it closes the gap between representation and presence, between testimony and truth, between language and experience.

Seeing the life in all things from an animist ethos further positions the narrative voice deeper in this reserved detachment, where the writer's "I/eye" is not central, but merely and crucially, again, a triangulating witness. For further context of her language use, her testimonial text, we may see, in *Oceanstory* as elsewhere, how Silko brings an Indigenous sensibility to language itself, in what many writers and critics have referred to as "the power of the word." As in Kiowa writer N. Scott Momaday's renowned work, "The Man Made of Words," or in Chickasaw writer Linda Hogan's terms ("Who Puts Together," 1983), language and reality here are so interwoven and mutually influential that by a certain use of language one may reverse-engineer reality, that is, influence reality by the power of prayer and song, again by the principle of consciousness as modern physics formulates the one who measures, the witness.

Hogan defines some of the related oral cultural dynamics: "These methods are characteristic of oral tradition, in which the word and the object are equal and in which all things are united and in flux. The distinctions between inner and outer break down" (p. 175). Hogan quotes Octavio Paz on returning language "to an earlier time 'before an abyss had opened between things and their names.' " Describing oral ritual, Hogan suggests that in oral performance and in Native writers' use of oral literary techniques:

> The life of the word and the fusion of word and object, by means of the visual imagination, return the participant or reader to an original source that is mythic, where something spoken stands for what is spoken about and there is [citing Momaday] "no difference between the telling and that which is told." ... Language used in this way becomes a form of dynamic energy, able to generate and regenerate ... As in the Orphic tradition, language creates the world and lets the world return through the song or the word. (pp. 175–176)

A "fusion of word and object" insists on a real meaning, a truth, "where something spoken stands for what is spoken about." Hogan helpfully demystifies this relationship between word and thing by citing power relations, where language "becomes a form of dynamic energy, able to generate and regenerate." Language is alive. In an animate world, language is another spirit, as are formative, generative stories.

Silko's literary testimony thus draws deeply on animate, Indigenous modes of expression, and we may recognize her dynamics through another analytical step, a rethinking of semiotics. Eduardo Kohn, in *How Forests Think: Toward an Anthropology beyond the Human*, further explains these Indigenous functions of semiotics beyond human language. He draws on Charles Peirce to make distinctions between three modalities of representation, of standing for something else: (1) symbolic in contexts of human conventional usage; (2) iconic, which is onomatopoetic or direct; and (3) indexical, which conveys unmistakably without social conventions. Thus, these human words on this page are symbolic, deriving meaning from a system of conventions. However, the word "crash" is iconic, more directly embodying something else, the sound of a crash. Further, a tree actually crashing and falling in the forest is indexical, an indicator, an index of danger to any perceiver, plant, human, or other animal. The tree and the forest, and each creature in it, including humans, are thus capable of both giving and receiving animate expression, where action and being are indexical, representational, expressive, and communicative. Thus, a tree can talk, whether falling or standing rooted; it can represent. Such analyses emerge in attempts by Western thinkers to understand non-Western, Indigenous ways of thought and language usage. These different forms of representation embody and explain that "earlier time, before an abyss had opened between things and their names," though we may amend such a linear view and consider such an "earlier time" as circular and synchronic rather than linear and diachronic.

Tied deeply to such animate expression, Silko uses language in ways that feel around that synchronic abyss between word and object. In her direct though lyrical style, the reader feels the immediacy or reality. Thus, toward the end of *Oceanstory*, the protagonist-narrator, adrift on a seaweed island, closely watches the water, and then speaks to the waves themselves:

I watched very small waves that lapped at the seaweed stems and at my face as if they were wild beings drawn near by curiosity to examine the seaweeds and me..."Be strong, seaweeds! Waves and winds be gentle please!" These words repeated themselves in my head over and over until the wind gradually diminished. (Loc 871)

Not only does she speak to the water, but the water also speaks to her. As the protagonist wanders the mile of sand at low tide on El Golfo (what U.S. visitors call the Sea of Cortez), she writes:

I found the writing the waves left behind on the fine white sand meanders and spirals. I found big spiral shells then and smooth stones in patterns that might be read like writing. I sat and watched the ocean heaving, shivering and breathing...The wave motions and sounds, the energy in the ocean air, the mists of pure oxygen lifted my consciousness. (Loc 382)

Indeed, her self-reflexive awareness seems requisite for this kind of perception of an animate world, a mutually participatory language: "I listened. I listened for something I could not name, but I knew would come from the intersection of El Golfo with the pale sand dunes and the dark plateau of black volcanic peaks asleep above the topaz ocean" (Loc 119).

Oceanstory, echoing *Almanac of the Dead*, is a novella about such listening amid the noise of economic machinations and corruption flowing south of Tucson, and back across the border. The story moves through grim realities of modern exploitation and alienation, but here, unlike much of *Almanac*, the healing power of water rises off the page. Scenes of animate nature continually balance scenes of debased humanity in a pattern of healing.

This balanced pattern applies to a larger rhythm in Silko's publications across her career. Language is followed by witness and witness is followed by language, and on and on. Text is followed by image, and round and round. One may say that the voices of animism are followed by the silence of the land. Always the land.

Thus, it is significant that after each of her major novels, after each of her major, epic efforts at articulating witness in fiction, after *Ceremony*, *Almanac*, and *Gardens*, Silko has followed with publication on smaller scale, often in nonfiction, focused on the ground beneath her feet, and often more imagistic in its medium. Following *Ceremony*, she turned to local material and shorter passages in *Storyteller* with its mixed media, especially to photographs and local stories of the land and of the people of the land. Similarly, directly following *Almanac*, she published *Sacred Water: Narratives and Pictures*, a photographic, autobiographical work on the arroyos and rocks of her natural neighborhood near Tucson. (Soon thereafter, as an extension of this pattern, she also published another nonfiction collection, *Yellow Woman and a Beauty of the Spirit: Essays on Native American Life Today*.) And following *Gardens*, she turned to nonfiction memoir in *The Turquoise Ledge*, also set in her Tucson Mountains. This geographical and biographical pattern in a major writer's life reveals not only the rhythms of her creative energies, moving in a sense from epic to lyric, fiction to nonfiction, from text to image, from language to picture. It also underlines this key structure in her work, as in her life, of witness and the testimony of vivid, vitalizing language, watching and speaking the truth, each as necessary steps to justice.

Looking at structure and substance, we have seen that witness and testimony are interpenetrating forms of silence and sound, spirit and matter, in Silko's prose, just as animism and land are interwoven content of spirit and matter. This interlacing of matter and spirit, of "delicacy and strength of lace," is key to the compelling quality of Silko's work.

Notes

1   Because there are numerous excellent biographical essays in print, including especially Silko's own introduction to *Yellow Woman* (1996) and Robert Nelson's insightful essay "A Laguna Woman" in Barnett and Thorson (1999), I will confine my biographical comments in this introduction to some salient events in Silko's life that bear on key themes. See also the list of Further Reading.

2   See, for example, Jace Weaver's assertion of "communitism" as the defining literary dynamic in *That the People Might Live: Native American Literatures and Native American Community*; as well as my discussion of this controversy in my chapters on identity and community in *That Dream Shall Have a Name: Native Americans Rewriting America*.

3   See Gercken's chapter in this book for a clear summation of William Bevis's "homing in" theory.

4   As a further dimension of this context of respect, it is worth noting that Becca Gercken's chapter in this book registers Indigo as "the strongest of all of Silko's characters" in terms of her "ability to maintain her cultural heritage and to learn and adapt quickly in both worlds."

5   Thanks to Northern Arapaho scholar Angelica Lawson for the clarity of her analysis through these terms: Resistance and Resilience (Lawson, 2010).

6   See Schüssler Fiorenza (1992).

7   For instance in my 1994 work, "Decolonializing Criticism: Reading Dialectics and Dialogics in Native American Literatures."

8   My 1999 work, "Silko's Blood Sacrifice: The Circulating Witness in *Almanac of the Dead*," addressed this dynamic of witness more fully, and these scholars have usefully expanded on that analysis.

9   See, for instance, Hugh Kenner's classic critique of this modernist aesthetic in point of view in *Joyce's Voices* (1979, p. 103).

References

Evers, L. and Molina, F. (1986), *Yaqui Deer Songs/Maso Bwikam: A Native American Poetry*. Tucson: University of Arizona Press.

Hogan, L. (1983), "Who Puts Together," in Paula Gunn Allen (ed.), *Studies in American Indian Literature: Critical Essays and Course Designs*. New York: MLA, pp. 169–177.

Keats, J. (1817, 1899), *The Complete Poetical Works and Letters of John Keats*, Cambridge edition. New York: Houghton, Mifflin and Company.

Kenner, H. (1979), *Joyce's Voices*. Berkeley: University of California Press.

Kohn, E. (2013), *How Forests Think: Toward an Anthropology beyond the Human*, Kindle edition. Berkeley: University of California Press.

Lawson, A. (2010), "Resistance and Resilience in Ofelia Zepeda's *Ocean Power*: Aesthetics and Ethics in a Tribally Specific Work." *Kenyon Review*, 32:1, 180–198.

Mellas, L. (2006), "Memory and Promise: Leslie Marmon Silko's Story." *Mirage* (University of New Mexico Alumni Magazine) (Spring), 10–14.

Moore, D. L. (1994), "Decolonializing Criticism: Reading Dialectics and Dialogics in Native American Literatures," in *Studies in American Indian Literatures*, 7–33. Reprinted in John Purdy and James Ruppert (eds) (2001), *Nothing But the Truth: An Anthology of Native American Literature*. Upper Saddle River, NJ: Prentice Hall, pp. 94–119.

Moore, D. L. (1999), "Silko's Blood Sacrifice: The Circulating Witness in *Almanac of the Dead*," in J. Thorson and L. Barnett (eds), *Leslie Marmon Silko: A Collection of Critical Essays*. Albuquerque: New Mexico University Press, pp. 149–183.

Moore, D. L. (2013), *That Dream Shall Have a Name: Native Americans Rewriting America*. Lincoln: University of Nebraska Press.

Nelson, R. M. (1999), "A Laguna Woman," in J. Thorson and L. Barnett (eds), *Leslie Marmon Silko: A Collection of Critical Essays*. Albuquerque: New Mexico University Press, pp. 15–22.

Nelson, R. M. (2004), "Settling for Vision in Silko's Ceremony: Sun Man, Arrowboy, and Tayo." *American Indian Culture and Research Journal*, 28:1, 67–73.

Olivo, B. (2010), "Author Silko Isn't Concerned about Time." *Express News* (25 July). [Online] http://www.mysanantonio.com /entertainment/books/article/Author-Silko-isn-t-concerned-about-Time [Accessed: July 22, 2013].

Owens, L. (1994), *Other Destinies: Understanding the American Indian Novel*. Norman: University of Oklahoma Press.

Rosen, K. (1974), *The Man to Send Rain Clouds: Contemporary Stories by American Indians*. New York: Vintage Books.

Rosenblum, B. and Kuttner, F. (2013), *Quantum Enigma: Physics Encounters Consciousness*, Second edition, New York: Oxford University Press.

Schüssler Fiorenza, E. (1992), *But She Said: Feminist Practices of Biblical Interpretation*. Boston: Beacon Press.

Silko, L. M. (1977, 1997), *Ceremony*. New York: Penguin.

Silko, L. M. (1981), *Storyteller*. New York: Seaver Books.

Silko, L. M. (1991), *Almanac of the Dead*. New York: Penguin.

Silko, L. M. (1996), *Yellow Woman and a Beauty of the Spirit: Essays on Native American Life Today*. New York: Simon & Schuster.

Silko, L. M. (2010), *The Turquoise Ledge*. New York: Viking.

Tillett, R. (2013), "On the Cutting Edge: Leslie Marmon Silko," in A. Velie and A. R. Lee (eds), *The Native American Renaissance: Literary Imagination and Achievement*. Norman: University of Oklahoma Press, pp. 74–87.

Weaver, J. (1997), *That the People Might Live: Native American Literatures and Native American Community*. New York: Oxford University Press.

Part One: *Ceremony*

"Accept this offering": Introduction to Part One

David L. Moore

Many readers, writers, and critics, Native and non-Native, regard *Ceremony* as the preeminent Native American novel. Spokane literary phenom Sherman Alexie, Acoma poet and essayist Simon Ortiz, and Creek poet and musician Joy Harjo are among the prominent Indigenous writers who have lavished superlatives on Silko's 1977 publication. Cherokee novelist and academic, Robert Gish, says it well:

> Momaday had influenced me. Welch, especially *Riding the Earthboy 40* and *Winter in the Blood*, was tremendous. But Silko's *Ceremony* was everything that a book could be, everything that literature was supposed to be, the realization of all the adages and quips, all the epigrams and sayings that I had heard and had quoted to students. Indeed, I did feel like Keats when first reading Chapman's Homer. I had found what Dickinson and Frost and Sandburg and company had said "poetry" was supposed to do. (Barnett and Thorson, 1999, p. ix)

Silko's first novel realizes EuroAmerican literary ideals while adapting Indigenous oral traditions of storytelling. That combination and her skillful blending of those modes are part of its power. The novel draws fluidly on history, myth, psychology, and spirituality to paint a picture of disease and healing at the heart of the twentieth century. It is both lyric and epic.

Famously mapping her novel like a spider's web, and voicing Thought Woman or Spider Woman of her Keres traditions, Silko does not lay out a linear plot line, but weaves a circle of many narrative strands. Via a semi-omniscient narrative point of view, vignettes in the novel leap from narrative strand to strand through stream-of-consciousness, a style that matches the earlier Modernists, but that pulsates with mythic imagery on the storied land of the Southwest. Those strands of stories are tangled around the mixed-blood protagonist Tayo, a young Laguna veteran of the Second World War whose shell-shocked grief over losing his cousin Rocky while he survived the Bataan Death March is woven with his disoriented guilt over cursing the Pacific island rains as a prisoner of war and thus bringing drought to his Laguna homeland. As he tries to heal, the ancient witchery continues to tangle him in threads of war, of the atomic bomb, of alcohol, of racism, of abandonment, of poverty, and of violence. To help him untangle himself, his family and his Laguna community find a mixed-blood Navajo medicine man, Betonie, who sets him on a quest, and he finds the love of two women, Night Swan and Ts'eh. These nearly mythic characters reintroduce him to himself as a mythic being on the land, like a patient standing in a sand painting. His challenge is to not fight with the destroyers, to not take the violent bait of the ancient witchery, but to neutralize their evil plans of blood-letting by remaining as a witness rather than another violent drunken Indian. Quite simply, he breaks the stereotype.

The climactic scene at the Jackpile Mine near Laguna Pueblo, where the uranium for the first atomic bomb was actually mined, contains one of the most resonant silences in twentieth-century literature, a blank space on the page, where Tayo disciplines himself to witness the witchery:

> But Tayo stayed on his knees in the shadows. Leroy had a knee on Pinkie's throat, and he could hear raspy choking sounds. Emo was laughing loudly, pointing at the body hanging stiffly, swaying a little in the gusts of wind, then pointing at Leroy kneeling on Pinkie's throat.

> The moon was lost in a cloud bank. He moved back into the boulders. It had been a close call. The witchery had almost ended

the story according to its plan; Tayo had almost jammed the screwdriver into Emo's skull the way the witchery had wanted, savoring the yielding bone and membrane as the steel ruptured the brain. Their deadly ritual for the autumn solstice would have been completed by him. (1977, p. 253)

By any reckoning of Indigenous fiction, beside that uranium mine, in the space where "the moon was lost in a cloud bank" stands the destructive history of the modern era, the rise of colonial capitalism since the Renaissance. The oppositional dynamics of colonial thinking, the material dialectics and domination of gender, class, and race are suspended where that moon was lost. Modern material history is the immediate context of this mythopoetic text. Tayo's refusal to play into those hierarchical dualisms of white supremacy satisfy his healing and the healing of the land—but only "for now." "…its witchery/ has returned upon it…It is dead for now" (p. 261).

This anticlimactic passage in *Ceremony* also happens to include one of the greatest printing typos in modern literature: "autumn solstice"—a celestial phenomenon that does not exist. The autumn *equinox* comes round every year, as do the summer solstice and the winter solstice, and of course the spring equinox. But there is no such thing as "autumn solstice." I do not point out this printer's and copy editor's error for a minor chuckle—rather to acknowledge how it strangely fits with and furthers the themes of the novel.

The typo points us quite synchronistically to a major thematic quality of *Ceremony* and, indeed, of Native American oral and written literature: balance. An equinox is a balance point, whereas a solstice is an extreme, a polarity, so this apparent error is actually a balance of extremes. Dramatically, the narrative had reached a solstice, an extreme, a winter, but thematically it has resolved into the balance of equinox, thus an "autumn solstice." Unlike the witchery that wants oppositions to destroy each other, *Ceremony* brings them into balance, hence the "autumn" part of the typo when an equinox would actually mark the balancing point between dark and light. Yet, it has been a "solstice" indeed, because of the extremity of the historical drama. Good and bad, life and death, Indian and white, all are part of the circle into which Tayo reintegrates himself, and like the seasons, these oppositions find balance in this novel. Thus, the penultimate page of *Ceremony*, "It is dead for now," a solstice of sorts, leads to the circular finale, "Sunrise,/ accept this offering,/ Sunrise" (p. 262), mapping a relative equinox. The darkest hour has occurred just before this dawn, the extreme has brought us to a balance point, so it is both an equinox and a solstice. Because it happens in autumn, the actual season of the equinox, things remain in equilibrium and balance. But because things have reached an extreme, the moment is rightly called a solstice, a zenith, a solstice in the cycle, and things now must cycle back. Thus, Sunrise.

The introduction to this book noted not only the best-seller status of *Ceremony* across decades, but also some of the ways that the novel works with Silko's founding dynamics of witness and testimony, especially through the Arrowboy myth of her Keres pueblo traditions. The three chapters that follow focus on other key dynamics.

Extending a generation of critical theory in gender studies, Kimberly Gail Wieser turns the lens onto masculinity in *Ceremony* and thereby illuminates vital dimensions of the narrative, the characterizations, and the themes. In "Healing the 'Man of Monstrous Dreams': Indian Masculinities in Silko's *Ceremony*," Wieser contrasts Tayo's and Rocky's different responses to the impact of assimilationist policies as those policies would socialize genders. Rocky is killed by trying to be a "good" man in the Western sense because of his mother's own imbalanced behavior from a Laguna perspective; whereas Tayo's breach with his mother is healed on the mountain, and he is able to internalize what Uncle Josiah teaches. This contrast gets at the heart of Tayo's quest.

Mascha Nicola Gemein extends and merges a different set of interdisciplinary critical perspectives in her chapter, "'Branched into All Directions of Time': Pluralism, Physics, and Compassion in Silko's *Ceremony*." Explicating a value of pluralism, Gemein links the novel's drama of Indigenous healing and interconnection with advances in the contemporary science of consciousness. Through this stimulating theoretical analysis, she also clarifies a vital literary context for this book, drawing connections between Silko and N. Scott Momaday, Simon Ortiz, Paula Gunn Allen, Louise Erdrich, Linda Hogan, and others. She shows how *Ceremony* indeed illuminates transitions between Western and Native sciences, as she unravels questions of space–time dynamics, agential realism, and the intrinsic power of compassion in the text. These dynamics move the narrative of healing toward pluralism.

In "The Lost Women of Silko's *Ceremony*," Carolyn Dekker offers a gift of crucial archival scholarship to long-running conversations about *Ceremony* as she reveals and analyzes an unpublished manuscript in the Silko papers at the Beinecke Library and compares it to the published novel. As she dug into Silko's papers, Dekker found more than what Silko herself had referred to as "notes and false starts" of a "stillborn novel" that preceded *Ceremony*. As Dekker explains, the "150 holograph and typescript pages surviving in the collection of Yale's Beinecke Library yield considerably more interest than is implied under the heading of 'notes and false starts.'" Not only is the manuscript set in Albuquerque, Gallup and Laguna; not only does it work out key themes; not only does it establish the form that she ultimately uses in *Ceremony*, that is, the famous structure of the novel *as a ceremony*; and not only is it built around a mixed-race protagonist, Angelina or Angie; but also the fact that the draft protagonist is a woman, also in need of a healing ceremony, provides perspectives on gender issues that have been circulating about the final published version.

Through gendered lenses of both the masculine and the feminine, as well as through a certain quantum politics of compassionate pluralism, these three intriguing chapters open new doors into the world of *Ceremony*, one of the major novels of the twentieth century.

References

Gish, R. F. (1999), "Silko's Power of Story," Preface to L. K. Barnett and J. L. Thorson (eds), *Leslie Marmon Silko: A Collection of Critical Essays*, Albuquerque: University of New Mexico Press, pp. vii–xi.

Silko, L. M. (1977), *Ceremony*. New York: Penguin.

1

Healing the "Man of Monstrous Dreams": Indian Masculinities in Silko's *Ceremony*

Kimberly Gail Wieser

Once there had been a man who cursed the rain clouds,
a man of monstrous dreams.

(SILKO, 2006, p. 38)

Introduction: Gender in American Indian Studies versus American Indian realities

Within American Indian Studies (AIS), many scholars have explored Silko's *Ceremony* (considered the most widely studied and taught novel of the American Indian literary renaissance) focusing on gender; among them are Paula Gunn Allen, Edith Swan, Susan Castillo, Judith Antell, and myself. While males are certainly mentioned in this criticism, only Swan in "Laguna Prototypes of Manhood in *Ceremony*" and Thomas Lynch in "What Josiah Said: Uncle Josiah's Role in *Ceremony*" have explored masculinities in *Ceremony* to any real degree. In response, this article focuses specifically on Indian masculinities in *Ceremony*, attempting to take a pragmatic approach toward healing for American Indian men and their relationships with women and other men, drawing on Sam McKegney's *Masculindians: Conversations about Indigenous Manhood* and on Eduardo and Bonnie Duran's *Native American Postcolonial Psychology*, among other studies.

Despite problematic depictions of males in *Ceremony*, most of the writing on gender, including my own, has overwhelmingly focused on female characters and the Feminine, perhaps because of the huge impact of Silko's cousin, the late Paula Gunn Allen, on American Indian literary studies and on AIS in general, with her foundational Red Feminist text *The Sacred Hoop: Recovering the Feminine in American Indian Traditions* in 1992—a significant year for AIS, the five-hundredth year of European occupation of these lands. Moreover, Allen also published an early article on *Ceremony*, "The Feminine Landscape of Leslie Marmon Silko's *Ceremony*" (1983). Currently, though, in the development of our field, as we attempt, in Craig Womack's words, "to mature as a discipline," we, to my mind, ought to consider the impact of Allen's work. She has perhaps inordinately given our field so much of a focus on women's and Two-Spirit issues, as we examine gender and its intersections with oppression, that it has elided study of the impact of colonization on the gendering of straight males. While certainly anthropology and history long-focused the colonial lens on heterosexual American Indian males for the purpose of scrutinizing, dichotomizing, dissevering, and controlling notions of who these men were and *are* in a manner supporting the ongoing paracolonial occupation of these lands, in ways that objectify and, in fact, disempower, our male relatives, AIS as a discipline has largely failed to do the same kind of counteractive, empowering, emancipatory, and decolonizing gender study that we have done in reaction to the historical and ongoing oppression of females and LGBTQI community members. As Sam McKegney says:

> Although Indigenous feminist and queer/Two-Spirit theories have effectively destabilized biological determinism and recovered the fluidity of gender concepts within many Indigenous worldviews, these theories have tended to retain a celebratory posture toward the feminine that has not been shared in their discursive engagements with the masculine. (2014, p. 8)

In part, this phenomenon is understandable considering the statistically horrifying conditions that surround women and LGBTQI people as vulnerable segments of our communities. According to the Indian Law Resource Center,

> Indian women are 2½ times more likely to be assaulted and more than twice as likely to be stalked than other women in this country. Today, one in three Native women will be raped in her lifetime, and six in ten will be physically assaulted. Even worse, on some reservations, the murder rate for Native women is ten times the national average.

Two-Spirit American Indian women seem to be at particular risk for sexual violence. According to the National Indian Country Clearing House on Sexual Assault,

> American Indian/Alaska Native LGBTQI women... suffer some of this nation's highest rates of sexual violence. In a recent study of 152 American Indian/Alaska Native Two-Spirit women, 85 percent reported being sexually assaulted at least once during their lifetimes.

However, the lack of focus on heterosexual American Indian males in American Indian literary studies is also perhaps due to an anger no one wants to discuss regarding the degree of overt and observable lateral racism directed at American Indian women and Two-Spirits by some straight Indian men. While an estimated 70–88 percent of violence against American Indian women is perpetrated by non-Indians, many of them domestic partners, the remaining 12–30 percent of the violence American Indian women experience is enacted by Indians, many of them male, many of them intimate partners or spouses. As Louise Bernice Halfe (Cree) suggests, the loss of men's traditional roles due to colonization and ongoing oppression leads to "rage" that "accumulates and the closest place that they have to expel that rage is within their immediate family. It becomes internalized. That family violence becomes laterally projected within the community" (McKegney, 2014, pp. 53–54). Statistics regarding the violence that impacts American Indian/ Alaska Native LGBTQI women are even more telling in regard to Indigenous male-enacted sexual violence in the community:

"Seventy-four percent of the perpetrators of this sexual violence were family members or acquaintances. Thirty-eight percent of the surveyed Two-Spirit AI/AN women reported experiencing both physical and sexual assaults by both strangers and family members" (The National Indian Country Clearing House on Sexual Assault).

Yet, as with other populations, one of the things we know about perpetrators is that they are generally also victims. Much of this sexual violence, in fact, can be attributed directly or indirectly to boarding/residential school trauma.[1] Duran and Duran's *Native American Postcolonial Psychology* explains that the result of government- and church-run Indian boarding/residential schools:

> was the systematic destruction of the Native American family system under the guise of educating Native Americans in order to assimilate them as painlessly as possible into Western society, while at the same time inflicting a wound to the soul of the Native American people that is felt in agonizing proportions to this day. (1995, p. 27)

Basil H. Johnston (Anishinaabe) claims children "were made to feel unwanted…never hugged, never caressed when they wept, never told 'I love you…'." There were "students who were violated, students who were raped by their own kind, by older Native students, fifteen or sixteen, and by the priests immediately after mass, by brothers in the various workplaces." He continues:

> Abuse is too mild a word. It is a violation of the worst kind. It violates not only the body, but also the spirit. And you live with this fear of death and fear of being dispatched to Hell. And I thought, and many of us thought, that we were the only victims. (McKegney, 2014, p. 42)

Even many who did not experience abuse in boarding schools directly are indirectly impacted by intergenerational trauma (Duran and Duran, 1995, pp. 30–35).

For this reason and more, discussing American Indian perpetrated domestic and/or sexual violence can feel disloyal to family and community; many American Indian women feel that people in the mainstream will perceive American Indian men on the whole negatively, despite the many, many good men in our communities, if we publically address these issues. We fear, rather than change and healing taking place, stereotypes will be reinforced and racist attitudes will be perpetuated. Speaking out is complicated for those who have been victimized. Addressing abuse and violence is painful; a collective shame arises due to the interwoven American Indian sense of identity we have with our families and communities—if one of us can do this, we all feel mortified and embarrassed. Moreover, because of our love for our imbalanced relative, we also feel great pity for that person. Discussing the brokenness at all, much less with anyone outside of the situation or, worse, outside of the community, seems like the last thing anyone would want to do from many American Indian perspectives. But as Richard Van Camp (Tlicho Dene First Nations) says of this domestic violence and abuse, "If we're not talking about it, it's killing us and it's wounding us and it's harming us" (McKegney, 2014, p. 189). We can no longer ignore Indian masculinities as we discuss gender in the academy if we wish our work to be in line with the needs of the community—communities do not heal if we isolate individuals from families, if we do not recognize that the trauma experienced by American Indian women and LGBTQI community members is part and parcel of the same trauma cycle American Indian straight males are caught within. As Bonita Lawrence says, "Empowerment for women means…we need to talk about empowering our men" (McKegney, 2014, p. 6).

American Indian men are *part of* their families, communities, and nations, and these families, communities, and *nations* have been the victims of violence. As the US Department of the Interior Indian Affairs Victim Services suggests in regard to statistics on Indian women,

> In looking at this information, it is important to view violence against Native American women as a continuum of crime—crime experienced from birth through death. Babies hear the domestic violence in the home, and are assaulted or abused; children are molested, beaten, neglected and abused; teens suffer date rape or date violence; young women are raped, abused or assaulted; married women suffer all forms of domestic violence and sexual assault; and seniors face elder abuse and financial fraud.

According to the US Department of Justice "Special Report: Hate Crime Victimization, 2003–2011," American Indians, male and female alike, are second only to people of two or more ethnicities in being the victims of hate crimes, crimes that are roughly twice as likely statistically to be based on race rather than on sexual orientation or gender. Moreover, on the whole, American Indians are, according to the Bureau of Justice Statistics report "American Indians and Crime," twice as likely as the national average to be the victims of violent crimes in general. In particular, Indian men are subject to violence by the state, in part due to what Sam McKegney calls the projection of "hypermasculine stereotypes of the noble savage and the bloodthirsty warrior (as well as their ideological progeny—the ecological medicine man, the corrupt [tribal] councilor, and the drunken absentee)" (2014, p. 1). In regard to how they are perceived by mainstream society, stereotypes such as these also serve as an excuse by the dominant culture for their historical elimination of Indian men and for eliminating Indian men today— justifying violence against them. Taiaiake Alfred (Mohawk) says, "There's no living with it [these hypermasculine stereotypes] because it's not meant to be lived with; it's meant to be killed, every single time. They're images to be slain by the white conqueror" (McKegney, 2014, p. 79). Consequently, American Indian males are those *most* likely to be killed by law enforcement, according to the Center on Juvenile and Criminal Justice, as Indians comprise only 0.8 percent of the population, but 1.9 percent of police killings.[2] Just as the hypersexualization of Indian/First Nations/Chicana women by mainstream society has served as an excuse to enact violence upon Indigenous female bodies from Canada to Mexico, stereotypes of Indian men have increased their risk for being the victims of violence from the state both historically and today. If we are *all* at risk, both inside of our homes and communities and out, then we must first find healing within ourselves, our families, and our communities in order to draw upon our common strength to impact and change the world. Community healing, by its very nature, must be inclusive of straight Indian males. Traditionally, they are our providers and protectors. Otherwise, too many of them will never fulfill these roles in healthy ways, and without that the rest our communities cannot heal.

Traditional Laguna manhood

The work done on masculinity in *Ceremony* has rightly centered on the convergence of gender and ethnicity, gendering being a culturally bound concept governing roles and relationships. In Laguna tradition, Josiah and Rocky as well as Josiah and Tayo are *anawe*. According to Swan:

> the maternal uncle possesses the male jural role for the matriline. Prior to marriage, a man stays with his sister(s) and mother; afterwards, he leave[s] his wife's house periodically return[ing] to his natal family … to execute obligations due his maternal kinfolk. He has authority over the children of his sister rather than his own biological offspring, who in turn belong to the clan of his wife. There they would fall under the jurisdiction of her brother, his brother-in-law. To his sister's children, mother's brother is their primary teacher, guardian and disciplinarian; he is the source of their inheritance, makes arrangements for their marriages, and has responsibility for collecting the brideprice for his nephews' marriages. (Swan, 1991–1992, pp. 40–41)

In rearing the boys, Josiah is being a good Laguna man. Regardless of Laura and Thelma's neglect of Tayo, Josiah does his job well, not begrudgingly. He teaches the boys what they need to know in order to fulfill their obligations to family through both transmitting oral traditions and through leading the boys in experiential learning. Lynch says that the overt focus on the feminine in previous studies on *Ceremony* has unfairly shifted focus away from Josiah, the fine job he does with his nephews, and the central role his teachings and stories play in Tayo's healing (1996, p. 138).

While Lynch points out more general life lessons that impart the wisdom needed to carry Tayo (or almost anyone) through life, here, for our purposes, the focus is on lessons that specifically guide Tayo and were intended to guide Rocky into being balanced Laguna male relatives. Three expressions of masculinity normalized for Laguna men of his time are mentioned heavily in the text: hunting deer; raising livestock (both of which have to do with providing for the natal family of female relatives to whom Laguna males are traditionally obligated); and interacting with nonrelative females as potential sexual partners. The word "hunt" is mentioned fifty times in *Ceremony*, "deer" fifty-three times, giving this more significance than we might have thought. Josiah teaches the boys the proper Laguna way men have traditionally provided for families for millennia, hunting respectfully. Tayo makes this clear in the scene where he and Rocky approach a deer they have shot: "He approached the deer slowly ... it was so beautiful that he could only stand and feel the presence of the deer; he knew what they said about the deer was true" (Silko, 2006, p. 50). When Rocky begins to clean the deer with what is disrespect from a Laguna perspective, Tayo removes his jacket to cover the deer's head, knowing Rocky knows just as well as he why he is doing this. Laguna cultural practice dictates this out of respect for the animal. This is reaffirmed by Josiah and Robert, who

> went to the deer and lifted the jacket. They knelt down and took pinches of cornmeal from Josiah's leather pouch. They sprinkled the cornmeal on the nose and fed the deer's spirit. They had to show their love and respect, their appreciation; otherwise, the deer would be offended, and they would not come to die for them the following year. Rocky turned away from them and poured water from the canteen over his bloody hands ... embarrassed at what they did. He knew when they took the deer home, it would be laid out on a Navajo blanket, and Old Grandma would put a string of turquoise around its neck and put silver and turquoise rings around the tips of the antlers. Josiah would prepare a little bowl of cornmeal and place it by the deer's head so that anyone who went near could leave some on the nose. (Silko, 2006, pp. 51–52)

Rocky, however, no longer believes in these cultural practices and makes a half-hearted argument for the non-Native practice of curing the meat by hanging it in a shed made frigid by the winter weather where it can "stay cold and cure properly," knowing his relatives would be unwilling to change their traditional ways in regard to hunting (p. 52). Rocky's identification with his teachers' Western scientific perspective makes him skeptical of his *anawe*'s ways of providing meat for their family and of showing the deer respect as a living entity and relative so that the deer will continue to offer itself in sacrifice that the people might live.

Prior to the war, Josiah had taught Rocky and Tayo how to adjust their Laguna ideals of manhood to the needs of changing times and yet support their family in a way grounded in tradition, which I define here as I do in my classroom as "continuity plus change in balance." In keeping with this paradigm, Josiah carefully breeds cattle he sees as both having land tenure from their ancestors, "the Mexican cattle," and other favorable characteristics from the cattle that are newcomers to the region: "Josiah said they would grow up heavy and covered with meat like Herefords, but tough too, like the Mexican cows, able to withstand hard winters and many dry years" (Silko, 2006, p. 80). However, Rocky's internalized "white ways"[3] also make him skeptical of his uncle's ideas about providing for the family even through the comparatively new method of raising livestock. The fact that the word "cattle" is mentioned one hundred times in *Ceremony*, "cow" forty-three times, and "sheep" fifty-one times shows the magnitude of this cultural adaptation to survival at Laguna. Raising livestock has become one of the most important roles of a Laguna man.

Both the Army recruiter's rhetoric and Rocky's confuse Tayo about his male duties. The recruiter's appeal to the "boys love [for] America," his promise of equal opportunity for positions such as pilots with great mainstream masculine cultural capital, and his very calling them "men" (Silko, 2006, pp. 64–65) are too much for Rocky to pass up, as Thelma groomed him to seek mainstream affirmation of his manhood. Rocky adds to this already persuasive rhetoric, calling Tayo a "brother" for the first time, making Tayo feel obligated.[4] After Rocky talks Tayo into signing to join the Army, Tayo remembers, "The understanding had always been that Rocky would be the one to leave home... But someone had to stay and help out with the garden and sheep camp. He had made a promise to Josiah to help with the Mexican cattle" (Silko, 2006, p. 72). Tayo had "felt proud when Josiah talked about cattle business. He was ready to work hard with his uncle... He was graduating in a month, and then he would work with Josiah and Robert (Silko, 2006, p. 74). Faced with conflicting notions of masculine obligations, Tayo promises Thelma, "I'll bring [Rocky] back safe" (Silko, 2006, p. 73), resulting in Tayo's feeling that he failed to achieve manhood on more than one level after he returns alone from the war.

Josiah also teaches Tayo to respect women's sexuality and bodily sovereignty through sexual initiation with Night Swan, whom Edith Swan suggests, drawing on Elsie Clews Parsons, "Laguna social mores" would have recognized as Josiah's wife, naiya to Tayo, had Josiah lived, appropriate in "the logic of matrilineal categories...without the negative overlay of western interpretation" of "apparent incest" (1992, p. 312). Swan claims Josiah negotiates this liaison appropriately as anawe to the boy (1992, pp. 314). Carolyn Niethammer explains in Hopi culture (related to Laguna and other Pueblo cultural groups), paternal aunts were often sexual partners with their nephews during the boys' puberty (1977, p. 211). Night Swan, Mexican like the cattle from her "cousin in Sonora" (Silko, 2006, p. 89), symbolizes the change that colonization makes unavoidable as things "Mexican" in this text quite often do, providing Tayo with sexual initiation in the absence of paternal aunts via his missing white father. While others disrespect Night Swan, Tayo approaches her sacred femininity in awe. The rigidly Catholic Hispanic women of Cubero malign her, threatened by her independent sexuality (Silko, 2006, pp. 87–88). Old grandma and auntie oppose her threat to Josiah's freedom to fulfill his responsibilities to his "natal" family as a good Laguna man should (Swan, 1991–1992, pp. 40–41). However, despite misunderstanding and resentment, Night Swan is sure of her status, demands respect, and has formerly refused objectification by a lover, literally dancing him to death, his horses responding to her ritual much as the weather responds to Ts'eh's (Silko, 2006, pp. 84–87). Before Tayo's encounter with Night Swan, he appeals to Spider Woman for rain (Silko, 2006, pp. 93–94). Oandasan notes that "by sowing plants and casting pollen upon the water, [Tayo] participates with the feminine sources of regeneration" (1993, p. 242). The liaison between Tayo and Night Swan (Silko, 2006, p. 96) is as much a result of his prayers as the rain is.

Rocky, however, rejects the guidance of Josiah, who would traditionally teach him to be a man as opposed to his father. Rocky is killed by trying to be a "good" man in the Western sense because of his mother's own imbalanced behavior from a Laguna perspective. If Rocky lived through the war, he would have been very frustrated by life with opportunity not nearly what his mother visualized. The era after the Second World War, after all, was the era of the American Dream, where white soldiers returned from war, got jobs, married, bought houses, had two children, put televisions in their households, and bought cars. By and large, these weren't opportunities open to American Indian men of that time, whether they remained home on reservations/tribal land or migrated to the city. In fact, the Relocation Era that shortly followed the Second World War proved this lack of opportunity. "The National Survey of Indian Vietnam Veterans" conducted by Tom Holm, Cherokee scholar and veteran, along with Harold Barse, Kiowa/Sisseton Sioux veteran, and Frank Montour, a veteran's center counselor from Lincoln Park, Michigan, confirms how this pattern continued for a later generation:

> For a significant number of Indian veterans the return to the United States was not what they had expected...If they sought acceptance by whites, they were disappointed. If they thought military service would bring them opportunity, they discovered it had only lowered their status within the American mainstream...In addition, despite the fact that many of them achieved relatively high educational levels after their military service, 46% remain unemployed. (Holm, 1994, pp. 24, 21)

When Rocky thought he "understood what he had to do to win in the white outside world," he was simply wrong, as Thelma had been wrong when she thought she was teaching him "what white people wanted in an Indian" (Silko, 2006, p. 51). In short, she sets him up for failure when she dissuades him from listening to his uncle. Although Rocky encourages him otherwise, Tayo is the one who internalizes what Josiah teaches, and he heals himself by following in Josiah's footsteps, acting as a "good" Laguna man to his relatives and in regard to his interactions with women outside of the family. First, however, he must survive a world of monsters.

Emasculation through colonization: Becoming "monstrous"

Carl Jung says in *The Psychology of the Unconscious*:

> It is a frightening thought that man also has a shadow side to him, consisting not just of little weaknesses and foibles, but of a positively demonic dynamism...But let these harmless creatures form a mass, and there emerges a raging monster. (1912, p. 35)

The notion of the monster is universal. From academic and Western mainstream perspectives, monsters are a metaphor for the dark side of the self and the ways in which darkness can escape the ego to manifest in individual and group violence. Our preoccupation with monsters of myths, fairytales, and movies is a way of exploring aspects of the self that are less savory or socially acceptable through worlds of "make-believe," a way of utilizing universal archetypes to avoid directly confronting warped, deformed, hideous, grotesque, frightening, violent aspects of human nature. Stories of monsters permeate Indian Country, as they do Western traditions. However, from traditional Native perspectives, these stories are our way of defining relationships to the *very real* rather than the archetypal; in Indian Country, ideas spoken become manifest, tangible. My Blackfoot relatives from Kainai and Piikani have stories of an old lady dragging her intestines behind her and eating children. They also see Bigfoot—whom my Comanche relatives call "Moopiits"— known by many tribal names. There are many varieties of "monstrous" creatures known to Indian people, most of whose names I won't even *write* despite the fact that I know them because I certainly don't wish to call them up.

My Cheyenne grandfather, Eugene Blackbear, Sr., used to tell a story about "Two-Face Man" that lived south of "Thomas, Weatherford, [Oklahoma,] kind of south-southeast from there. There's three little mountains, look like peaks, close toward the South Canadian River" around 1920. Some Cheyennes were camping in large groups still at that time, and a few women, curious, "got some calico, and they got some tobacco, and they went over there and took some gifts, to this place that was designated, where this monster had lived." The monster, wanting to be left alone, was angered, and attacked the camp. The people, fearful, all gathered in the tent of a medicine man, seeking advice from the Badger Spirit, who had pity on them, telling them to ask the Thunder Spirit to defend them. He drove the monster away, but while the people were fleeing the camp, a small girl fell:

> When she hit the ground, I guess she died. And they just left her there. What they should have done is they should have picked her up and carried her and buried her over there somewhere. But they left her body there. Maybe that monster could get her and

eat her or whatever. Anyway they left that little body there, that little girl's body.

This story bears a number of parallels to depictions of the monstrous in *Ceremony*. Most notably, when community is confronted with the monstrous, a girl ends up inadvertently sacrificed; something once pure, unsullied, and beautiful is left behind for the beast to consume, or in Laura/Reed Woman's case and the case of Helen Jean among others, for the beast to copulate with in a most objectifying manner—the female equated with territory in a cross-cultural alpha male battle for dominance. It is through such coupling that another parallel emerges as Laura gestates the offspring of the beast:

> The feelings of shame, at her own people and at the white people, grew inside her, side by side like monstrous twins that would have to be left in the hills to die. The people wanted her back. Her older sister must bring her back. For the people, it was that simple, and when they failed, the humiliation fell on all of them; what happened to the girl did not happen to her alone, it happened to all of them. (Silko, 2006, p. 69)

Tayo here not only becomes the culture hero whom Robert Nelson equates with one who will save his "mother"/Reed Woman (2008, pp. 4, 68–70), but also becomes "shame," twinned and personified. This twinning of shame, too, parallels not only the Two-Faced Man story above, but also functions particularly well to describe Tayo's condition. Duran and Duran say that "shame is akin to existential death" within the warrior tradition (1995, p. 39). As a Laguna man, Tayo is living with two significant instances of shame because of dual defeats—colonization and his failure to protect his brother Rocky in a war that falls outside of the parameters of his responsibility as a traditional Laguna man. According to Duran and Duran,

> defeat has deep psychological ramifications...even greater [because] the colonizer imposes a diametrically opposed mythology on the people and also on the land that the warriors are supposed to keep safe and alive within the traditional tribal worldview. Add to this the destruction of men's roles

in the traditional economy and you have men divested of meaningful cultural roles…a deep psychological trauma of identity loss occurs…The fact that the conquerors remain is a continual source of aggravation and hostile feelings…feelings of helplessness and hopelessness are compounded to such a degree as to make the choice complete psychosis or splitting of the ego into at least two fragments. The split ego, then, will keep one aspect of the person in touch with the pain and one aspect identifying with the aggressor…This identification with the aggressor by Native American men is of a quality that has as a core a desire to gain the aggressor's power…At a deep level the acquisition of the aggressor's power has the ultimate goal of destroying the aggressor and restoring the community to a pre-colonized lifeworld. Because removal of the colonial forces is not realized, the repressed rage has no place for cathexis except to turn on itself. (1995, pp. 35–37)

Both of these twin states are manifested in the male characters in the novel—a split identity that can flip in an instant to become psychosis. Identification with the aggressor in the world of this novel translates into identification with the destroyers and witchery, not merely settler-colonialism, characterized as the simple by-product of a greater evil: "white people are only tools that the witchery manipulates" (Silko, 2006, p. 132).

Exposure to Western styles of warfare as an inappropriate and in fact toxic substitute for the lost role of traditional warrior ways seems to be the greatest common denominator in making these male characters monstrous. After all, neither Emo, Pinkie, Leroy, nor Harley is characterized as a "half-breed…[w]hite son of a bitch," as Tayo is (Silko, 2006, p. 252). Tayo's monstrosity, predicted because of his paternity and the circumstances surrounding his conception, actually comes to fruition through his military experience, not because he is half-white. In what traditionally should have been his passage into manhood, his "quest" to bring something good back for his people, his first journey into the underworld of warfare, Tayo becomes instead the "man who cursed the rain clouds," someone who deprives his people of their basic needs by his actions. Duran and Duran explain that transgressing one's cultural ways and values is a way of causing illness to the self in American Indian worldviews (1995, pp. 20–21). In despair, Tayo defaults to internalized mainstream cultural values, acting against the Laguna teachings of his uncle. In doing so, Tayo becomes the "man of monstrous dreams" (Silko, 2006, p. 38), on the verge of becoming the foretold offspring of the beast rather than a son of the People. This monstrosity would be because of his direct exposure to witchery through Western warfare, through the rendering of humans into things in acts of unnatural, imbalanced violence without virtue. Furthermore, the "medicine" that creates the darkest power of this evil war is made through the rape of Tayo's homeland, an act we must equate with the taking of territory and women by colonialism:

> The gray stone was streaked with powdery yellow uranium, bright and alive as pollen; veins of sooty black formed lines with the yellow... But they had taken these beautiful rocks from deep within earth and they had laid them in a monstrous design, realizing destruction on a scale only they could have dreamed. (Silko, 2006, p. 246)

In mainstream warfare, men are "toy" soldiers, objectified and controlled by their "superiors," not autonomous warriors fighting battles of their own choosing. Men are "things," considered both disposable and interchangeable.

When Ku'oosh attempts to heal Tayo, he is completely unaware of these differences. Traditional warfare meant hand to hand combat in which the warrior knew whether or not he had killed his enemy just as a hunter knew he had killed an animal as prey. Soldiers in mainstream modern warfare

> kill[ed] across great distances without knowing who or how many had died... the old man would not have believed anything so monstrous. Ku'oosh would have looked at the dismembered corpses and the atomic heat-flash outlines, where human bodies had evaporated, and the old man would have said something close and terrible had killed these people. Not even oldtime witches killed like that. (Silko, 2006, pp. 36–37)

After his return to the States, Tayo is hospitalized for psychosis, which Duran and Duran say can emerge from fractured identity in taking on the role of the aggressor. Moreover, even after Tayo is released from hospital and returns home, he and Harley fail

miserably at taking care of sheep when their families give them
what they perceive as easier jobs. They both return home suffering
from posttraumatic stress disorder, making them less effective male
relatives. They have no useful roles in their families.

Learning to objectify themselves and other men on and off of the
battlefield, they are also bad relatives to each other. While each of
the men is guilty of this to varying degrees, Emo epitomizes those
who internalize the aggressor. Emo, a witch, "reverses and twists
the teachings and beliefs of his people" (Silko, 2006, p. 247). He
"liked what they showed him…some men didn't like to feel the
quiver of the man they were killing; some men got sick when they
smelled the blood" (Silko, 2006, p. 62). Emo's monstrosity leads to
his dark ritual with the teeth he took from the Japanese soldier, his
"war souvenirs," with which he calls up darkness and bad things
for his people (Silko, 2006, pp. 60–61). Ultimately, this behavior
is what leads to his fighting with Tayo (Silko, 2006, p. 53) and to
Emo's witchery at the end of the book as he leads Leroy and Pinkie
to sacrificially mutilate Harley, then turns on them as well (Silko,
2006, pp. 250–253).

Having been made monstrous through the process of internalizing
settler-colonial values, these veterans express their brokenness in
their interactions with each other and their families. Moreover, they
have tried to remake themselves as simulations of white men to
avoid feeling like "things" themselves while objectifying nonrelative
women in general:

> One time there were these Indians, see. They put on uniforms, cut
> their hair. They went off to a big war. They had a real good time
> too. Bars served them booze, old white ladies on the street smiled
> at them…These Indians fucked white women, they had as much
> as they wanted too. They were MacArthur's boys; white whores
> took their money same as anyone. (Silko, 2006, pp. 41–42)

The very language used to describe these women objectifies them:
Tayo's "blond girl" (Silko, 2006, p. 41), Harley's "two blondes in
bed with him" (Silko, 2006, p. 43), the "blond cunt," which is equal
in importance only with "the cold beer" (Silko, 2006, p. 42). Emo
tells this story about himself and his Army buddy O'Shay going into
a bar, loosening up with "a few drinks," then approaching "two
white women" who were "alone":

> One was kind of fat
> She had dark hair.
> But this other one, man,
> She had big tits and
> real blond hair.
> I said to him.
> "Hey buddy, that's the one I want.
> Over there."
> He said, "Go get 'em, Chief"...
> The fat girl had a car,
> I sat in the middle, grabbing titties
> with both hands...
> Yes, sir, this In'di'n
> was grabbin' white pussy
> all night. (Silko, 2006, pp. 57–59)

The terms the veterans use internalize white culture and destroyer mind-sets. These relationships shame both men and women. Even Emo is embarrassed about the time he had "a titty in [his] mouth," and a white man yelled "Geronimo!"—because the white woman in bed with him figured out he was an Indian and fainted (Silko, 2006, p. 60). In this situation, he too is transformed by the word into an object—an "Indian," rather than a "man." This imbalanced sexual behavior is neither isolated to this text nor the time period it represents. If anything, in reality today things are worse. Van Camp notes that "really demeaning, humiliating, gruesome" websites are where "many of our male youth are learning about sex now. That it has to be something that's punishing or it has to be power over someone or it has to be humiliating or women are meant to be objectified" (McKegney, 2014, p. 189). Our communities, like the one in this novel, need healing.

Tayo's path to healing

Healing community starts with healing relationships between individuals and the Earth. To do this in the novel, Tayo has to realize his own agency, must take control of the narrative he is living. He must realize he is not the "thing" white men have made him out to be. Neither is he the brown white man that boarding school tried to make him into. Tayo must counteract the story of the destroyers by choosing instead to return to living the story of the People. Like generations of culturally Laguna men before him, Tayo must continually redefine the action of his very "being," what it means to be a Laguna man, to be *hadztse*, in Keresan terms. As Duran and Duran point out, American Indian traditional ways are "a systematic approach to being in the world…" a process of "thinking, as opposed to the content thinking" of mainstream culture (1995, p. 15). In the process of being Laguna again, Tayo not only takes up manhood that Josiah modeled to him, taking care of his maternal family through caring for livestock, going on the mountain in his quest, but he also returns to their traditional model of hunting—coming into contact with one of the Laguna archetypes of masculinity, Mountain Lion, the prototypical hunter. Tayo becomes a traditional warrior fighting on his own land for that land and for the people who belong to that place when he takes on the Texans.

Janice C. Hill Kanonhsyonni (Mohawk) suggests missing rites of passage for American Indian young men today contribute to an inability to see themselves as men: "If they're not provided with the ceremony and the understanding that it is time for them to move into the next stage of life…we have grown men who are really like babies" (McKegney, 2014, p. 19). Tayo enacts for himself new rites of passage after Betonie guides him through what I describe elsewhere as a symbolic re-entering of the womb and rebirth (Wieser, 2002, p. 74). He comes of age as a man again through encounters with Ts'eh, his entry into sacred space of Tse-pi'na, Mt. Taylor, and in his victory over the Texans and retaking of his family's cattle, thus his entry into the proper sphere of warfare. Through this course of action—ceremony— Tayo joins the healed, the mature, what Thomas Yeahpau (Kiowa) calls in *X-Indian Chronicles: The Book of Mausaupe*, "the man clan" and what Van Camp calls "the Tribe of Man," effectively reversing the process of assimilation regarding his gendered behavior. He does this by returning to traditional teachings, rejecting imbalanced dominant culture worldviews imposed on him through schooling and his experiences in the hegemonic warfare of the outside world. Lynch says, "In learning how to heal himself and how to properly function as a man in gynocentric Laguna culture, Tayo's most valuable guide is his uncle Josiah" (1996, p. 139). Rejecting the predictions regarding his birth, he does not have to be monstrous: Tayo is not destined to be his father's son. As a Laguna man, he is the cultural offspring of his *anawe*, Josiah.

Josiah has taught Tayo to be provider and protector, to respect women's sexuality and bodily sovereignty, and that part of being a man is balancing within oneself some qualities usually associated with the Feminine, nurturing others and being responsible for bearing culture. Duran and Duran say,

> The regression of tradition in the [American Indian paracolonial] male has been based on the male's inability to become pregnant. Since humans interpret psychological and spiritual reality through physical perception, the issue of pregnancy or the carrying and giving of life becomes symbolically important. If we accept that males can be psychologically and spiritually pregnant, then we can expect the male to carry and give birth to the spiritual life in the community. (1995, pp. 37–38)

Tayo's symbolic pregnancy with this story at the beginning of the novel represents the fact that his culture has been born to him by Josiah—he indeed does carry within him the ability not only to heal and rebalance himself, but also to pass that healing and balance on to others. With the absence of physical offspring in the text, we can only read ourselves, the readers, as the inheritors of the story that he births. Through Silko's midwifery, we ourselves are reborn through our processing of this text as Tayo is when he emerges from Betonie's ceremony. It is up to us to engage in our own healing relationships based in our own balanced ways, grounded in our own traditions. We only have to "remember the story" (Silko, 2006, p. 102).

Notes

1   This policy was adopted by both Canada and the United States, with "boarding schools" referring to the experiences of American Indians and "residential schools" referring to the experiences of First Nations people.

2   According to the US Department of Justice report "Policing and Homicide," the overwhelming majority of victims of police shootings are male for all groups.

3   "Ways" is the colloquial term used widely among American Indians
     to describe particular tribal or individual behaviors consistent with
     one's belief and value system as the outward manifestations of
     philosophical and spiritual constructs and are inclusive of daily life
     behaviors, rituals, and ceremonies. Following "ways" leads to living
     in balance and achieving healing.
4   Though the text makes it clear Rocky has not done this because
     Thelma actively discouraged it (p. 65). The reader needs to be aware
     that Rocky's not calling Tayo brother is alienating behavior in social
     context of Indian Country. Cousins are considered brothers and
     sisters almost everywhere, much more first cousins who were reared
     together in Laguna culture. Moreover, even close friends are often
     taken as siblings.

References

Allen, P. G. (1983), "The Feminine Landscape of Leslie Marmon Silko's
    Ceremony," in P. G. Allen (ed.), *Studies in American Indian Literature:
    Critical Essays and Course Designs*. New York: Modern Language
    Association, pp. 127–133.
Allen, P. G. (1992), *The Sacred Hoop: Recovering the Feminine in
    American Indian Traditions*. Boston: Beacon Press.
Blackbear, E., Sr. and Gail Wieser, K. (2008), *Heóevékése: The Life of
    Yellow Bird, Eugene Blackbear, Sr*. Unpublished manuscript.
Center on Juvenile and Criminal Justice (2014), "Who are police
    killing?" [Online] http://www.cjcj.org/news/8113 [Accessed:
    February 2, 2015].
Duran, E. and Duran, B. (1995), *Native American Postcolonial
    Psychology*. New York: SUNY Press.
Holm, T. (1994), "The National Survey of Indian Vietnam Veterans."
    American Indian and Alaska Native Mental Health Research, 6:1,
    18–28.
Indian Law Resource Center (2010), "Violence against Native women
    gaining global attention," [Online] http://www.indianlaw.org
    /safewomen/violence-against-native-women-gaining-global-attention
    [Accessed: December 18, 2014].
Jung, C. G. (1953), *The Psychology of the Unconscious*, in C. G. Jung,
    The Collected Works, Vol. 7. New York: Pantheon.
Lynch, T. (1996), "What Josiah Said: Uncle Josiah's Role in *Ceremony*."
    North Dakota Quarterly, 63:2, 138–152.
McKegney, S. (2014), *Masculindians: Conversations about Indigenous
    Manhood*. Winnipeg: University of Manitoba Press.

The National Indian Country Clearing House on Sexual Assault (2015), "Traditionally, American Indian/Alaska Native Lesbian, Gay, Bisexual, Transgender, Questioning, and Intersex (LGBTQI) people were held in high esteem by their communities," [Online] http://niccsa.org/lgbtqi/ [Accessed: January 3, 2015].

Nelson, R. M. (2008), *Ceremony: The Recovery of Tradition*. New York: Peter Lang.

Niethammer, C. (1977), *Daughters of the Earth: The Lives and Legends of American Indian Women*. New York: Macmillan.

Oandasan, W. (1993), "A Familiar Component of Love in *Ceremony*," in R. F. Fleck (ed.), *Critical Perspectives on Native American Fiction*. Washington, DC: Three Continents Press, pp. 240–245.

Silko, L. M. (2006), *Ceremony* (Penguin Classics Deluxe Edition). Penguin Group US. Kindle Edition.

Swan, E. (1991–2), "Laguna Prototypes of Manhood in *Ceremony*." *MELUS*, 17:1, 39–61.

Swan, E. (1992), "Feminine Perspectives at Laguna Pueblo: Silko's *Ceremony*." *Tulsa Studies in Women's Literature*, 11:2, 309–327.

US Department of Justice (2013), *Special report: hate crime victimization, 2003–2011*. [Online] http://www.bjs.gov/content/pub/pdf/hcv0311.pdf [Accessed: December, 19 2014].

US Department of Justice, Bureau of Justice Statistics (1999), *American Indians and crime*. [Online] http://bjs.gov/content/pub/pdf/aic.pdf [Accessed: December 19, 2014].

US Department of Justice, Bureau of Justice Statistics (2001), *Policing and homicide*. [Online] http://www.bjs.gov/content/pub/pdf/ph98.pdf [Accessed: February 2, 2015].

US Department of the Interior, Indian Affairs (Bureau of Indian Affairs) (2013), *The honor is to serve: victim services*. [Online] *http://www .bia.gov/WhoWeAre/BIA/OJS/VictimServices/index.htm* [Accessed: December 19, 2014].

Wieser, K. G. (2002), "Sacred Sexuality in Leslie Marmon Silko's *Ceremony*." *Red Ink*, 11:1, 70–77.

Yeahpau, T. (2006), *X-Indian Chronicles: The Book of Mausaupe*. Cambridge: Candlewick Press.

2

"Branched into All Directions of Time": Pluralism, Physics, and Compassion in Silko's *Ceremony*

Mascha N. Gemein

Only humans resisted what they saw outside themselves.
Animals did not resist. But they persisted because they
became part of the wind.

(SILKO, 1977, p. 27)

Ceremony is the first of three novels in which Silko elaborates on webs of identity, storytelling, and self-determination on the one hand, and the pressures and oppression of imperialist ideology on the other. Published in 1977, *Ceremony* also is a testimony of the resurgence of Indigenous literary voices toward a pan-Indian communication about past and present affairs. Importantly, this conversation of political and literary voices contributed to a more inclusive, culturally pluralistic reconsideration of U.S. America's imperial legacy. Some of the themes, motives, and the method of performative writing in *Ceremony* resonate with other contemporary works, for instance the earlier *House Made of Dawn* (1968) by N. Scott Momaday and Gerald Vizenor's *Darkness in Saint Louis Bearheart* (1978) that share the use of a seemingly oral storytelling event as the narrative frame. All three authors emphasize the power of visions and dreams as well as healing through understanding ceremonial principles. Paula Gunn Allen explains that Momaday and Silko's contribution was the exploration of an "Indian consciousness" (Allen, 1992, p. 151), meaning an "achronicity" both within the story and as narrative strategy, which distinguishes them from many earlier Native American novelists. Their works embody what Vizenor has more recently termed "survivance," that is, the survival of Indigenous people and also their resistance to colonial dominance through the continuance of stories, both in their narrative structure and as contributions to a larger intertribal communication: "Native stories are the sources of survivance...prompted by natural reason, by a consciousness and sense of incontestable presence that arises from experiences in the natural world" (Vizenor, 2008, p. 11).

As Elaine Jahner writes, *Ceremony* educates the reader about "not only what happens to Tayo but how and why it happens" (Jahner, 1979, p. 44), thus sharing Laguna tribal perspectives, ethnohistory, and a contemporary assertion of cultural sovereignty. It has been best known for its mythological framework and biocultural outlook on environment, gender, local cultural heritage, and spiritual renewal. The reader "learns to relate myth to immediate action" (p. 44) and may acknowledge the need for new stories, meaning adaptive practical and spiritual approaches. Silko writes that while "the land was telling the stories in the novel," it was "so difficult to convey this relationship without sounding like Margaret Fuller or some other Transcendentalist" (Silko and Wright, 1986, p. 27). This statement illustrates Silko's effort in translating a Laguna ecological and cosmological perspective into effective associations for readers of other ethnic backgrounds without compromising tribal particularities. It also indicates her appreciation for the effect American Transcendentalism has had on Anglo-American biocultural perceptions. Silko's later novel, *Gardens in the Dunes* (1999), is a result of her consideration of American Transcendentalism and her acknowledgment of culturally pluralistic exchange and negotiation. Both *Almanac of the Dead* (1991) with its focus on strategic, heterogeneous alliances and *Gardens in the Dunes* with its exploration of compassion and the historical layers of local cultural heritage provide a fresh context for a rereading of *Ceremony* as more than the popular plot of a mixed-blood or culturally alienated Native character finding fulfillment through the return to his/her tribal worldview. Rather, Silko's first novel anticipates the need for and potential of pluralism, cultural integration, and alliance that are emphasized in her consequent works.

Since much scholarship has explored the cultural matrix of mythological entanglements in *Ceremony*, this chapter will explore how two aspects move beyond and interlock with cultural particulars, namely the roles of space and time and the notion of compassion as the best form of resistance against harmful forces. The multidirectional movement between sky and earth in *Ceremony* relates to the role of gravity in space–time geometry and the possibility of the distortion of space and time, as evidenced by modern physics. Space–time dynamics and the agency of mountains in the novel also relate to the theory of agential realism as formulated by theoretical physicist and philosopher Karen Barad (2007). Finally, recovering space and time from simplified conventions of the dominant society—both through Indigenous and Western science perspectives—allows a constructive, creative approach to history and cultural landscapes.

Silko's concept of witchery stands for the complexity and at times elusiveness of destructive and oppressive structures as experienced through colonization and capitalist, neoliberal globalization. What it takes to loosen this grip of witchery, Silko suggests, is compassion, because compassion drives an individual effort toward change. Silko's novels feature diverse individuals who seek to defy the imperial odds, to survive and thrive despite the powerful, overwhelming presence of colonial legacy and institutionalized ideology. In *Ceremony*, Laguna medicine man Ku'oosh says that "the story behind each word must be told so that there could be no mistake in the meaning of what had been said; and this demanded great patience and love" (pp. 35–36). The novel begins with Thought-Woman and the acknowledgment, "You don't have anything/if you don't have the stories" (p. 2), which refers to the stories of Tayo and historical persons, those who made similar experiences, the old and the contemporary stories of the Laguna people, the stories of Indigenous peoples, and ultimately everyone's stories (Silko, 1997, pp. 49, 52–53). Creative alliances and pluralistic movements require that everyone's story is told and the meanings are mutually understood. Everyone has to recover stories, become compassionate about others and patiently clarify meaning within one's community and across worldviews.

In *Ceremony*, Silko illuminates decolonization within a Laguna framework as a first step toward the more intercultural and global approaches of her later works. *Gardens in the Dunes* relates the cultural histories of places in Europe to Indigenous ones and features culturally and geographically diverse individuals striving for change through compassionate exchange and alliance. *Almanac of the Dead* deals with the development of larger activist groups and alliance formations. Yet Silko does not suggest transnational alliances uncritically; she describes unease among collaborators and strategic alliances that are limited in time and purpose (Ray, 2013, pp. 8–12). The novel illustrates how large movements are inherently pluralistic with ever changing internal dynamics. Ku'oosh's statement above brings that to the point: compassion and care for the right stories and meaningful understanding are prerequisites for pluralist communities within and across cultures that can lead to healing on a larger scale.

Tayo's complicated process of recovery and healing in *Ceremony* illustrates this notion of compassion as the key to larger social change. His mental, emotional, and at times physical resistance against rejection, abandonment, poverty, loss, and trauma initially keeps him too alienated from the ability to experience compassion to find healing by himself or to articulate his internal struggle to others. However, Old Betonie's postcolonial ceremonial practice and Ku'oosh's ability to relate Tayo's ceremonial experiences to Laguna Pueblo cosmology provide the functional structure for Tayo's healing. In turn, female characters evoke Tayo's ability to feel compassion and model a caring and self-determined life for him. Tayo finally grasps why his uncle Josiah said that animals persisted because they did not resist (Silko, 1977, p. 27). He eventually experiences the totality of space and time, understands how the tenets of tribal cosmology apply to his situation, and with that decides to let go of resistance as a forceful reaction. He replaces it with loving care, understanding that creative and constructive action is a better way to persist and weaken the impact of destructive influences.

Between the sky and the earth: Physics and tribal cosmology

Silko's three novels explore possibilities for the initiation of compassion, healing, and meaningful alliance. Due to the deep impact of imperialism on space and time perceptions—place names, for instance, or borders of settler colonial nation-states, and the one-sided control over the interpretation of history—Silko is concerned with these very factors and writes toward compassionate, just, and pluralistic reconsideration. Her approach to adaptive and creative decolonization in recognition of each landscape's pre-imperial cultural heritage applies to all peoples, including those identified as carriers of colonization and corporate globalization.

Cardinal directions in Silko's novels illustrate such inclusive outreach. *Almanac of the Dead* climaxes in a south-north revolutionary movement and transcends time by means of a multilayered map, the "Five Hundred Year Map" of what is now the greater Southwest, and its annotations about Indigenous prophecy and ongoing resistance. As Arnold Krupat has analyzed, the map counters the east-west story of EuroAmerican empire-building in North America and "shifts the axis of *where* is important, thus shifting the axis of *what* is important" (Krupat, 1996, p. 53, emphasis in original). The map is part of a larger movement toward Indigenous mapping, in this case meaning the overall efforts of speakers, writers, and scholars to recover Indigenous conceptualizations of physical and cultural landscapes by emphasizing Indigenous notions of space and time, the ontological characteristics of physical phenomena, and the integration of the history and products of colonization and globalization into Indigenous ontologies.

In turn, *Gardens in the Dunes* reverses the EuroAmerican east-west story with a Native American visiting Europe and more importantly a EuroAmerican recovering and returning to her European homeland. On this occasion, Silko feels the pulse of the Old World back to pre-Roman times. Motives associated with the Ghost Dance connect distant places and ancient peoples whose heritages converge to envision alternative pathways to self-determination. *Ceremony*, in turn, explores the self-contained cosmos "between the sky and the earth" (Silko, 1977, p. 219).

The movement between zenith and nadir is bilateral because Tayo's ceremonial journey follows a star pattern and yet seems characterized by the notion of gravity and grounding. Moreover, Tayo increasingly overcomes the sense of chronological time and with it the fear of absolute loss. Robert M. Nelson (2002) has analyzed the text's intricate connections between places, durations, and mythological points of reference. The convergence of time and space in the novel is indeed characteristic of the motif of ceremonial activity within the tribal cosmos, but it also relates to space–time geometry as presented through the Laguna Pueblo spiritual lens.

Gravity, space, and time depend on each other, as physicists have shown in the twentieth century. In *Ceremony*, Tayo experiences a gravity that pulls him toward earth and the center. In a moment of utter exhaustion, Tayo feels the "magnetism of the center" (Silko 1977, p. 201) and wonders if "he would seep into the earth and rest with the center, where the voice of silence was familiar and the density of the dark earth loved him" (pp. 201–202). With Ts'eh, who reminds Tayo of compassion and lets him recover the feeling of love, Tayo experiences the sense of "gravity emanating from the mesas and arroyos" (p. 227). David L. Moore writes about gravity in *Ceremony* as "the cosmological force of attraction [that] is the energy of identity in Silko's ground" (Moore, 2013, p. 214); the land serves as a literal and cultural ground for identity (p. 211). According to the origin story, the Laguna people emerged from the earth (Silko, 1998, pp. 13–14). The nadir of the Laguna cosmos points toward the space of preemergence, the origin of a people. However, the center of gravity is not just explained through gravity in direction of nadir; zenith is equally significant. Tayo's journey is outlined in the sky, and height seems to elevate his strength. Even before his ceremony formally begins, Tayo feels particularly strong when reaching what seems to be the "highest point of the earth" in the Chuska Mountains (Silko, 1977, p. 139). Jahner has analyzed Tayo's growing attention to his biocultural surroundings, identifying the sunrise after his first meeting with Ts'eh as a first key event of both "convergence and emergence" (Jahner, 1979, p. 38). While one may argue that Tayo's emergence or beginning of his ceremonial journey already took place during Betonie's ritual practice, the notion of convergence is highly useful. At sunrise, Tayo's physical senses are sharpened, and he reaches a state of mindfulness that lets him perceive everything from the stars to the Ka't'sina near the river and his horse's "dim memory of the blood when horses had been wild" (Silko, 1977, p. 183). Tayo is drawn up and across the land as well as back in time. His experience is an embrace of sky and earth, a reintegration into the physical cosmos and tribal cosmology.

The predominant feature of the sky or zenith is the star constellation that is first drawn in the sand by Betonie, who saw it in a vision together with Josiah's cattle, a mountain, and a woman. As will be seen, the constellation functions as a cultural map and also provides practical directional guidance for Tayo's journey and process of healing. Tayo later finds the cattle on Mount Taylor, a sacred mountain for the tribe, and meets the mysterious Ts'eh (p. 152). The star map indeed appears in a picture in Ts'eh's house, and Ts'eh knows about Betonie's vision (pp. 176–179). That night, Tayo also sees the star constellation to the north in the night sky (p. 178), indicating that he should look for the cattle in the north, even though it usually moves southward (pp. 79, 186). Strikingly, a two-dimensional drawing of the stars appears in the text of the novel at this point (p. 179). As the only image in the novel, it emphasizes the importance of the zenith and the notion of mapping in its general sense of spatial orientation and visual representation. It also invites the reader with the book his/her hands into Tayo's ceremonial journey at that point.

Tayo later returns with his truck to pick up the found cattle and finds Ts'eh's house deserted, but an old shield showing the star map was left behind (pp. 214–215). And in the final night of Tayo's ceremony, map stands against map. At the shaft of the old uranium mine, Tayo identifies the "witchery's final ceremonial sand painting" (p. 247). It draws "the lines of cultures and worlds" so that "human beings were one clan again, united by the fate the destroyers planned for all of them" (p. 246). Tayo here understands the connection between uranium mining, the atomic bombs of the nearby Trinity Site, Hiroshima and Nagasaki, and his hallucination of seeing his uncle's face on a Japanese soldier executed during the Second World War. He understands both the Laguna people and the Japanese as victims of a larger scheme of witchery and all people united in the face of destruction via the policies of nation-states. Tayo also identifies Betonie's star map in the night sky and recognizes that he is about to complete his ceremony if he escapes the witches' map:

> But he saw the constellation in the north sky, and the fourth star was directly above him; the pattern of the ceremony was in the stars, and the constellation formed a map of the mountains in the directions he had gone for the ceremony. For each star there was a night and a place. (p. 247)

While Nelson associates the star constellation with a relationship between inner and outer realignment (Nelson, 2002, p. 141), the notion of vertical dynamics and space–time geometry is equally intriguing. The general theory of relativity explains that if one observes an event in the vicinity of a very large mass, the closer to a strong gravitational center the event takes place, the more space and time around it will be distorted. Space is stretched toward the center of gravity, the environment closes in, time slows down, and, at the edge of a black hole, finally even comes to a standstill. These black hole effects, known as the tidal force and time dilation, were predicted a century ago by Albert Einstein and Karl Schwarzschild and are described in accessible form by Al-Khalili (2011, pp. 68–71) and Hawking (2008).

A similar scenario is drawn in Silko's novel as space and time converge. The appearance of the star constellation in two different nights, in a sand painting, as a picture, as an image on a shield, and as part of the publication itself connects and distorts space and time, even beyond the narrative. The stars' appearance through multiple media, at various places, and at different times contributes to a gradual development of a constellation in the sense of a cosmic installation that transcends time and space. The center of gravity in *Ceremony* is not just Earth and its mythological embodiment, but the holistic entity of the Laguna Pueblo cosmos. Tayo's physical movement across the land, the notion of gathering mountains, as will be discussed next, and the feeling that time converges evolve as Tayo comes closer to grasping the tenets of the tribal cosmos, and this process may be associated with a particle moving into a black hole, witnessing space and time distortion.

As mentioned, the mountains play an active role. Beyond their physical features and function as settings for certain action in the novel, the mountains are also part of Betonie's Navajo sand painting and the star map. They thus exist in different dimensions and elevations, actively transcending space between earth and sky, nadir and zenith. Once Tayo fully comprehends the sand painting, he notices that "there were no boundaries ... The mountains from all directions had been gathered there that night" (Silko, 1977, p. 145). Jahner comments on this quotation saying that "time and space, inner and outer come together" (p. 43), but there may be more at work than inner and outer realities. In "Interior and Exterior Landscapes" (1998), Silko writes about the agency of seemingly less animate things in that "rocks and mountains were known on occasion to move" (p. 7). The notion of mountains that gather implies movement and a dynamic toward a center of gravity. It also corresponds to what Barad has termed "agential realism" (Barad, 2007, pp. 132–185), the understanding that everything emerges from "intra-acting agency" (p. 139), that is, from dynamic relationships. Tayo experiences the dynamics of the cosmos, the "ongoing materializing of different space-time typologies" (p. 141) in Barad's words, through the lens of Laguna ontology. Just before Tayo's last encounter with his fellow veterans and the showdown at the uranium mine, he experiences such cosmic agency again:

> All things seemed to converge there ... at that moment in the sunrise, it was all so beautiful, everything, from all directions, evenly, perfectly, balancing day with night, summer months with winter. The valley was enclosing this totality, like the mind holding all thoughts together in a single moment.
> The strength came from here, from this feeling. It had always been there. (Silko, 1977, p. 237)

From within tribal cosmology, Tayo increasingly sees through the network of agencies, of good versus evil forces, of witchery and resistance versus creative adaptation. Barad writes that knowing is "an ongoing performance of the world" (2007, p. 149) that pairs responsiveness and accountability. Tayo begins to realize that he can act upon and change dynamics, rather than just react and reinforce existing agency. Tempted to participate in violence at the uranium mine, he assumes accountability and decides to walk away. His ability to refrain from violent reaction results from experiencing the holistic entity of the cosmos when sky, earth, the mountains, and time converge. Tayo overcomes chronological time toward a more inclusive sense of all time being contained between sky and earth, slowing down as space stretches toward the center of gravity. Allen calls such a phenomenon "achronicity," that is, the "kind of time in which the individual and the universe are 'tight,'" (Allen, 1992, p. 150), where past and future come together. This climax is indicated early on. It starts before Tayo is drafted by the military, when he meets the enigmatic Mexican flamenco dancer Night Swan. As she seduces Tayo, she becomes ageless "like the rain and the wind" (Silko, 1977, p. 98). The ageless appearance elevates her from the boundaries of chronological time. Night Swan's association with rain also alludes to the mythological Reed Woman and Corn Mother whose presence provides rain in the poetic tribal stories referenced throughout the novel (pp. 13–14, 49). Tayo himself increasingly transcends Western time between the start of the ceremony at Betonie's place and its completion at the uranium mine. Looking for the cattle on Mount Taylor, he soothingly feels that his "ride into the mountains had branched into all directions of time," and as his memories converge, he realizes that "this night is a single night; and there has never been any other" (p. 192). Again the text mirrors modern physics: the mountains converge into a "totality" (p. 237), which could be interpreted as a parallel concept to the state of singularity beyond the event horizon of a black hole. Time culminates into one present that swallows past and future, slowing down so much that it appears not to pass anymore.

Thus, *Ceremony* is constructed as an oral storytelling event within a mythical context that makes for a nonlinear—in Allen's words, achronistic—narrative; it transcends boundaries of time and place. Therefore, it calls for the same approach that Barad has identified as overdue, that is, "something like an ethico-onto-epistem-ology—an appreciation of the intertwining of ethics, knowing, and being" (Barad, 2007, p. 185). On this level of basic conceptualization, theoretical physics and tribal ontology interlock. In addition, Tayo's revelation, as quoted above, is indicative of another key aspect: "The strength came from here, from this feeling [of totality]. It had always been there" (Silko, 1977, p. 237). The strength Tayo feels is that of compassion for his homeland and all its diverse entities. Through his journey, ceremonial participation, and the help of Betonie and Ts'eh, Tayo relearns to love and care.

Only the capacity for compassion allows him to sense the totality of space and time; it is the moment in which he prepares to let go of resistance and no longer be distracted by it.

Becoming part of the wind: Learning compassion and letting go

If everything is contained between earth and sky and various actors actively influence a journey of healing, the key problem comes down to the individual's perception. Tayo requires a life-affirming reorientation that can recover his ability to be compassionate. An early passage in *Ceremony* is symptomatic of this issue. As Harley and Tayo are riding to a bar at the border of the reservation, Tayo— inarticulate, will-less and lost in time and space at this point— wonders why he feels that it takes such "a great deal of energy to be a human being" (Silko, 1977, p. 25):

> Tayo thought about animals then, horses and mules, and the way they drifted with the wind. Josiah said that only humans had to endure anything, because only humans resisted what they saw outside themselves. Animals did not resist. But they persisted because they became part of the wind. (p. 27)

While this passage deals with physical positioning and movement in wind, it also includes a deeper insight into the contrasts between the forceful motion of resistance and ability-oriented, constructive adaptation. What humans see "outside themselves" are changing circumstances, perceptions, and pressures that seem to demand a constant repositioning of the self, and Silko observes that humans tend to focus on aspects they can address with forceful resistance against whatever pressures they identify. This form of resistance may result in an eternal uphill battle against—and therefore likely restricted to—imposed boundaries and ontological definitions, which demands much endurance and bears few prospects. While *Almanac of the Dead* shows that forceful resistance may be necessary at times, Silko warns that it cannot be all of the solution and has to be enacted with the right mind-set, otherwise it might be self-destructive. Silko's protagonists learn to avoid focusing on conflict and confrontation and to turn to constructive and creative activity, choices that become particularly clear in *Ceremony* and *Gardens in the Dunes*. Becoming "part of the wind" to facilitate further movement and self-actualization allows the characters to explore and shape their own destiny and accept it.

Many characters in *Ceremony*, including Auntie, Rocky, and fellow veterans, practice forms of resistance, but experience unhappiness and pain. More often than not, their resistance proves destructive to the integrity of their family or community and their well-being. Tayo's Aunt Thelma, called Auntie, for instance, alienates her brother Josiah, her sister, and her nephew Tayo by contributing to the gossip and community dynamics from which she is suffering at the same time. According to Auntie's perception, part of the Laguna Pueblo community must have succumbed to colonial-blood politics, equating supposed race with identity while disregarding enculturation. These politics cause Auntie's anxiety about her nonconformist family (pp. 33–34), and she defines herself as a victim of her deceased sister's choices and behavior. Paradoxically, while she criticizes her sister for having a child with a non-Native man, she raises her own son, Rocky, within non-Native values. Even though Tayo is culturally engrained in the Laguna tribal culture that Rocky rejects, Auntie treats her nephew as the unwanted outsider because of his status as a mixed-blood child born out of wedlock (pp. 32, 65–71). Night Swan explains that such internalized racism results from the fear of change. While everything is inevitably changing, she says, people "think that if their children have the same color of skin, the same color of eyes, that nothing is changing… That way they don't have to think about what has happened inside themselves" (p. 100). Such communal fear can lead to forms of resistance that are self-colonizing. Navajo medicine man Betonie suggests that such harmful outer influences are often enhanced by uncritical community reaction: "Some people act like witchery is responsible for everything that happens, when actually witchery only manipulates a small portion" (p. 130). Therefore, individual contemplation and action are needed, which some members of Laguna Pueblo successfully demonstrate.

Josiah, Grandma, and the spiritual leaders of the community withstand racial politics and seek to understand Tayo's spiritual condition, the true essence of a Laguna person. Josiah is inclusive and sensitive as he educates Tayo in tribal knowledge before the

Second World War. When Auntie tries to keep him away from his Mexican lover Night Swan, Josiah does not openly resist, but humbly and silently continues his much criticized relationship (pp. 90–93). Through Night Swan's intervention, Josiah decides to buy a herd of Mexican cattle. Again, he does not forcefully resist—in this case scientific books about cattle breeding and BIA policies—but after careful consideration he quietly chooses the Mexican speckled-cattle over the more heavily domesticated Hereford cattle (pp. 74–76). When Tayo returns from war sick and confused, Night Swan and the cattle are key ingredients for his spiritual recovery. Yet, it is Grandma who is the first to sense that Tayo's main problem is his lost ability to relate to others. She remains surprisingly marginal to Tayo's life, possibly because in the last prose passage of the novel she indicates that his experiences are not as unique as they may seem and "don't get [her] excited any more [*sic*]"; she claims, "it seems like I already heard these stories before… only thing is, the names sound different" (p. 260). However, at a crucial point in time, Grandma reaches out to the religious leader Ku'oosh, knowing from experience how to classify the nature of Tayo's problem. While the elders at first remain unsure of Tayo's identity, they are ready for dialogue (p. 233). Yet Ku'oosh understands that Tayo and the other veterans suffer from foreign influences and that some things cannot be cured in the old way: "I'm afraid of what will happen to all of us if you and the others don't get well" (p. 38). Therefore, he recommends the nonconformist Navajo singer Old Betonie (pp. 116–118), hoping that Betonie could break through the wall of resistance and inarticulate struggle that does not allow Ku'oosh to get through to Tayo.

Old Betonie initiates Tayo's cure through his postcolonial approach to ceremonial practice that is influenced by intercultural alliances. Betonie has found his own way of selective adaptation and ongoing self-determination, focusing his strength and effort on creative persistence instead of open resistance. His Mexican grandmother initiated the adaptation of traditional Navajo chants, first together with Betonie's grandfather and later himself alone. Betonie explains that "the ceremonies have always been changing… things which don't shift and grow are dead things… The people mistrust this greatly, but only this growth keeps the ceremonies strong" in the face of colonialism and fast changing history (p. 126). Betonie's archive of materials and his use of sand paintings are forms of adapted Indigenous mapping and postcolonial appropriation because they include various non-Native items that are aligned along the directions of Navajo cosmology (pp. 119–120). Betonie embodies what Sharon Holm has pointed out for *Ceremony* in general, namely that Silko insists on the tribal "uncompromising relationship with place while also acknowledging that a complex historical and contemporary interrelationship with differing epistemological, political, and economic practices affects how both a 'spiritual system' and a contemporary political viability of place can be maintained" (Holm, 2008, p. 251). Betonie's creative integration makes his ceremonies successful for those who deal with changing life circumstances and pluralistic influences, such as the identity politics of colonialism and modern warfare.

Thus, Betonie's character anticipates the idea of creative cultural inclusion based on self-determined appropriation that is continued by European characters in Silko's later novel. His communally grounded, yet highly individual attempt to integrate layered cultural landscapes, including cosmological and colonial ones, is a phenomenon that the characters Aunt Bronwyn and Laura in *Gardens in the Dunes* illustrate within a European context. Bronwyn and Laura practice a similar approach, just in the opposite direction of time and history. While Betonie includes the recent, intercultural history, Bronwyn and Laura include the regional cultural history of medieval times, European antiquity, and even pre-antiquity. Moreover, Betonie practices the alliances and exchange that Silko explores further in her later novels. His partially Mexican genealogy points at the south-north dynamic that plays out in *Almanac of the Dead*. His acceptance of and care for others no matter their ethnic identity echoes in the loose network of compassionate individuals presented in *Gardens in the Dunes*. Betonie explains the core issue: "We have all been waiting for help for a long time. But it never has been easy. The people must do it. You must do it" (Silko, 1977, p. 125). Healing, persistence, decolonization, and self-determination are all aspects that can only be reached communally if the individual takes action and leaves his/her previously accepted boundaries. As Betonie's and Tayo's situations illustrate, and as Silko later shows with Bronwyn and Laura, such a journey may look different for each person and require some experimentation and learning along the way.

Liberation from immediate, forceful resistance for the sake of persistent, creative adaptation is more than a mixed-blood dilemma; it is a basic human condition. In Tayo's case, the initial habit of forceful resistance is multilayered and inconsistent. It began in his childhood due to poverty, abandonment, and disdain, and climaxes due to posttraumatic stress syndrome from his Second World War experience, including the Bataan Death March and the loss of his cousin Rocky. As long as Tayo focuses on fighting his memories and dreams, he suffers physically and mentally. He remains inarticulate, disoriented, and unclear about his identity. Tayo's suffering, however, leads to a gradual reorientation toward culturally conditioned intuition and tribal knowledge with regard to problem-solving: "Fear made him remember important things" (p. 242). He realizes: "The dreams had been terror at loss, at something lost forever; but nothing was lost; all was retained between the sky and the earth, and within himself. He had lost nothing" (p. 219). In Laguna Pueblo cosmology, Silko indicates, the universe is self-contained. Well-being depends on one's individual and communal positioning in relation to other forces and actors in the universe; it is a process, a state of becoming. When Josiah notes that animals persist because they become part of the wind, he refers to this philosophy. A sole focus on resistance and confrontation, paired with the inability to accept the death of loved ones, poses an obstacle to healing. Tayo may recognize this dynamic, but he struggles to act upon such guidance because his aunt's accusatory behavior, Josiah's passing away during Tayo's absence, Rocky's violent death at war, the war memories at large, and the self-destructive impact of troubled veteran buddies surround Tayo with forceful resistance at all times.

The slight memory of compassion allows Tayo to escape the drinking and storytelling of the veterans, a "ritual" (p. 43) used to channel the aggression from their resistance against painful memories and current disorientation. A physician quotes a report saying that alcohol use and violence among Indian veterans were rampant, but Tayo intuitively recognizes that it is something "going on for a long time" (p. 53). He senses a larger change of mentality that alienates people socially and spiritually. His own memories are characterized by moments of compassionate illusion, for instance seeing Josiah's face in a Japanese prisoner who is to be executed during the Second World War (pp. 7–8). While the soldiers define Tayo's terrified reaction as "battle fatigue" (p. 8), it really is a flash of compassion that keeps Tayo humane enough to be healed later. His veteran peers, especially their leader, Emo, have lost their ability to relate to others; they cannot break out of the increasing cycles of alcohol and violence. Even though, as Betonie warns, witchery "only manipulates a small portion" (p. 130), people can lose themselves in a spiral of violent resistance. Based on that premise, witches and witchery remain abstract, without or reaching beyond a specific body or identity, a placeless and timeless force known only through its symptoms. The key in escaping the lure of witchery lies in a lesson Tayo remembers from Josiah: "Nothing was all good or all bad either; it all depended" (p. 11). Ts'eh explains that the destroyers aim to block people's emotions and make them forget, which Tayo identifies with his experience of losing the "sensations of living" (p. 229). The novel contains a poem that describes how "white people"—an intentionally vague term—were created as a tool for evil during a contest of Indian witches (pp. 132–138). Yet Silko stresses that both Indian and white people had been fooled and tricked into believing lies (pp. 191, 204), meaning that both groups have the opportunity and need for liberation and healing. Tayo eventually realizes that lies are keeping each group from healing individually and jointly because "as long as people believed the lies, they would never be able to see what had been done to them or what they were doing to each other" (p. 191) and see the potential for compassion and self-determination.

Identifying the problem as believing in "lies," however, is insufficient in the absence of compassion as a key toward recovering alternative knowledge and a more wholesome focus. Both Night Swan and Ts'eh, two enigmatic characters in *Ceremony* who are closely connected to mythology and the landscape, appear adaptive to changing circumstances, focus on creative, compassionate activities, and assert their self-determination. They model the philosophy that lets go of violent reaction for the sake of creative and caring action. In that function, they are key figures in changing Tayo's focus from colonial impacts to tribal cosmology and adjusting his mental state from resistance to persistence.

Night Swan is mostly associated with the ability to love. Spiritually, she predicts that Tayo is part of a larger scheme (p. 100), a reference to his role both in the witches' desired map and in Betonie's ceremonial star map. Emotionally, she prepares Tayo for the insight that love never ceases and that "nothing was ever lost as long as the love remained" (p. 220), a key message that helps Tayo accept and process the death of his relatives. Practically, Night Swan sets up Josiah's initiation into cattle ranching as if knowing that the cattle could later be a major point of reference in Tayo's attempt to regain orientation and purpose. The search for the cattle also leads Tayo to the woman nicknamed Ts'eh, who identifies as "a Montaño," Spanish for "mountain-" (p. 223). Ts'eh is associated with a central figure within Laguna cosmology (p. 257) and with the sacred mountain Tse-pi'na, Mount Taylor. Her blue silk shawl connects her to the dark blue shadow of the large image of a pregnant she-elk—annually repainted by the Laguna priests (pp. 230–231)— and to Betonie's Mexican grandmother who also wore a blue shawl (p. 221). Jennifer Brice has illustrated the possible connections between Night Swan and Ts'eh as incarnations of Ts'its'tsi'nako, Thought Woman, and between Tayo's sexual encounters with both of them as cause for rain that relieves the land from drought (Brice, 1998, p. 136).

Ts'eh demonstrates how compassion and holistic biocultural relationships manifest in mundane and humble activities of daily life. Here is her true teaching moment with Tayo: Ts'eh carefully arranges stones and plants and teaches Tayo to gather and transplant plants based on traditional ecological knowledge (Silko, 1977, pp. 183–184). She explains, for instance, "This one [plant] contains the color of the sky after a summer rainstorm. I'll take it from here and plant it in another place, a canyon where it hasn't rained for a while" (p. 224). This example illustrates the principle of creative activity as a more effective form of resistance against oppressive environments. Ts'eh's biocultural approach to care for stones and plants is most strongly echoed in the non-Native character of Bronwyn in *Gardens in the Dunes*. Silko favors female approaches not as superior, exclusionist, or even specifically Indigenous, but as the most likely and creative response to the male dominance of capitalist–imperialist ideology. Both Ts'eh and Bronwyn model choices and behaviors that replace forceful resistance with creative adaptation. Ts'eh's compassion and love restore the rhythm of Tayo's world, make him feel whole (pp. 219–220), and allow him to engage in basic actions of environmental care (p. 227).

Throughout her novels, Silko stresses that healing is about repositioning oneself between sky and earth, about reemerging into one's cultural identity and reality. Silko writes that emergence for the Laguna people meant more than an act or action, but the process of a people's "emergence into a specific cultural identity ... a journey of awareness and imagination" characterized by the effort of people "differentiating themselves" (1998, pp. 14–15) and finding a "viable relationship" to their physical surroundings (p. 16). For Tayo, it begins with abandoning thinking in boundaries (1977, p. 145) to find healing in "something great and inclusive of everything" (p. 126). After the ceremony with Betonie, Tayo realizes in a dream that it is his task to recover Josiah's stolen cattle. Tayo's effort to relate to the cattle and to retrieve them from the thieves eventually provides him with an opportunity to relate to his physical surroundings. He feels that boundaries are melting and that the mountains of the four directions have come together, an indicator of a healing world (p. 145). Tayo thus gains a purpose, yet he has to "recognize himself again" (p. 154), which occurs later during a climax of physical exhaustion. Tayo can steal back Josiah's Mexican cattle, but his horse slips and falls with him, leaving Tayo behind, numb and then harassed briefly for trespassing by ranch hands. Prostrate with exhaustion, Tayo thinks that if he allowed himself to sleep,

> the resistance would leak out and take with it all barriers, all boundaries; he would seep into the earth and rest with the center, where the voice of silence was familiar and the density of the dark earth loved him. He could secure the thresholds with molten pain and remain; or he could let go and flow back. It was up to him. (pp. 201–202)

Tayo's ponderings illustrate the idea of resistance as reinforcing boundaries. Resistance is tempting as one desires to "secure the thresholds" for fear of loss, but it does not allow for an alternative to the endless struggle. Tayo feels the gravity pulling him toward the tribal place of emergence, to a new attempt at differentiating himself as a person, as part of a people, and as an actor within a cosmological network of agencies. His multidirectional movement between nadir and zenith and his understanding of cosmological forces that correspond to the scientific notion of an agential realism allow him to liberate his mind and explore alternatives. Tayo has to "let go and flow back," like the animals who drift with the wind. With the support of intercultural allies, including Night Swan, Old

Betonie, and Ts'eh, Tayo learns to creatively work around and counter oppressive and destructive forces. During the showdown at the uranium mine, he understands this process of change even better: "He cried the relief he felt at finally seeing the pattern, the way all the stories fit together...He was not crazy. He had only seen and heard the world as it always was: no boundaries, only transitions through all distances and time" (p. 246). At that point, Tayo achieves letting go and not interfering violently with a scene that urges him to resist. Instead, he turns to watch the stars and eventually walks away, no longer distracted from constructive mindfulness and a meaningful way of life.

Tayo's journey toward healing is indicative of the strong sense of optimism that Native American authors of the 1970s and 1980s expressed in regard to the regeneration of tribal cultural sovereignty and the reconciliation between humans and nonhuman members of the biocultural community. With the dynamic and pluralistic perspectives of Betonie and Tosamah, both Silko and Momaday employ characters who practice cultural integration, albeit on their own terms, as Simon Ortiz has stressed in "Towards a National Indian Literature" (Ortiz, 1981, p. 11). The elusiveness of Betonie and Tosamah and the ability for dynamic adaptation of the protagonists Tayo and Abel contrast with the less successful healing of the characters in James Welch's novels of that time. In *Winter in the Blood* (1974) and *The Death of Jim Loney* (1979), Welch's characters miss their chance—if they ever had one—of biocultural repositioning, have no female assistance in recovering compassion, and are ultimately unable to adapt constructively. Allen further claims that Welch's characters do not overcome their alienation because they remain caught in chronology as reflected in the narrative structure (1992, p. 151). They are caught in boundaries and resistance patterns, unable to experience agential realism and the possibility of time–space convergence.

All these authors indicate that the dynamism, adaptability, and compassionate inclusiveness inherent in Native cultures—the becoming "part of the wind"—are a key for survivance and an escape from imposed stasis and sterility (Owens, 1992, p. 167). Yet, while landscape and mythology in Momaday's and Vizenor's novels are significant—in both cases even including human–animal shape-shifting—biocultural reorientation and spiritual renewal do not include strong feminine input as in Silko's novel. In fact, Silko's focus on female perspectives and compassion is not fully taken up again until Louise Erdrich and Paula Gunn Allen's writings in the 1980s. Erdrich's character of Fleur Pillager in *Tracks* (1988) and other novels contributes a strong biocultural approach. Silko's stories about the triangle of meaning between women, environment, and mythology as well as biocultural, postcolonial, and even postnatural ethics particularly relate to Linda Hogan's works in the 1990s and 2000s. In *Dwellings: A Spiritual History of the Living World* (1995), Hogan discusses "the different histories of ways of thinking and being in the world" (p. 12), meaning culturally different knowledges (plural!) and sciences, which relate to Silko's long-time contemplation on Western perspectives, for instance Transcendentalism, and the possibility of intercultural dialogue and alliances. In fact, *Ceremony* illuminates transitions between Western and Native sciences regarding space–time dynamics, agential realism, and the intrinsic power of compassion to facilitate constructive healing and the sharing of stories, meaning, and knowledge in pluralistic communities.

References

Al-Khalili, J. (2011), *Black Holes, Wormholes and Time Machines*, 2nd edition. Boca Raton: CRC Press.

Allen, P. G. (1992), *The Sacred Hoop: Recovering the Feminine in American Indian Traditions*. Boston: Beacon Press.

Barad, K. (2007), *Meeting the Universe Halfway: Quantum Physics and the Entanglement of Matter and Meaning*. Durham and London: Duke University Press.

Brice, J. (1998), "Earth as Mother, Earth as other in Novels by Silko and Hogan." *Critique: Studies in Contemporary Fiction*, 39:2, 127–138.

Erdrich, L. (1994), *Tracks*. London: Flamingo, 1988.

Hawking, S. (2008), "Into a Black Hole," Lecture. Web. Stephen Hawking homepage. http://www.hawking.org.uk/into-a-black-hole.html [Accessed: November 15, 2014].

Hogan, L. (1995), *Dwellings: A Spiritual History of the Living World*. New York: W. W. Norton.

Holm, S. (2008), "The 'Lie' of the Land: Native Sovereignty, Indian Literary Nationalism, and Early Indigenism in Leslie Marmon Silko's *Ceremony*." *American Indian Quarterly*, 32:3, 243–374.

Jahner, E. (1979), "An act of Attention: Event Structure in *Ceremony.*" *American Indian Quarterly*, 5:1, 37–46.

Krupat, A. (1996), *The Turn to the Native: Studies in Criticism and Culture.* Lincoln and London: University of Nebraska Press.

Momaday, N. S. (1968), *House Made of Dawn.* New York: Harper & Row.

Moore, D. L. (2013), *That Dream Shall Have a Name: Native Americans Rewriting America.* Lincoln: University of Nebraska Press.

Nelson, R. M. (2002), "The function of the landscape of *Ceremony*," in A. R. Chavkin (ed.), *Leslie Marmon Silko's Ceremony: A Casebook.* Oxford: Oxford University Press, pp. 139–173.

Ortiz, S. J. (1981), "Towards a National Indian Literature: Cultural Authenticity in Nationalism." *MELUS*, 8:2, 7–12.

Owens, L. (1992), *Other Destinies: Understanding the American Indian Novel.* Norman: University of Oklahoma Press.

Ray, S. J. (2013), "Environmental Justice, Transnationalism, and the Politics of the Local in Leslie Marmon Silko's *Almanac of the Dead.*" *Journal of Transnational American Studies*, 5:1, 1–24.

Silko, L. M. (1977), *Ceremony.* New York, NY: Penguin Books.

Silko, L. M. (1991), *Almanac of the Dead: A Novel.* New York: Simon & Schuster.

Silko, L. M. (1997), *Yellow Woman and a Beauty of the Spirit: Essays on Native American Life Today.* New York, NY: Simon and Schuster.

Silko, L. M. (1998), "Interior and Exterior Landscapes: The Pueblo Migration Stories," in S. J. Ortiz (ed.), *Speaking for the Generations: Native Writers on Writing.* Tucson: University of Arizona Press, pp. 2–24.

Silko, L. M. (1999), *Gardens in the Dunes.* New York: Simon & Schuster.

Silko, L. M. and Wright, J. (1986), *The Delicacy and Strength of Lace: Letters between Leslie Marmon Silko & James Wright.* St. Paul, Minnesota: Graywolf Press.

Vizenor, G. (1978), *Darkness in Saint Louis Bearheart.* St. Paul: Truck Press.

Vizenor, G. (2008), "Aesthetics of Survivance: Literary Theory and Practice," in G. Vizenor (ed.), *Survivance: Narratives of Native Presence.* Lincoln: University of Nebraska Press, pp. 1–23.

Welch, J. (1974), *Winter in the Blood.* New York: Harper & Row.

Welch, J. (1979), *The Death of Jim Loney.* New York: Harper & Row.

3

The Lost Women of Silko's *Ceremony*

Carolyn Dekker

In the preface to the thirtieth anniversary edition of *Ceremony*, Silko writes of what she calls "the notes and false starts" of a novel she worked on before she tried a comic story about Harley:

> I tried twice to develop a young female protagonist to be the main character of a novel; but I found I was too self-conscious and failed to allow my fictional woman to behave independently of my image of myself. (Silko, 2006, p. xvi)

Set primarily in Albuquerque, Gallup, and Laguna in the 1970s, the unfinished novel follows a mixed-race woman named Angelina or Angie, and focuses on her need for a healing ceremony. The 150 holograph and typescript pages surviving in the collection of Yale's Beinecke Library yield considerably more interest than is implied under the heading of "notes and false starts."[1] In 1990, Silko implied a closer connection between the Angie drafts and *Ceremony* when she spoke of two "stillborn novels" not as attempts to write "a novel" but as attempts to write "the novel," *Ceremony*:

> What caused the first two attempts at the novel to be stillborn was that I had a narrator who was a young woman, about my own age. And it just did not work. It just becomes yourself. And then you have to look at how limited you are, and so the only

way you can break out of your personal limitation is to deal with a fictional character. (Silko, 2002, p. 245)

In the same interview, Silko points to the section of *Ceremony* set in the riverside camp in Gallup as "the only surviving part" of the stillborn novels. The Angie drafts, however, are far more richly and crucially entangled in the drafting of *Ceremony* than these statements indicate. In them, Silko works out key themes, as well as the form that she ultimately uses in *Ceremony*: the famous structure of the novel *as a ceremony*. The drafts thus constitute a third origin story for *Ceremony* alongside the funny story about Harley and Silko's own longing for the Southwest during her Alaskan exile.[2]

Silko understates her own achievements in the Angie drafts. Particularly when compared with female characters in *Ceremony* (whom Silko herself admits are "not as fully realized as the men"), Angie emerges as a three-dimensional, strong, provocative, flawed, sensual, seeking female character (2002, p. 243). Her rich characterization brings considerable pressure to bear upon the problematics in *Ceremony*'s representation of its ordinary human women who serve as debased foils to figures such as Ts'eh and the Night Swan. Angie is all the more remarkable because *Ceremony*'s weak female characters are part of a larger paucity of female protagonists and well-developed female characters in Native American literature. Judith Antell attributes this lack to a problem of audience: the Indian male "excit[es] romantic nostalgia in the minds of readers," neatly slotting into the role of the "vanishing savage," and thus, she concludes, male protagonists "best illustrate the alienation and despair which Indian people have experienced in the 20th Century" (Antell, 1988, p. 214). If female characters have so seldom been tried, however, and if their rarity is driven by mainstream (white) market preferences, it seems premature to conclude that male protagonists have a special ability to best illustrate the alienation and despair of Indian people. Writing in 1988, Antell allows notable exceptions for Paula Gunn Allen's *The Woman Who Owned the Shadows* (1983) and Louise Erdrich's *Love Medicine* (1984). Angie represents a prior attempt at such a female character, and one through whose drafting and discarding Silko raises the question of whether and how female pain can be universalized.

When these drafts, vastly different from *Ceremony* though they are, take their place in *Ceremony*'s genealogy, they invite us to consider the effect of some of the most fundamental variables in the work's construction. Most startlingly, Tayo was once (in some way) a woman named Angie. He was once a Vietnam veteran. *Ceremony* began a generation later, had traffic with cities, and attempted to be a Chicana novel as well as a Native American one. In ultimately electing the protagonist and setting that she did, Silko flung her novel's radius of geographic concern outward, reaching toward Japan, toward the atomic bomb, and through it to the trans-historical problem of genocidal and ecocidal violence. The Angie drafts show what she sacrificed for this vision.

He wondered if it was important: Female pain in Angie's story

Two versions of a single scene in the Angie drafts make for particularly uncanny reading because in them Angie makes the uphill trudge that Tayo makes in *Ceremony*, walking to his tense first meeting with the unconventional Navajo medicine man, Betonie, above Gallup. Silko experiments with Angie's timeline as she brings her to this crucial meeting. A page of notes identifies her as twenty-five years old and pregnant in August of 1973 when she seeks the help of a medicine man at Zuni. It is a year of drought. The medicine man watches from a mesa as a woman drives to the foot to see him. In one version, she comes in an old Dodge, and she brings $200 worth of offerings for his services: soft white buckskins, a sheep to butcher, turquoise, and silver. As in *Ceremony*, the medicine man's eyes reveal his mixed heritage, with Angie seeing that his eyes are brown and concluding, "Somewhere a white or a Mexican in his past."

In a second version of the same scene, she drives up not in an old Dodge but in a new pick-up truck, "shining chrome all around and yellow paint." She wears a velvet skirt and turquoise and silver rings. She is married now and has at least one surviving child. The medicine man observes her as she walks up. "The woman was young and had beautiful eyes, brown eyes. He wanted to like her, but he could also see that she was rich. Rich and beautiful. What more did she want?"

What the medicine man does not know is that the list of painful events in Angie's life is staggering. The first of Angie's wounds is the death of her mother. In two different versions of the same scene, Angie witnesses her mother's murder. In one, her mother is stabbed by a john; in another, two black women storm into the apartment, wielding big knives and yelling that her mother is a "fucking no-good Indian whore." The police arrive and render no first aid but speak words that haunt Angie for years: "Serves them right." One way or the other, the stabbing was related to her mother's work as a prostitute, but her death was attributable to police racism and indifference.

Following their mother's death, Angie's sister, Marie, is adopted by a white family in Colorado, while Angie is sent to Laguna to live with her uncle. After a girlhood comprised of equal parts heartbreaking half-acceptance by her family and cattle-working idyll, she falls in love with a cousin whose family will not allow him to marry a half-breed woman. She has a baby at sixteen with a bull-riding, alcoholic Navajo boyfriend who turns out to be married. Her child either dies at birth or is stolen and ritualistically murdered by Navajo witches. Angie and Marie are reunited in young adulthood the following year and live together in Gallup until, in the course of her own career as a prostitute, Marie is found dead. Angie moves to Albuquerque and supports herself by working at a bar and taking men home for money. Then she becomes pregnant again and goes home to Laguna (either marrying and coming into money, or not) before she comes to meet the proto-Betonie at Zuni.[3]

As he watches her walk up, the medicine man "wondered if it was important, whatever it was that brought her to him." Even this terrible tally—the loss of a mother, a first love, a sister, and a child—does not add up enough to make her legible to others as a sufferer. He "want[s] to like" this woman but feels prevented from doing so by her beauty and wealth and the easy life both imply. In this conflicted impulse, he voices the experiment that Silko makes in the two versions of the scene. Is Angie worth healing if she is poor and alone? If she is rich and married?

No matter her social or marital status, each of Angie's losses has a small radius, taking place in the domestic space of a family. When Silko ultimately discards Angie and gives the planned healing ceremony to Tayo, she throws Angie over in favor of a maximally legible and worthy sufferer, the traumatized male veteran. Tayo brings geographic mobility through his involvement in the great national project of a world war, the many suffering miles he walked in the Philippines, and his preoccupation with the long reach of modern weaponry, some of which he has seen firsthand. His is a vastly spacialized trauma, in contrast to the small social and domestic spheres within which Angie suffers. Ultimately, Tayo's replacement of Angie provides a dispiriting answer indeed to the medicine man's question of whether womanly pain is worth caring about, and to the question of whether this pain can be universalized in the way in which Silko ultimately strives to universalize Tayo's.

The Angie drafts are aesthetic and literary-historical events separate from *Ceremony* and significant to both Silko's career arc and the history of Southwestern and Native American literature. They are, however, also part of *Ceremony*'s story, and make possible a reading of *Ceremony* that is aware of what John Whittier-Ferguson calls "the burden of the draft" (1997, p. 315). When Ku'oosh speaks in *Ceremony*, Tayo explains that "the reason for choosing each word ha[s] to be explained with a story" (Silko, 1977, p. 32). By reading *Ceremony* through the Angie drafts, I hope to follow Ku'oosh's example of including in the narrative the story of its own becoming. The Angie drafts illuminate more of *Ceremony*'s story, of the acts of memory, accretion, combination, and deletion that make *Ceremony*'s meaning. They help especially to enable an imaginative mapping of the losses, absences, and near misses within Silko's text, speaking voids that are not readily apparent because of the novel's vast richness and scope.

A page of notes suggests that Silko initially planned for Angie to win over the medicine man. In a large hand, Silko jots:

<u>Healing Ceremony</u>
cut into story
[Ed.: underlining in Silko original]

The suggestion (or imperative to herself) that the healing ceremony will cut into the story seems to imply the prose and verse structure that emerges in *Ceremony*. Silko further notes the purpose of the ceremony, or the structure, as "bringing two worlds together." What are those two worlds? To the left of these notations, she has circled

"A visit to the valley of the lavender she-elk" and drawn an arrow to the ceremony. To the right of the notations, she has boxed a list: "peyote/dreams/darkness/frenzy/witchcraft." The two worlds may be those of the generative symbol of the she-elk and the witchery listed opposite one another here. The two worlds could also refer to the mythic world of traditional story in verse and the prose sections containing Angie's and Tayo's (prosaic) existences. These worlds of verse and prose finally converge and interpenetrate in the final scenes of *Ceremony*, and, in their convergence, make Tayo whole and mark his reintegration into Pueblo community.

No draft of Angie's visit to the valley of the lavender she-elk exists in the archive, but this visit does occur in *Ceremony*. In that scene, Ts'eh and Tayo stand before the elk, "her belly swollen with new life as she leaped across the yellow sandrock, startled forever across the curve of cliff rock, ears flung back to catch a sound behind her" (1977, p. 214). It is not hard to imagine Angie as the page of notes projects her. Angie stands before the elk, also nearing the culmination of a healing ritual, and perhaps enjoying a special connection with the rock painting because her own belly is swollen with new life in defiance of all of the darkness, frenzy, and witchcraft that has stalked her. There is power in this vision of Angie and in this story. So much power that Silko took its structure, its "Healing Ceremony/cut into story," and gave it to Tayo's story. Silko rendered Angie's novel incompletable not when she sold its papers or when she decided that she had "failed to allow [Angie] to behave independently," but when she removed from it its very skeleton and used it as the armature for Tayo's *Ceremony*.

They were losing her: No ceremony for Helen Jean

Perhaps as a result of long and tiresome questioning, Silko's stance regarding her decision to use a male main character in *Ceremony* is defensive. She points to her childhood in "the Pueblo matriarchy" as providing examples of female empowerment and observes that "male novelists write about female protagonists all the time" (Silko, 2006, p. xviii). Silko's contention that a female novelist ought to be free to write of male protagonists rings deeply true, but does not explain the particular kinds of women missing from the novel. Thanks to Ts'eh and the Night Swan, with their glorious, generative sexuality and their ability to exert supernatural influence on the lives and world around them, *Ceremony* has no lack of positive and powerful female figures. What it lacks are richly drawn and sympathetic female characters who are merely human in the ways in which Tayo is so successfully, deeply, and ambiguously human.

This characterization of Tayo, and the corresponding lack of it for Helen Jean and other women, is a key component in understanding *Ceremony*'s structure. Paula Gunn Allen contends that there are two kinds of people in *Ceremony*: one category who "belong to the earth spirit and live in harmony with her," and a second group who are associated with "human mechanism" and serve the witchery. Allen is correct as far as *Ceremony*'s women go: they exist in stable categories. There is no danger of the Night Swan or Ts'eh becoming "inimical to all that lives" (Allen, 1986, p. 118). Tayo, however, is fitted to be the novel's protagonist precisely because he is a round and dynamic character. Allen sees Tayo as always unconsciously knowing his place in the world and needing only to come to know it consciously. Helen Jaskoski also underplays Tayo's complexity and peril when she asserts that Tayo "exemplifies the pastoral figure of the shepherd, the exemplar of a materially simple life sought in harmony with nature" (1991, p. 162). I would argue that Tayo is far from exemplary at many moments in the novel. Tayo's allegiance and the reader's interpretation of him both hang in the balance.

Ceremony has two great, driving questions: the plot-based question of what will befall Tayo and the metatextual question of how the reader is to interpret him. Tayo admits to Betonie, "I've been sick, and half the time I don't know if I'm still crazy or not" (Silko, 1977, p. 115). Readers are invited to share his uncertainty, especially when he interacts with the earth spirit, Ts'eh. When Tayo lies down across a pool from her, sleeps, and dreams of making love to her, he wakes with his fists full of sand, feeling "shaky inside" and fearfully wondering, "What if there were no traces of her?" (1977, p. 206).

Tayo spends the summer in healing communion with Ts'eh, but, seen from another angle, Tayo spends the summer sleeping in the hills, companioned by a woman whom only he can see (and that only sometimes). His community, his family, and even the traditional medicine man, Ku'oosh "think [he] might need the doctors again" (1977, p. 212). As Tayo prepares to escape those doctors, the reader must confront the knowledge that every available outside observer finds Tayo's actions erratic and possibly pathological.

Within *Ceremony*'s 1977 post-Vietnam war context, Silko is toying with the cultural figure of the tripwire veteran. One may ultimately conclude that Tayo's summer in the hills makes him literally and generically pastoral, but much of the novel holds forth a darker reading. Tayo's affinity for undomestic space makes him literary kin to the now-archetypal Rambo, the protagonist of David Morrell's 1972 novel, *First Blood*, which follows a former Vietnam prisoner of war on a flashback-fueled killing spree.

The Angie drafts provide a textual history for Tayo's resonances with Vietnam in the person of a character named Lighteagle, a Vietnam draftee whose grandfather dies while he is at war. Lighteagle confides in Angie, "He was going to teach me about the Sun Dance and visions. Just like he taught me to fish and to hunt." Angie understands that, with his grandfather's passing, "any chance of ever being close to the inner circle of the traditional way had been stolen was gone from him as it had been taken from her too. Lighteagle was tormented with blame." This is an early working-out of Tayo's predicament, in which Josiah's death while he is at war in the Pacific Theatre cuts Tayo off from his most likely religious sponsor and initiator.[4] "Lighteagle was tormented with the blame" not only because he was not with his grandfather when he died, but also because his absence broke the chain of transmission of traditional knowledge. He concludes, "I guess it is my fault anyway. For not knowing all that stuff in the first place." By projecting Lighteagle backward in time and reimagining him as Tayo, Silko draws upon the cultural figure of a suffering Vietnam veteran whose pain has the potential to destabilize and jeopardize his entire community.

Is Tayo a peaceful shepherd or a murderous Rambo? Tayo sees himself with this double consciousness when, at the novel's climax, he considers attacking Emo in order to save Harley. He knows that his act of violence would cause him to lose control of how his life's story was represented:

> He would have been another victim, a drunk Indian war veteran settling an old feud; and the Army doctors would say that the indications of this end had been there all along, since his release

from the mental ward at the Veterans' Hospital in Los Angeles. (Silko, 1977, p. 235)

The stereotypes of the drunk Indian, the violent veteran, and the mental patient stand open to receive and interpret him. The heroic intentions of his violence would disappear into them without a trace. In pushing down the temptation toward violence, Tayo wins the right to create himself through story, which he exercises before the elders in the kiva. The elders accept his interpretation, knowing Ts'eh was not a corporeal woman or a mad hallucination, but a powerful and benevolent spiritual being, and the verse and narrative prose portions of *Ceremony* briefly converge:

> They started crying
> the old men started crying
> 'A'moo'ooh! A'moo'ooh!'
> You have seen her
> We will be blessed
> again

(1977, p. 239)

The novel thus resolves its two main questions with Tayo surviving to be embraced by his community and with the narrative thoroughly endorsing the reading of Tayo as mentally and spiritually sound.

The rich indeterminacy of Tayo's characterization stands in stark contrast with that of Helen Jean, one of the novel's few non-mythic women. The bare outlines of Helen Jean's life point to a woman who should be worthy of readerly engagement and sympathy. Armed with typing skills, professional ambition, and dreams of supporting her younger sisters, she moves to Gallup but is quickly disillusioned when she can only find work as a janitor. Soon even that work comes with a manager who sexually exploits her, and she quits the job and turns to hanging around the bar when the veterans' disability checks come in, sleeping with men and asking them to help her out with a few dollars. She maintains for her roommates the illusion that she leaves each morning for work as a secretary, a daily dissimulation that enacts the distance between the life that her desires and skills fit her for and the life that Gallup's racist and sexist horizons circumscribe for her. So why does the novel handle her with such savage finality?

The Helen Jean section comes just before Tayo's first meeting with Ts'eh, setting up the two characters as foils for one another and slotting them neatly into that binary that Paula Gunn Allen names: Ts'eh belongs to the earth spirit, while Helen Jean serves the witchery. There is no room for Helen Jean to be of dual nature, or to be, like Tayo, a character who is offered a choice of whether to belong to the earth or the witchery. Helen Jean's internalized racism is such that her sense of self-worth is based upon being unlike other Indian women—"at least [her hair] wasn't long or straight" (1977, p. 154). Her preference for curly permanent waves becomes a symbol of her betrayal of her native identity. She is a woman lost to her own community because, like Tayo's mother a generation before, she has acceded to the notion that to do her lipstick and her hair "perfectly" is to do them "exactly like the white girls" (1977, p. 63).

Despite the fact that Helen Jean, like Tayo, is able to see the performance of war stories by the Indian veterans as a pathetic attempt to recall a time when "they had been treated first class," Helen Jean and Tayo regard each other with wariness (1977, p. 153). He is nauseated by her heavy, rose-scented perfume and the insincerity of her flirtation with Leroy, as she rubs her leg against him but "star[es] out the window while she did it, as if her mind were somewhere else" (1977, p. 144). He is disturbed by this detachment, even while Helen Jean, with instincts sharpened by violent encounters with other men, is disturbed by Tayo. She sees him, "the quiet one," as potentially dangerous. Her decision to ditch Harley and Leroy and leave the bar with the Mexican man, which Tayo reads as coy and faithless, is actually a calculated decision to put as much distance as possible between herself and the ominously silent Indian veteran who "acted funny" (1977, pp. 149–150). Despite Helen Jean's good reasons to detach and flee, both Tayo and the novel treat her actions, like her perfume and lipstick, as reliable markers of corruption.

Angie's story: Her mother had lived something like this

Given *Ceremony*'s negative representation of Helen Jean, it is notable that Angie, another young woman working as a prostitute, is well drawn and sympathetic. Silko's description of Angie's life in Albuquerque has a languid and sensual quality, not a degraded one.

She slept from 6, when the men usually left, until 2 o'clock, when the afternoon Santa Fe Chief went north. She always woke up then, and if she felt like it, she would drag out the long galvanized tin tub–the Mexican bath tub of her youth–and start filling it with hot water from the little sink. She bought perfumed bath salts in expensive flower-covered tins, and she lathered her hair in perfumed soap. She had soft thick towels with colored bright designs on them. It was like Marie always said, cheap rent and plenty of men [and] you could enjoy a lot of nice things.

Despite Angie's blithe tone, the memory of Marie's fate dispels any endorsement of prostitution as an occupation. But this is no tragic, fallen-woman tale. Silko doesn't shy away from showing Angie enjoying the consolations of this dangerous but self-chosen path. Perhaps she is astray, and "nice things" are nothing from which to make a life, but the reader identifies with Angie rather than judges her as they all but join her in her bath. The use of the second person in Angie's paraphrase of Marie invites the reader to enjoy the nice things, too: to pleasure in the hot water, the perfume and the doubled adjectives in the experience of "soft thick towels with colored bright designs." Likewise, there is no sense that Angie is irredeemably lost to herself: the tin "Mexican bath-tub of her youth" is a poignant reminder of her rural upbringing that shows she is connected to her past and her identity while living in the city.

Angie has come here to live Rocky's dream "to get away from the reservation…to make something of himself. In a city somewhere" (1977, p. 121). In *Ceremony*, the cities can never fulfill this promise. From his vantage in the heights above Gallup, Betonie looks down and tells Tayo, "They are down there. Ones like your brother. They are down there" (1977, p. 121). In contrast to such distant and often deterministic glimpses of urban Indian life, the Angie drafts use careful attention to Angie's living space to represent her ability to shape her own life. She rents the loft above a hide warehouse near the railroad tracks after being unable to bear the thought of living in an apartment building. On the iron stairs outside her warehouse loft she can sit and look east over the tracks to the Sandia mountains, "hazy blue in the afternoon sun." She fills the space with potted geraniums, and looks up through the many industrial windows at the stars, thus finding a way to be connected to both earth and sky.

That view of the sky helps her place her own life in the context of the lives of other women she has known, making common-feeling out of her solitude:

> Occasionally she would wake up and lay on the mattress and look up at the sky through the rows of little square windows and she would realize that Marie had lived this way too, and that her mother had lived something like this, except that she had been older and had them to look after.

As the rows of square windows assemble a vision of the night sky, Angie seeks to assemble a shared vision of female experience from the glimpses of the separate lives of women she has known. Angie's sky-gazing identifies her as a person looking in the right place for direction and solace, as Ts'eh and Betonie teach Tayo to look up at the sky for guidance during his healing journey.

Such moments undo one of the binaries familiar to readers of *Ceremony*: the divide between the rural and the urban. Cities in *Ceremony* are corrupt and draw the corrupt to them. Angie's Albuquerque is not a space of deculturation or witchery but is a complex meeting place for peoples. It explores intertribal relations between Pueblos and Navajos; the negotiations of urban and reservation Indian life, and possibilities of intercourse or mobility between Indian and Chicano/a worlds. Soon after moving to Albuquerque, Angie attends a party with Indians who have spent more time in the city. Being around them makes her self-conscious about her faded jeans, calico shirt, and worn tennis shoes. This clothing marks her as having recently arrived from the reservation, while they dress to distance themselves from reservation Indians:

> The women ... liked Western style clothes and elaborate hair[dos]. The men liked cowboy boots and sport coats; they didn't wear Western shirts because that's what reservation Navajo men wore, the ones who could hardly speak English, and these men did not want to be mistaken for them.

Angie believes that the urban Indians' self-expression (like Helen Jean's in *Ceremony*) emerges from distaste or hatred for other

Indians. The Albuquerque Indians dress like "rich white ranchers and Texas rodeo stars," choosing to assert themselves by projecting the image of the culture that represents the theft of tribal lands as a way to mark themselves as unmistakably urban, educated, and middle class.

This party scene from inside a thriving community of happily assimilated or acculturated Indians plays interestingly with the parameters of half-breed literature. Patricia Riley asserts that "acculturated full-bloods can also qualify for a kind of mixed status" and quotes Paula Gunn Allen, who says that "The breed (whether by parentage or acculturation to non-Indian society) is an Indian who is not an Indian." Allen describes a classic tragic-mulatto scenario in which the breeds "are a bit of both worlds, and the consciousness of this makes them seem alien to traditional Indians while making them feel alien among whites" (Riley, 2002, p. 59). Angie's story complicates this trope when it places Angie, the traditional Indian, in a room full of acculturated Indians (many of them more full-blooded than she) and it is she who is left alienated and self-conscious, even as she offers a withering reading of their fashion choices. Angie removes herself from this crowd, but not from Albuquerque. She believes some other path is possible, even in the city.

For a time, she pursues this other life in a multiethnic rather than an Indian context. Angie's most important lover is a Chicano man named Viviano. His wooing takes a serious turn when he asks her if she knows she is beautiful and she answers, "Sometimes I think so. But it depends. There are people who don't like to see mixed bloods." To this, he offers, "I thought you were chicana. Until I heard you talk. ~~You look like us except'~~ he hesitated, 'you are not quite 'right'. He looked into her eyes + smiled–'You're an Indian all right." Silko's in-line editing softens Viviano's initial comment, but both versions suggest that Angie's voice, either her reservation accent or her lack of a Chicana one, reveals her as a non-Chicana. Otherwise, she might pass. Indeed, Viviano's observation shows that Angie is a character who is to some extent always passing, whether it be by staying silent and allowing herself to be taken for Chicana or by asserting herself as linguistically or culturally Indian.

Viviano is not the first to make the observation. "You don't look like an Indian," her boss, Primo, says when he hires her as a bartender. Angie is insulted but "did not bother to answer," consoling herself with the thought, "All he was, she knew, was a mixed-blood Indian raised in Spanish ways." This sentence was initially drafted to read: "All a chicano was, she knew, was a mixed blood Indian raised in Spanish ways." Angie senses Primo holding Indians below Chicanos and displays a desire to take him down a peg by asserting that "all he was...was a mixed blood Indian." As the story unfolds, Primo becomes a dependable friend to Angie, and her initial aspersion about Primo being a mixed-blood Indian becomes a foreshadowing of the connection that the two enjoy. As the bar endures a plague of graduate students, Primo tells old stories of people who don't cut their hair and suffer infestations of black widow spiders. Angie "always smiled at Primo's stories" because "they reminded her of the stories she'd heard all her life about children who touch prayer sticks at the shrines and children who kill toads and frogs." Though Angie and Primo assert different racial, ethnic, and cultural identities, the common thread of their stories serves as a marker of true—perhaps even truer—kinship.

If a breed is an Indian who is, for one reason or another, not an Indian, then Angie's story also presents at least one other type of half-breed: a Chicano who is not a Chicano. Viviano is first introduced (in one version of this narrative) as one in an interchangeable series of lovers who fit into stable ethnic categories: "a homosexual Navajo" and "the big Pawnee" are replaced when she "found a big Chicano." But this identity is destabilized by Angie's assertions about Chicanos, mixed-blood Indians, and Spanish ways, as well as by Viviano's cultural and social associations. Viviano has rural roots—an uncle with a ranch north of Ojo del Padre—but he is "writing his doctoral dissertation on the economic impact of the white man on rural Chicanos in New Mexico" and his work is supported by a National Science Foundation grant. At the bar where Angie works, Primo and the regulars stare at him, making him "uncomfortable to be a college chicano" drinking with other graduate students. Through his research, he has set himself up in the historically Anglo role of sociological or anthropological observer of the rural community. In a different iteration, Viviano is married to a white woman and employed by the City Hall in an alcoholic counseling program. At night he weeps in Angie's bed because "he was a tormented man living a life he believed he should live, but not his life." In trying out these different lives for Viviano, the Angie drafts explore the experience of the alienated Chicano alongside that of the alienated Indian, portraying a multiethnic Southwest on a Chicana-Native American axis that will become more characteristic of Silko's later work in *Almanac of the Dead*.

The reason for choosing each word had to be explained with a story: Uses of archival knowledge

What are we to do with the knowledge that Tayo was once a woman? That *Ceremony* held but abandoned considerable investments in Chicana identity, in urban life, and shades of acculturation? By outlining the trajectory of a composition process, drafts can be indicative of important variables in a finished work. The Angie drafts show that (despite Silko's efforts to deflect it) considerable pressure can be brought to bear upon the choice of a male protagonist for the novel and upon the shallowness of its representation of human women, as well as upon the choice of a 1940s setting, and even on the rural setting and the novel's form.

Ceremony was a novel about healing from trauma before it became a novel about war. Veterans' reintegration and posttraumatic stress disorder or combat fatigue are important lenses through which to read *Ceremony* in its historical setting, its initial moment of publication, and its present-day context, but we should also recall Angie, Marie, and their mother as we have these conversations. Veterans and posttraumatic stress disorder are closely linked in the public mind, but the lost women of *Ceremony*'s Angie drafts can remind us that, though many veterans suffer from PTSD, the majority of PTSD sufferers are not veterans: they are women. A veteran's chances of coming home from Operation Iraqi Freedom with the disorder were around 14 percent, but just living as a female in America puts one in the path of so much physical and sexual trauma that women's lifetime incidence of PTSD is 9.7 percent.[5] These numbers would assuredly only grow more alarming if they were broken down along racial or socioeconomic lines to isolate women of a similar background to Angie's. There is more than enough violence in women's lives to carry off a story about trauma and healing.

Indeed, there is trauma enough in women's lives in *Ceremony* to tell such a story, but, despite Helen Jean's sympathetic history as a victim of workplace discrimination, sexual exploitation, and her essentially accidental descent into prostitution, Helen Jean's curls and her thick, red lips are signs enough for Tayo to invite readers to see her as fully lost to what Allen calls human mechanism or witchery. Perhaps the vision of Angie, the unrepentant, sensualist former prostitute, so terribly misread by Betonie as having it all and deserving no healing, can invite us to re-see Helen Jean, to imagine room for her within the novel's healing ceremony and to reach for an additional strain of meaning in *Ceremony*. We might lament how one type of suffering should breed empathy for another, but often fails to do so.

This strain of meaning can in turn inform our readings of the nuclear and geopolitical in *Ceremony*, highlighting as it does the novel's near misses of empathy as key moments for measuring Tayo's affliction and recovery. The first of these occurs very early in the novel when Tayo, newly released from the veteran's hospital, collapses in a Los Angeles train depot and is bent over by a Japanese-American mother and child. Their natural expression of human concern leaves him reeling and asking, "Those people. I thought they locked them up" (Silko, 1977, p. 16). The depot man's response, "Oh, that was some years back. Right after Pearl Harbor," obliquely evokes one of the classic prophylactics to empathy offered in postwar discourse about the atomic bomb, while Tayo, himself a survivor of the Bataan Death March, embodies the other. After all he has suffered, hatred and fear are lodged within Tayo like an illness. He vomits again and again into a trashcan, not trying to rid himself of this hatred and fear, but trying consciously to "vomit that image from his head" of "the face of the little boy, looking back at him, smiling" (1977, p. 16). The little boy reminds him of Rocky in their shared boyhood, but Tayo resists that moment of familial identification and his dawning knowledge that this boy and his mother have also suffered, just as he resisted the vision of Josiah that made his murdered enemies his kin.

When Tayo emerges from his healing ceremony, his vision leaps across space and time to bring him into expansive sympathy with people devoured "in cities twelve thousand miles away, victims who had never known these mesas, who had never seen the delicate colors of the rocks which boiled up their slaughter" (1977, p. 228). Tayo's newfound ability to see his own suffering as one part of the destroyers' great plan, a part which links him to other sufferers across the globe, is the achievement of a generous capacity for vision that marks both his healing and his full maturation. This maturity underlies his ability to choose nonviolence instead of attacking Emo just a few hours later.

Tayo's decision not to attack Emo is not merely a metaphor glorifying pacifism. Peace and war are called up in this moment because the nuclear vision that emerges in *Ceremony* is an interpersonal geopolitics. Silko's relentlessly intersectional, capacious vision deploys similar moments of near-empathy between the men and Helen Jean and in discussions of various characters' treatments of animals, as in the stirring Tayo feels along his spine when he hears Harley laughing about the thirty sheep and the good sheepdog who died under his care. Tayo was chilled because his friend scoffed at the commercial value of the sheep and "didn't seem to feel anything at all" (1977, p. 22). Tayo's quest in *Ceremony* is to find a way to feel without being incapacitated by feeling, to learn to heed rather than shout down those moments when human experiences come near converging and humanity intrudes upon habitual wartime stances of inhumanity.

When Silko elects to use Tayo as protagonist and 1940s Laguna as the setting, she accesses the atomic bomb as a symbol for her vision of humanity and convergence, tapping a powerful cultural practice of seeing the bomb as an inflection point in history. To examine the Angie drafts is to glimpse an alternate universe of choices and opportunities foregone: the subtler, social meetings of Indian and Chicana, the habitable city, and the shades of cultural change or acculturation unflattened to witchery and harmony. Perhaps the richest lesson of the Angie drafts is about the questions we ask novelists. We so often demand, how did you get the idea or the inspiration for your book? The Angie drafts remind us that it can be misguided to ask for a singular original moment for a complex work of fiction. The alternate origin story provided here in the Angie drafts shows that *Ceremony* began not only as an historical trauma—Second World War service and its aftermath—but also as a great wilderness of intersecting cultural traumas in need of literalization. Much was found, as well as lost, along the way.

Notes

1 All archival materials quoted are from the untitled work in Box 2 of the Leslie Marmon Silko Papers, Yale Collection of American Literature, Beinecke Rare Book and Manuscript Library. These materials were acquired in June of 1992 and do not yet have folder numbers.

2 In the most repeated account, Silko tells how she set out to write a humorous tale about the lengths to which an alcoholic veteran (Harley) will go for a cold beer, but the story was invaded by Tayo (Silko, 2006; Silko, 2002; Silko, Undated [*Ceremony*]). In the preface to the thirtieth-anniversary edition, she reiterates this account and adds another when she emphasizes that she wrote the great Southwestern novel while homesick in Ketchikan, Alaska, and that its vivid landscape descriptions resulted from her efforts to write herself home (Silko, 2006).

3 It is noteworthy how this brief early outline contains resonances and forecasts of plot and character with *Almanac* (Seese's child), and with *Gardens* (the sister relationship of Indigo and Salt), as well as with *Ceremony*.

4 Edith Swan reaches the same conclusion via early twentieth-century anthropologist Elsie Clews Parsons, who asserts that for the Laguna, "religious identity and access to ideology formally pass through men" (1988, p. 236).

5 A 2008 RAND Corporation study placed the percentage of Operation Iraqi Freedom veterans then suffering from PTSD at 13.8 percent. The US National Comorbidity Survey Replication conducted between 2001 and 2002 put the lifetime prevalence of PTSD for men at 3.5 percent and for women at 9.7 percent.

References

Allen, P. G. (1986), "The Feminine Landscape of Leslie Marmon Silko's *Ceremony*," in *The Sacred Hoop: Recovering the Feminine in American Indian Traditions*. Boston: Beacon Press, pp. 118–126.

Antell, J. (1988), "Momaday, Welch, and Silko: Expressing the Feminine Principle through Male Alienation." *American Indian Quarterly*, 12:3, 213–220.

Jaskoski, H. (1991), "Thinking Woman's Children and the Bomb," in N. Anisfeld (ed.), *The Nightmare Considered: Critical Essays on Nuclear War Literature*. Bowling Green: Bowling Green University Press, pp. 159–176.

Riley, P. (2002), "The Mixed Blood Writer as Interpreter and Mythmaker," in J. Brennan (ed.), *Mixed Race Literature*. Stanford: Stanford University Press, pp. 57–69.

Silko, L. M. (Undated), Untitled Work. Leslie Marmon Silko Papers, Box 2. Yale Collection of American Literature, Beinecke Rare Book and Manuscript Library, New Haven, CT.

Silko, L. M. (Undated), [*Ceremony*]: [preface?] Written for promotional department at Viking, Leslie Marmon Silko Papers, Box 2. Yale Collection of American Literature, Beinecke Rare Book and Manuscript Library, New Haven, CT.

Silko, L. M. (1977), *Ceremony*. 2006 Edition. New York: Penguin.

Silko, L. M. (2002), "Interview by Laura Coltelli," in A. Chavkin (ed.), *Leslie Marmon Silko's* Ceremony: *A Casebook*. New York: Oxford University Press, pp. 241–256.

Silko, L. M. (2006), Preface to *Ceremony*. New York: Penguin, pp. xi–xix.

Swan, E. (1988), "Laguna Symbolic Geography in Leslie Marmon Silko's *Ceremony*." *American Indian Quarterly* 12: 3, 229–249.

Whittier-Ferguson, J. (1997), "The Burden of Drafts: Woolf's Revisions of *Between the Acts*." *Text*, 10, 297–319.

Part Two:
Almanac of the Dead

"Indian Country":
Introduction to Part Two

David L. Moore

Almanac of the Dead has been compared to Dante's *Commedia*, to Joyce's *Ulysses*, and to Melville's *Moby Dick*.[1] The vast scope of Silko's novel certainly invokes similar historical and mythic dimensions across centuries, and its political critique is pointed, now on the colonial capital of the modern era. Yet its affirmation of Indigenous revolution is unique. Reaching such an affirmation in this magnum opus is another aspect of the author's role of witness, the text's semi-objective, semi-omniscient point of view, and of the reader's participation in that role that together bring the book to life.[2] It is a tough read, because the content is so grim, so the reader must step back into the role of witness in order to maintain distance—but in so doing, when one understands Silko's usage of the Arrowboy myth and her positioning of the author and the reader on the turquoise ledge of witness (as we discussed this role in the introduction), then that role allows a different kind of engagement, a deeper participation than merely "suspension of disbelief." Through the combined immediacy and detachment of witness, the reader's belief that this story is "too real" becomes a commitment to the issues Silko exposes.

The novel has a basic thesis, inscribed on the map that opens the book: "The Indian Wars have never ended in the Americas.

Native Americans acknowledge no borders; they seek nothing less than the return of all tribal lands…The ancient prophecies also foretell the disappearance of all things European" (1991, pp. 14–15). Amid the 763 pages of varied characters who live and die among terrorist bombs, failing bulletproof vests, snuff films, international trade in body parts, arms and munitions, and a catalog of drug-laced sex and violence—as well as encouraging elements such as barefoot prophets, sacred macaws, people's armies, and the sudden appearance of a giant stone snake near the uranium mine tailings at Laguna—the novel articulates a remarkable vision:

> The old people had stories that said…that it was only a matter of time and things European would gradually fade from the American continents. History would catch up with the white man whether the Indians did anything or not. History was the sacred text. The most complete history was the most powerful force. (p. 316)

That force is the relentless spirits of the earth:

> The forces were harsh. A great many people would suffer and die. All ideas and beliefs of the Europeans would gradually wither and drop away…The white man would someday disappear all by himself. The disappearance had already begun at the spiritual level. (p. 511)

The confidence in telling this story of return, this act of testimony and of witness, constitutes radical action generated by the novel itself. The reader is invited to participate. As Wacah, one of the Indigenous Mexican prophets, proclaims:

> all human beings were welcome to live in harmony together. People from tribes farther south, peasants without land, *mestizos*, the homeless from the cities and even a busload of Europeans, had come to hear the spirit macaws speak through Wacah…the people were protected by the spirits and needed no weapons. The changes might require another hundred years, until the Europeans had been outnumbered and the people retook the land peacefully. (pp. 709–710)

It takes a detached witness in the reader to dig through the novel's grim "realities" and to find such prophecies of gradual peace, promising actual resolutions to the colonial era's imbalances, but that seems to be the point of the novel: to point to those prophecies. Where "the ancestors" spirits were summoned by the stories, "the stories or 'histories' are sacred"... "within 'history' reside relentless forces, powerful spirits, vengeful, relentlessly seeking justice" (p. 316). Thus, the novel ends in a vision of rebirth: "... the giant snake had returned now ... The snake was looking south, in the direction from which the twin brothers and the people would come" (p. 763).

In 1981, Silko was awarded the MacArthur Foundation fellowship, or "genius grant," allowing her to work for the next decade on *Almanac of the Dead*. This work of fiction stands among the many original MacArthur projects working creatively to change the world. As discussed in the introduction, *Almanac of the Dead* is in some ways an extension of themes in *Ceremony*, and a precursor to themes in *Gardens in the Dunes*, though each is radically different in tone. They link not only through the Arrowboy myth of witness, but also by the eventual return to the spirits of the land, on personal, continental, hemispheric, and global scales, with mythic resonance for the body politic. As the story of an almanac and its keepers across generations, *Almanac* accounts for the brutalities of history as well as its long arc toward justice.

Penelope M. Kelsey makes visible some vital dimensions of Silko's second novel through "Indigenous Economic Critique in Silko's *Almanac of the Dead* and Gaspar de Alba's *Desert Blood*: Against a Philosophy of Separatism." She shows how Silko uses Pueblo worldview and narrative frameworks as tools to critique modern capitalism, but Kelsey further complicates this straightforward juxtaposition of Indigenous and settler-colonial patterns with a nuanced gender analysis through third and fourth genders in Pueblo culture. Silko's familiarity with these alternatives, according to Kelsey, portrays abject sexualities in *Almanac* as not entirely negative, even as they remain necessarily part of capitalism's toxic modes of production and exchange. In the first part of her chapter, Kelsey thus contextualizes Silko's portrayal of queer subjectivities in the larger cosmology that the novel invokes and narrates. Then Kelsey brings *Almanac of the Dead* into conversation with Alicia Gaspar de Alba's mystery novel, *Desert Blood: The Juárez Murders*. In Gaspar de Alba's critique of capitalism through an exposure of

the border politics of the actual Ciudad Juárez femicide, an assault
on Indigenous women, Kelsey finds another fiction based on real
histories painfully resonant with Silko's material in *Almanac*. In the
context of her gender analysis, Kelsey maps the ways these two
novels form a coherent critique of resource extraction economies
and capitalism through Indigenous worldview. She shows how
both lay bare a EuroWestern philosophy of separation that makes
such exploitation possible. In further contrast, she clarifies how
Silko imagines Indigenous peoples might heal from the aftermath
of genocide. We see how Silko's novel embraces alternative futures
hewn from Native economic principles of responsibility, right
relationship, and community.

Deborah L. Madsen's chapter, "Silko, Freud, and the Voicing of
Disavowed Histories in *Almanac of the Dead*," grounds the link
between the novelist and the founder of psychoanalysis in a 1992
interview where Silko describes how she overcame a writing block
by setting aside her manuscript of *Almanac of the Dead* in order
to read Sigmund Freud. "About two-thirds of the way through,
I just finally had to stop and read Freud, and I read all eighteen
volumes, one right after the other." Madsen also pursues Silko's
own comparison of the writing process to psychoanalysis: "It's like
do-it-yourself psychoanalysis. It's sort of dangerous to be a novelist.
I really learned it with this one—you're working with language
and all kinds of things can escape with the words of a narrative."
However, rather than analyzing the author, Madsen does important
textual work by exploring the role of Freudian theories of language
in *Almanac of the Dead*. Madsen's chapter asks how the cluster
of issues explored by Freud has been used narratologically by
Silko. Looking at the novel's heteroglossic style, Madsen analyzes
the role of *Almanac*'s narrative voice as a means of translating an
Indigenous epistemology into the conventions of English language
literature. Madsen applies Freud's late work, especially *Moses
and Monotheism* (1939) in which he develops the theory where
personal and social dysfunction originate in guilt inherited from
a foundational historical act of violence. Freud argues that the
historical transformation of such inherited guilt informs cultural
ritual and figurative language, most intensely in the development
of religious practices but also in patterns of social violence and
compulsive neurotic behaviors. As Madsen offers this profoundly
suitable lens for understanding characters and narrative structures

in *Almanac*, we see how Silko not only applies Freudian principles to settler-colonial patterns, but she also presages twenty-first-century studies of intergenerational trauma in Indigenous populations.

Beth Piatote illuminates visionary possibilities in Silko as she focuses on a key trope in the novel, with "Seeing Double: Twins and Time in Silko's *Almanac of the Dead*." Tracing a fundamental structure of correspondences, she pushes the function of witness to the larger act of "seeing." Indeed, she specifies the specular process in the act of witness. As Piatote explains, from the start of the narrative, all things have similarities to be seen and discerned; the agentive force of "things" demands a careful eye. The mixing of "old blood" and "new blood" hints at a theme that emerges through the book: time (as past/old and present/new) gains materiality in the body. The embodiment of time and the agency of "things" reflect a world that is unstable, in which there is no fixed point of orientation, either temporally or materially. While the activities of the characters differ—mixing, cleaning, and counting—all of the characters are visually tracking each other, pointing to the dominant interpretive practice of the book: seeing. To make meaning of this world, one must see its elements in relation to each other, one must discern fine differences, one must distinguish between twins. The novel is filled with twins, both biological and metaphorical, and it is incumbent upon the reader to recognize and discern them, including the most terrifying twins of all: capitalism and colonialism.

Through this binocular lens, Piatote's chapter helps us to understand the remarkable dynamics that link *Almanac of the Dead* as fiction to its own twin reality as history. Piatote explains how all things in this book bear a resemblance to something else. An almanac, after all, is a compendium of days in which correspondences are assumed. Based on past occurrences and patterns, an almanac predicts when a certain set of forces is expected to converge again and produce a new day that is very much like a previous one, predicting which days are auspicious for various activities. As Lecha explains of old almanacs, they "don't just tell you when to plant or harvest, they tell you about the days yet to come—drought or flood, plague, civil war or invasion" (p. 137). Silko's novel, structured as a narrative almanac, offers episodic entries of past and present events that anticipate and predict the future. There is no single linear plot or central protagonist to follow, rather a cast of more than thirty characters who circulate through the book, engaging in various forms of warfare. Objects, too, express animate life and desires: "Knives, guns, even automobiles, possessed 'energies' that craved blood from time to time" (p. 512). The *Almanac* presents a world in motion, a world in which "revolution" is both an ideological call and a geophysical fact. This structure participates in the novel's critique of the Conquest of the Americas; by putting time and energy in motion, it contests the notion that Conquest is or ever will be complete. As the *Almanac*'s "Five Hundred Year Map" declares: "The Indian Wars have never ended in the Americas" (p. 15).

These three chapters bring fresh, courageous energy to the unprecedented reading experience that is *Almanac of the Dead*. New ways of seeing Silko's text in various contexts, of gender, of trauma, and of delicate perception between dualities in time, actually partake in the novel's "revolution" as another kind of participatory research. As Silko writes, "The energy or 'electricity' of a being's spirit was not extinguished by death; it was set free from the flesh. Dust to dust or as a meal for pack rats, the energy of the spirit was never lost." These scholars help to show how the narratives of death in *Almanac of the Dead* may set the spirit free, and "the energy had only been changing form, nothing had been lost or destroyed" (p. 719).

Notes

1   See, for instance, Janet Powers' piece in Barnett & Thorson (1996) in Further Reading.
2   Several pieces in the Further Readings section explore the role of witness in *Almanac*.

4

Indigenous Economic Critique in Silko's *Almanac of the Dead* and Gaspar de Alba's *Desert Blood*: Against a Philosophy of Separation

Penelope M. Kelsey

The United States created the border in violence and has maintained and regulated it through violence.

(ELIZABETH ARCHULETA)

Awash in a world replete with traditional Laguna Pueblo stories and Keresan language, though forbidden to speak the language in schools, Leslie Marmon Silko remembers that she only became aware of her difference as someone of mixed ancestry when non-Native adults came to her primary school and wanted to take pictures of "the Indian children," telling Silko to move out of the camera's view. This request came presumably because as someone of visibly mixed ancestry, Silko was not a "real Indian" and perhaps also served as an unwelcome reminder of the realities of racial intermarriage through the United States, but especially in New Mexico, where *mestizaje* is a normative state of being. Hence, from an early age, Silko felt the impositions of borders created by the colonial imaginary and perceived its efforts to police or discipline her own young body into already defined categories. This psychic wound would necessarily be exacerbated by Silko's own identity as Indigenous from both north and south of the U.S.-Mexico border— as both American Indian and Mexican Chicana—and the required exclusion of Indigeneity within the Mexican and American national imaginaries, an idea I will explore at greater length in this essay by bringing *Almanac of the Dead* into conversation with Alicia Gaspar de Alba's *Desert Blood*. In brief, American and Mexican notions of identity and legitimate claims to citizenship are predicated upon rigid notions of identity that Silko's work continually refuses; further, Silko's fiction actively disrupts and questions the maintenance of these settler-colonial exclusions, while Gaspar de Alba's novel implicitly acknowledges the tensions in U.S./Mexico imaginings of the Indigenous female other.

In contrast to the colonial categories of indigene versus alien, Silko writes of the integrity of the Laguna old-timers' definition of Laguna community and identity as delineated along a continuum of behavior:

> My physical appearance seemed not to matter to the old-time people. They looked at the world very differently; a person's appearance and possessions did not matter nearly as much as a person's behavior. For them, a person's value lies in how that person interacts with other people, how that person behaves toward the animals and the earth. (1996, p. 61)

Embedded in this definition of Pueblo cultural values and identity formation is a critique of consumer capitalism and its recourse to objectifying dynamic beings; furthermore, this separation between humans and the natural world informs the philosophy of separation from which borders arise, a process Eva Cherniavsky labels "capital's relentless tendency toward abstraction" (2006, p. 50). Thus, capitalism functions as an extension of colonialism and anthropocentric Eurowestern social constructs in Silko's writing. Further, Silko addresses the introduction of a capitalist economy as a causal factor in Indigenous investment in the colonial project's definition of the self, insofar as subjects of the colonial project become invested, intellectually and economically, in that definition of themselves (e.g., legal codes, settler-defined tribal governments, and restricting resource access to members sanctioned by the settler-colonial authorities). In fact, *Almanac of the Dead* clearly invokes the history of slavery and conquest as capitalist enterprise that defined racial categories (Black, Indian, mestizo) that the Américas are organized around to this day; the characters in *Almanac* then enact a prophecy whereby Indigenous and tribal peoples (American and African) can reclaim sovereign space and self-definition within decolonial categories.

In a related example, Silko has been addressing the issue of the border patrol in the Southwest in her writing for over two decades; specifically, Silko decries the police state that enforces classificatory, carceral definitions of citizen and alien. In her 1994 work, "The Border Patrol State," Silko describes the heavy surveillance of the U.S.-Mexico border and the palpable impact it has had and continues to have upon her day-to-day life as a person of Mexican and Laguna ancestry living along the border. Silko writes,

> Manifest Destiny may lack its old grandeur of theft and blood—
> "lock the door" is what it means now, with racism a trump card
> to be played again and again, shamelessly, by both major political
> parties. "Immigration," like "street crime" and "welfare fraud,"
> is a political euphemism that refers to people of color … Even in
> the days of Spanish and Mexican rule, no attempts were made to
> interfere with the flow of people and goods from south to north
> and north to south. It is the U.S. government that has continually
> attempted to sever contact between the tribal people north of the
> border and those to the south. (1996, p. 121).

Silko's essay makes plain that for Indigenous peoples of the Américas, the border is a highly politicized space writ over with an imposed settler-colonial geography not hewn of Indigenous worldview. Whether one is Diné or Ráramuri, Mexicano with no conscious claim to being *Indio* or a self-identified Chicana/o[1] with an embrace of Aztec and other tribal ancestries, the border continually discriminates against those who appear to be Indigenous to this hemisphere and who lack visible markers of being members of the *gringo* society.[2] In fact, in an essay on *Almanac of the Dead*, Elizabeth Archuleta contends that visible Indigeneity has been inseparably entwined with criminality in settler society:

> The United States still perceives American Indians as foreign
> and potentially criminal with their allegiances lying elsewhere.

Therefore, drug and immigration laws that ascribe criminality
to people of color reinforce colonialist attitudes about American
Indians and other dark-skinned individuals crossing and traveling
near border areas. In the Southwest, race, space, and identity
became intertwined, resembling the South where Jim Crow laws
created a "black" identity and the "black" space of segregation.
(2005, p. 118)

Archuleta's historicizing of the Southwest places the border of
Silko's fiction and nonfiction in its cultural context and highlights
key themes of nativity, origins, and border policing that resonate
within *Almanac* and in ongoing popular racial discourse, such
as current media coverage of Central American migrant children
at the Texas border.[3] Archuleta's observations also highlight
the interrelationships between African American and Native
American experiences of carcerality in the western hemisphere, of
policing categories borne of the capitalist endeavors of conquest
and slavery; similarly, this legacy is interwoven in plot elements
bridging the Américas and Africa via characters such as Clinton
and Menardo.

Silko's 1991 epic novel, *Almanac of the Dead* was published
on the eve of the quincentennial anniversary of Cristobal Colon's
"discovery" of the Americas at Guanahani, and, not surprisingly,
borders in the novel, particularly those between settler state and
Indigenous nations throughout North, Central, and South America,
produce a continuing tension as a signifier of conflicts between
claimings and inhabitance of contested geographies. Similarly, Alicia
Gaspar de Alba's 2005 novel *Desert Blood* is set in a singularly
significant border town, El Paso or Ciudad Juárez, and the novel
portrays the collisions of Northern exploitation with always-already
colonized experiences of Mexicanos, Tejanos, and Chican@s in that
border town. Using the perspective of Chican@ lesbian academic
Ivon Villa who has returned home to El Paso to adopt a child, the
reader experiences a jolting awakening to the grim realities faced
by *maquiladoras*, or young female laborers, who work in factories
along the border. Seeking initially to adopt the child of a fifteen-
year-old pregnant factory worker, Ivon's endeavor is cut short when
the mother is murdered, leaving Ivon childless, but motivated to
bring the murderer to justice. In the course of her self-appointed
investigation, an inquiry that Ivon undertakes precisely because

of the failure of existing justice systems to successfully solve the Juárez femicide, Ivon discovers the unsolved murders of (now) hundreds of *hijas del sur* ("daughters from the south"), young, dark women with dark straight hair who are employed in the border *maquilas* under dangerous conditions for very little pay and who are fired at will when they get pregnant. In fact, the market forces that consume these young women, leaving their raped and dead bodies in unmarked graves in the desert to be found by activists leading *rastreos* (investigative searches), have many arms: U.S. businesses seek the cheap employment of impoverished young women (often girls) from southern Mexico to staff their factories; a misogynist and anti-Indigenous transborder culture contributes to and normalizes staffing the management of the factories with men who often sexually harass these young women who themselves are far from their families; drug, prostitution, and pornography rings take advantage of the incoming supply of young, attractive bodies and employ these young women in their activities by force or other persuasion; the police and border patrol are complicit and ineffective in their enforcement of legal protections for these young women both while living and after death; finally, El Paso's identity as the destination for sexual predators who are relocated to the city after their release from prison markedly underscores and encourages the disproportionate violence against Mexican and Chican@ women in Juárez and El Paso, highlighting their particular precarity in a legalistic, jurisdictional, and developmental borderland.

Indigeneity is ever-present but unvoiced in Alba's novel: the primary targets of the Juárez femicide are phenotypically young Indian women from the lower classes and, usually, the undeveloped south of Mexico, which has a high Indian population, marking them as figuratively tribal if not actually Indigenous in communally recognized ways. Color, skin tone, language, hair, facial features, and body frame are all returned to in Alba's descriptions; however, Alba never makes the overt point that *las hijas del sur* are most assuredly Indigenous women, a fact that imbricates the Juárez femicide with a larger pattern of attacks on Indigenous peoples. Both Silko and Alba present critiques of capitalism and its misogynist and colonial effects through the lens of the novel; both foreground pathology and perversity by way of establishing the rationale for such exploitation, using differing vantage points (from within and without); both situate the border and Indigenous peoples and spaces as central to the novels' conflicts, while Alba does not give this perspective voice or provide a lexicon for this conceptualization; and both conspicuously position queer identities as having significance for their visions, though with vastly differing articulations.

In *Almanac of the Dead*, Silko uses Pueblo worldview and narrative frameworks as tools to critique capitalism; this literary engagement of Pueblo narrative has precedent in *Storyteller* and *Ceremony*. Using the Pueblo witchcraft narrative, certain figures in *Almanac* are necessarily demonized, although they are not inherently negative figures within traditional Pueblo worldview (i.e., gays, addicts), *nor within the novel itself* if placed within the trajectory of Pueblo narrative as defined by Silko. Meanwhile, Gaspar de Alba similarly performs a critique of capitalism that is deeply informed by border politics and Indigeneity; however, her Indigenous figures are implicitly Indigenous, not explicitly so: their Indianness is never provided a voice, though the conditions of their Indianness are inherently tied to their oppression in *Desert Blood*. Together, these two novels form a panoramic critique of capitalism replete with Indigenous worldview, providing deeply situated histories and analyses in the specific locales of Tucson and Cuidad Juárez/El Paso, and enacting two different models of queer Indigenous representation as social critique.

Queerness, toxicity, and *Almanac of the Dead*

Almanac of the Dead is a markedly ambitious novel, encompassing three continents, countless countries, numerous Indigenous territories, and the Fifth World of Hopi prophecy. This geographic expanse is all unified through a consistently changing narrator, though the most important one who functions as a point of departure is Sterling, a Laguna Pueblo man who has been expelled from his community as a scapegoat for the exposure of a sacred stone snake that mysteriously appeared at Laguna several months prior to the arrival of a Hollywood film crew; Sterling has been entrusted with the oversight of the filming and makes an irrevocable misstep when he accidentally leads the crew to this sacred site. Sterling's expulsion is also fueled by familial jealousies of his relationship to his aunt who dies soon after his sentencing. Sterling is an unmarried man with profound ties to his elderly aunts; he works off of the Pueblo for years on the railroad and returns in his retirement, during which he is soon employed as the tribal cultural protection officer for a Hollywood film being shot at Laguna. Sterling acts, if not as a moral compass, as a mediator for the novel's readings, one with clear ties to Laguna traditions, but also one who has experienced the fracturing of boarding school education and colonial assaults on culture. In fact, Sterling identifies his reason for never marrying as a failure to find a woman who would measure up to his powerful and matronly Laguna aunts who signify the cultural continuity and resilience of earlier generations at Laguna. Meanwhile, the death of his parents during childhood and his early departure for boarding school have acted to arrest Sterling's development figuratively: in part, he maintains his solid relationship with his aunts because boarding school has prevented his full maturation to adulthood as a Laguna man, in addition to leaving him without the cultural sensitivity to know when to intervene in the filming.

Sterling acts as a normalizing agent, who is not completely consumed with varying expressions of colonial toxicity, and a voyeur, of sorts, who provides the reader with a lens for approaching the myriad horrors to which *Almanac* will subject them. Sterling's constant immersion in *True Detective* crime magazines of the 1950s and their narrative of early twentieth-century criminal icons, such as John Dillinger, acts as a narrative frame for approaching the crime readers witness in the novel and also affirms a much longer trajectory of criminal behavior in American society: the truism that the United States was founded by criminals and outcasts hereby is continually alluded to and thematically developed as the demise of Dillinger and others and the locales they frequented recur in Sterling's reflections and in the action of the novel. Further, John Trudell's observation that justice is unobtainable on stolen land is also underscored by the recurring leitmotifs of settler crime, massacre, and lawlessness. As Zeta observes, "no legal government could be established on stolen land" (Silko, 1992, p. 133). The action of *Almanac* embodies and performs the tradition of corruption conceived with initial land theft and proceeding through the contact period to the present.

Seese, a non-Native addict whose child has been abducted and who, like Sterling, is employed by Lecha, Zeta, and Ferro at the compound outside of Tucson, also provides readers with a metric for navigating the morass of dysfunction, addiction, and crime that the novel washes over the reader. If Sterling's greatest crime is a failure to possess deep cultural knowledge and facility with engaging non-Natives in a Laguna context, Seese's failing is her lack of grounding in the love triangle formed by her photographer boyfriend David, his former lover Eric, and herself, with the added fourth leg of Beaufrey, a cocaine and pornographic film dealer who is strongly attached to David. Seese's own addiction clouds her judgment, leading her to fail to apprehend the lengths to which Beaufrey will go, in order to confirm his claim on David. Thus, Beaufrey's growing jealousy of Seese's bond with David via their son Monte leads to the kidnapping and (presumed) death of the child. Seese's search for Monte leads her to Lecha, a renowned psychic who is consulted by police in unsolved criminal cases; however, much as with David, Seese again makes a misstep in not apprehending that Lecha, though a talented psychic, has "bought" Seese's loyalty as an employee through a false promise of finding the child, when, in fact, the child is likely dead. This lie, however, allows Seese to continuing living with some shred of sanity, and furnishes Lecha with a much needed assistant as she finishes her restoration of the almanac.

Like Seese's relationship to Lecha, all of the novel's five major narrative threads are connected by webs of settler colonialism and Indigenous struggle as well as critiques of capital. The first thread includes some of the Tucson area characters, Lecha, Zeta, Ferro, Paulie, and Calabazas. These figures embody both the integrity and restoration of Indigenous knowledge and lands, with an inflection of the consequences of growing away from the earth and the feminine principle.[4] Lecha is responsible for the restoration of the almanac, a Mesoamerican book of glyphs that predates contact and that has been fragmented by the loss (sale and otherwise) of pages in the codex. Zeta is her twin and the adoptive mother of Lecha's son Ferro who runs a drug business based in the family's ranch compound outside of Tucson; Paulie is his minion and sexual partner. Calabazas is a trafficker in drugs and other illicit trade items, an allegory of reliable mapping, and one of the twins' clanspeople and thus a relative tying them back to their home village of Potam.

Like their German father, Zeta has inherited an internal emptiness that, according to Yoeme, the twins' Yaqui grandmother, is borne of having grown away from the earth and having violently taken its riches as well.

A second thread among the multiple patterns of *Almanac* interweaves the revolutionary activities and drug wars south of the border. These settings include a Marxist revolutionary school in Mexico City, which trains and prepares Indigenous Mexicans to prepare for the coming apocalypse. There are also two prophesied brothers from the south, a pair of twins, Tacho and El Feo, who act as harbingers of the coming Fifth World and the decolonization of the Américas. The affair between Menardo, a self-made *Indio* man, and Alegria, the *guera* architect who designs Menardo's wife Iliana's dream home on the edge of the southern jungle, highlights the entwinement of class and Indigeneity, given Iliana's upper-class origins and her need to validate Menardo's social standing through excessive displays of wealth. For North American readers, these segments provide context for the larger ideation surrounding Indigeneity in the Américas, which differs significantly from the blood-quantum-based thinking predominant in assigning Native identities in the United States and Canada.

A third thread of the novel is located in Africa, another colonial site deeply in need of decolonization. This set of conflicts functions largely as a tie to the Tucson homeless and veterans who are largely people of color, especially African Americans. This fourth narrative thread portrays a rising body of homeless people dubbed "the army of the homeless," which operates as a primary symptom of the real estate development and other capitalist ventures founded on stolen land. The leaders of the army are Native American and African American, which implies the connection between colonization of the Américas and forced abduction from Africa. Meanwhile, Max Blue and his wife Hannah Blue make unprecedented wealth from real estate development that is entirely unsustainable, pushing the desert's fragile ecosystem far beyond its limit. That these characters are making incredible wealth from capitalist ventures that "other" the earth, while people are living without homes on the streets of Tucson, illustrates the disjuncture between venture capitalism, human consumption, and the environment. That these criminals will be brought to justice seems a foregone conclusion as Silko's language highlights the ludicrous nature of this endeavor.

The final thread of the novel, which is a subset of the first, and is set largely in California, encompasses the relationships between Seese, David, Eric, and Beaufrey, and underscores how addiction lends itself to imbalanced behavior and is taken advantage of by capitalist, resource-extractive practices. The narrative arc continually interweaves Seese's flashbacks of her drug-addled days with David and Beaufrey and a portrayal of the vicious power dynamic in this triangle, though Seese finds herself necessarily distracted by the triangle between herself, Eric, and David. Both here and with the characters of Ferro and Paulie is where the novel earns its reputation for reinscribing stereotypes of abject queer sexualities; however, as this analysis will show, an approach to the novel that transits the Laguna cosmological tropes that Silko employs will illuminate how imbalances attributable to settler colonialism are truly the culprits in *Almanac*.[5]

Toxicity, abject sexuality, and the *kunideeyahs*

Almanac of the Dead has been critiqued, and perhaps rightly so, for its portrayals of toxic queers and abject sexuality. One is at a loss in reflecting on the book to identify a single, resilient, and positive LGBTQ representation. Beaufrey is a power maven who pursues David more for dominance than for love; Eric is a self-hating southern queer; David, while not entirely unlikeable, takes photos of Eric post-mortem and exploits a legal escape clause in his "modeling agreement" with Eric to the benefit of his career; Ferro abhors his mother, Lecha, who abandoned him at birth; Paulie is a subservient sycophant who has no identity beyond his self-imposed enslavement to Ferro. Pedophiles recur as disturbed male figures who assault boys and girls alike, and Lecha is called in by the police to help find missing boys who have been buried on a beach by one such deviant. It's an ugly lot. But, by and large, when characters are fully developed and have more than a momentary lifespan on the page, and when those fully developed LGBTQ characters are situated in their larger context—and they are all men—the abject nature of their behavior has a rationale, however flawed.

In fact, many queer characters are relative moral paragons compared to those in their immediate environment: for instance, Beaufrey is encoded as queer with a palpable tie to David, which will not brook any threat (i.e., Seese, Monte, David, and Seese's baby), and he makes his living creating and distributing pseudo-snuff films for what, it would seem, Silko identifies as the "real" perverts. Beaufrey is merely there to make a profit. Similarly, while David seizes the opportunity to take photos of Eric immediately after his suicide, the reader never sees his emotional response as he does this, as we have limited omniscience in narration via Seese. Further, when the photographs have their opening in the gallery, David cannot bring himself to attend the showing and view them. Ferro is a stereotypical woman-hating gay, it would seem; however, his attitude is explained by Lecha's abandonment of him days after his birth and her ongoing ability to find humor in this event. Paulie has been marred by a traumatic past, but like others scarred by life, he finds meaning and validation in serving Ferro. In each abject case, the text provides mediating circumstances, despite its apparent cumulative effect.

Where an explication of toxic queer and abject sexual representations becomes enlightening is in reconciling Silko's own salvaged Pueblo narrative of witchery, which informs her larger body of work and, most certainly, the narrative arc and rationale of *Almanac of the Dead*. First introduced in Silko's 1977 novel *Ceremony*, most readers of Silko are now familiar with the central poem, which later appears in *Storyteller* (1981) as well. In brief, the poem's speaker recounts a witches' convention in North America in time immemorial that incites a "contest in dark things," culminating in one unknown witch, neither male nor female, of an unknown tribe, telling a story of the creation of white people, which sets the conquest in motion. The finale of this story is the discovery by white people of uranium in the hills above the pueblos:

Up here
in these hills
they will find the rocks,
rocks with veins of green and yellow and black.
They will lay the final pattern with these rocks
they will lay it across the world
and explode everything. (Silko, 2012, pp. 127–128)

While the other witches no longer think the story is funny and ask the storyteller to "call that story back," the witch says, "It's already turned loose./It's already coming./It can't be called back" (Silko, 2012, p. 129). This prophetic prose poem provides a fictional frame that recounts the history of uranium discovery and mining at Laguna Pueblo, a capitalist endeavor undertaken without the informed consent of the Lagunas.

This central lyric also forms the rationale for *Ceremony*: drought is brought to Laguna Pueblo because of the people's agreement to have uranium mined from their land, which fuels the bombs dropped at Hiroshima and Nagasaki. Tayo himself faces his own culpability as a colonial subject who kills other colonized peoples while serving in the Second World War; to restore balance again and complete the ceremonial circle, Tayo must resist fighting with the destroyers and not be lured into killing their victim outside the mine. This ritual cycle is repeated elsewhere in Silko's writing, and the witchcraft trope functions as an emblem for settler colonialism, resource extraction economies, the philosophy of separation (separateness vs. integration), and those who are its pawns (e.g., Emo). Similarly, the witchcraft cycle or function forms the rationale for the imbalances that are presented in *Almanac*: nearly any character who suffers from imbalance and who exploits the earth or human vulnerability for their own benefit is an agent of the witchery or *kunideeyahs*.

Silko makes a clear delineation between those who are implicated to one degree or another in the spread of the witchery and those who are its agents. For instance, Beaufrey makes his living creating films for pedophiles and "snuff" aficionados, but the narrator is clear that Beaufrey finds his customers disgusting and creates fake "snuff" films that satisfy his customers without actually harming the actors. Ferro clearly suffers from his abandonment by Lecha as a baby, so his pathology is clearly unlinked from his sexuality and the pathology's causality is in Lecha's failure as a mother. Other examples abound, but what is clear is that all characters in the text suffer and are toxic, which is a symptom of their condition as members of a settler-colonial state, whether oppressed or oppressors. As Jeff Berglund argues in *Cannibal Fictions*, "the errors of *all* of the cannibalistic characters in the novel—not just homosexual men—stem from the failure to meet other humans, Subject to Subject…[Further], Silko offers up no relationship between men and women that is mutually satisfying, that is not fractured by egotism" (2006, p. 158). Thus, *Almanac* is rife with toxic characters, and some of them are gay, which leads to negative representational consequences. However, this seeming reinscription of abject queer stereotypes is the consequence of an epistemic intervention on Silko's part via the witchery narrative, an idea that I will develop at greater length in the chapter's conclusion.

We'Wha, Lhamana, and two-spirited Pueblo identity

Reflecting on Silko's sizeable corpus of writing, her conversance in Pueblo oral tradition, story, and song is clear; thus, one may safely assume that Silko is familiar with Pueblo third- and fourth-gender roles among the Pueblos. Silko observes,

> In the old Pueblo world, differences were celebrated as signs of the Mother Creator's grace. Persons born with exceptional physical or sexual differences were highly respected and honored because their physical differences gave them special positions as mediators between this world and the spirit world...
>
> Before the arrival of Christian missionaries, a man could dress as a woman and work with the women and even marry a man without any fanfare. Likewise, a woman was free to dress like a man, to hunt and go to war with the men, and to marry a woman. In the old Pueblo worldview, we are all a mixture of male and female, and this sexual identity is changing constantly. Sexual inhibition did not begin until the Christian missionaries arrived. (1996, p. 67)

In this passage, Silko acknowledges her own awareness of traditional Pueblo acceptance of a range of gender expressions, and she affirms the integrity of that way of life before it was ruptured by Christianity. Thus, her own observations suggest other possible meanings for her inscriptions of seemingly abject queer characters.

A closer consideration of Pueblo gender formation sheds further light on Silko's queer representations. From an early age, young Pueblo children might show a transgender affinity for dress, behavior, and language that was part of a cultural process of "gradual acquisition of gender," as Will Roscoe explains in *The Zuni Man-Woman*. Regardless of whether a maturing child was biologically male or female, all individuals "acquired" gender identity through "cultural and ritual interventions" (1991, p. 132). Third- and fourth-gender individuals were referred to as Lhamana and were commonly observed among Pueblo people by outsiders until early in the twentieth century (p. 28). The most well known example in the non-Native world was We'Wha, a Zuni Pueblo, who was born a male, but was initiated as a Lhamana during adolescence.[6] We'Wha was considered the most important person in the Zuni Pueblo, and when the first non-Native missionary arrived, We'Wha served as a liaison and quickly learned English (Roscoe, 1991, p. 46). Later in life, anthropologist Matilda Coxe Stevenson visited the Pueblo and befriended We'Wha, eventually taking We'Wha to Washington, D.C., to represent Pueblo peoples. So convincing was We'Wha's presentation that Gage never suspected We'Wha was male and roomed with We'Wha for six months during that time (Roscoe, 1991, pp. 48–49).

Third- and fourth-gender roles, thus, are normative for traditional Pueblo culture, and Silko's writing reflects both a deep fluency in Pueblo oral tradition *and* a championing of the Pueblo principle that an individual's behavior (not blood quantum or other arbitrary characteristic of phenotype) determines their place within the community. As a result, considerations of queerness in *Almanac of the Dead* should be reframed and reconsidered through the Pueblo worldview that encompasses third and fourth genders and a range of sexualities as an important part of diversity and survival. That We'Wha formed an integral part of Zuni life and played a vital leadership role affirms that queer individuals form an irreplaceable part of Pueblo culture and society. Hence, given her clear embrace of Pueblo oral tradition, portrayals of queerness that appear abject in Silko's *Almanac* must be closely examined, in order to disentangle queerness from any assumed pathology, as colonial pathology constitutes a new post-contact norm for all characters in *Almanac*. In fact, dismissing queer characters as toxic flattens a potentially robust understanding of toxicity as a mode in which all characters in *Almanac* operate and may prevent a clear understanding of Silko's critique of capital, which forms the framework of the entire novel.[7]

Other toxicities and critique of capital

Louis Owens invokes "other destinies" as a way of framing contemporary Native American literature and film and the ways their narrative arcs do not conform to Western fictional conventions; similarly, Silko operates in a mode of "other toxicities" to dramatically underscore the pathology of capitalism and its pervasive aftereffects in Indian Country.[8] *Almanac of the Dead* is a nearly exhaustive lexicon of toxic behaviors that are predicated upon the witchery trajectory: that non-Natives grow away from the earth, that they steal the land of the Natives, that they poison the land and water, and that they destroy the earth. That Silko's witchcraft narrative functions as a critique of capitalism has already been observed by Sharon Holm: "irrevocable socioeconomic and geophysical changes determined by the emerging ideologies of late capitalism in the form of mining and logging operations [in *Ceremony*] are the tensions that both underpin and unsettle the view of the land" (2008, p. 246). Capitalistic ventures that are encompassed in this toxic economy include pornography, drug rings, sex work, trafficking of contraband items, and real estate development. The pathology of the characters is predicated upon their engagement in these various illicit activities, although trafficking goods across the border is not inherently problematic, but rather represents Indigenous refusal to be contained by colonial borders. The greatest pathology present in *Almanac* is that of those whose greed moves them to grow away from the earth and to relate to others only as a means to feed the internal abyss created by this separation from the earth. A prime example is Zeta's and Lecha's father, a failed geologist, who was unable to correctly predict the location of precious metals and minerals any more, owing to his disconnection from the earth. Silko writes, "the condition had…been seen in persons who had been revived from drowning in a lake or a spring with an entrance to the four worlds below this world…The white man had violated the Mother Earth,…had been stricken with the sensation of a gaping emptiness between his throat and his heart" (1992, p. 121). Thus, his insatiable search for silver "dries" him up just as "the veins of silver had dried up," leaving him an "imperfect vacuum" or walking corpse (1992, p. 120). The twins' father lives for many years thereafter, but he no longer sleeps or eats and eventually falls prey to self-mummification. Thus, the twins' father is consumed by his own participation in rapacious consumption, and, in turn, his disorientation makes him incompetent at mapping, illustrating the earth's refusal to acknowledge him as he denies sentience to it. Importantly, Zeta carries this "emptiness inside her," which signifies her emotional kinship with her German father, the one who was incapable of seeing Indians, who "simply did not exist for him," or recognizing his wife, Amalia, as an Indian herself (Silko, 1992, pp. 119–120). Lecha, for her part, avoids the existential abyss that consumed her father and the maladjustment of separation that Zeta suffers from even as a girl. Thus, Silko's central characters exemplify the psychic losses incumbent upon indigenes who are marred by the economic and emotive consequences of a philosophy of separation (i.e., resource extraction).

Borderlands critique of capitalism in *Desert Blood*

Gaspar de Alba's novel, *Desert Blood*, takes as its topic the Ciudad Juárez femicide, the decades-long string of rapes and murders of *mestiza* and Chican@ women along the border of El Paso and Juárez, and like Silko, Gaspar de Alba pinpoints capitalism's rapacious consumption as the causal factor in the exploitation of and violence against Indigenous people.[9] Gaspar de Alba narrates the novel through the voice of Ivon Villa, a Chican@ academic who returns home to El Paso to adopt a child, but is swept up by a desire to unravel the mysterious deaths which is exacerbated when her teenage sister, Irene, is abducted from a fair on the Mexican side of the border. Ivon's unique position as an academic who has fled her hometown after graduating from high school marks her class identity when she returns, but that history also allows her leeway to cross borders and re-enter El Paso and Ciudad Juárez's seedier locales on her quest to adopt a child and on her search for her sister Irene after her disappearance. Thus, queerness, class, border identity, and sexism are prominent themes that emerge in the novel's narrative, much as they are in *Almanac*.

Gaspar de Alba crafts the novel to emphasize the uniquely exploitative nature of the overlapping relationships between *maquilas* and the femicide. In particular, Gaspar de Alba uses ASARCO (the American Refining and Smelting Company), a copper refinery established in 1899 and acquired in 1901 by Meyer Guggenheim, as a prominent geographic site in El Paso that ties together the leitmotif of pennies and the raped bodies of former *maquiladoras*. On numerous occasions on *rastreos* and during investigations, the bodies of murdered *maquiladoras* are found with pennies inserted vaginally or swallowed in the digestive tract: clearly the pennies signify the laboring brown bodies in a transnational neoliberal schema, but a roll of pennies also easily functions as a phallus, as observed by Ivon, making currency and its potential to violate an expression of a hierarchical system of patriarchy and globalization. During Cecilia's autopsy, the coroner finds pennies in her stomach, as if she had been forced to swallow them, and on a *rastreo* with Father Francis, Ivon and others spot pennies in a *maquiladora* victim's throat: "It's like Abe Lincoln's been shoved down her throat" (2005, p. 250). Ivon connects the pennies to those found at Cecilia's autopsy and prods Laura Godoy, a talk show host and activist, to share what she knows with the promise that it not be made public. Laure confesses that the autopsies have revealed pennies in the vagina, rectum, mouths, and stomach, and bowel of victims, a fact that she begs Ivon not to share publicly because of the risk to the coroner's job (2005, p. 251). Copper's color functions as a marker of Indigeneity in the circulation of capital in exploitative North/South relations. Finally, filling a body with copper coins before incinerating it ensures the complete destruction of any evidence. As Gaspar de Alba observes, she used "the images of American coins, particularly pennies, to signify the value of the victims in the corporate machine; the poor brown women who are the main target of these murders, are, in other words, as expendable as pennies in the border economy" (p. v). Those who seek to exploit these Indigenous, brown women are often associated with silver currency ("their faces, like large silver coins"), signifying how these individuals have been consumed with extractive rapacity, how their own identities and physicality mirror the larger global economy that privileges their gender and race, as higher than that of the women who are associated with a less valuable metal (Gaspar de Alba, 2005, p. 1). Gaspar de Alba is clear that her use of the coin symbolism was a conscious choice: "to my knowledge, none of the bodies of the actual victims was ever found to have had American pennies inside them" (2005, p. v). Thus, we can close read her use of coins in the novel as allegorizing her critique of the philosophy of separation and the rapacity of capitalism south of the border.

Coins and currency function as a symbolic system of exchange that is entirely dependent upon its users "buying into," or believing in, an agreed-upon value. Coins are also the end product of an extractive mining process that is labor-intensive and leaves a legacy of environmental poisoning at the site of the original mine *and* at the industrial site or refinery where the metal is smelted. In this regard, ASARCO's extraction and refinement process conforms entirely, as collectively ASARCO and Meyer Guggenheim have created multiple sites of environmental damage globally. Because Irene is held hostage in a barrack just hundreds of yards from the ASARCO refinery, ASARCO becomes a site representative of the nexus of power relations between the forces of capital unleashed by NAFTA, Indigenous women's exploitation in the *maquilas*, and the sexual predation that arises at their confluence. To be clear, the Ciudad Juárez murders began a couple of years after the signing of NAFTA, when the overall murder rate of Mexican women was notably low, lower than the United States and other developed countries. Thus, the femicide is a symptom of the transnational forces of global capital unleashed by NAFTA, a neoliberal fix presumed to stimulate and support the development of Mexico's economy, which instead placed undue duress upon the most vulnerable individuals in the border economy: Mexican women who are phenotypically Indigenous.[10] Gaspar de Alba and coauthor Georgina Guzmán write in *Making a Killing* that:

> The victims [of the Juárez femicide] are known colloquially as "*las inditas del sur*," the little Indian girls from the south of Mexico—poor, dark-skinned, and Indigenous-looking—who have arrived alone and disenfranchised in Ciudad Juárez to work at a twin-plant *maquiladora* and earn dollars to send back home. (2010, p. 1)

The primary targets of the femicide as portrayed by Gaspar de Alba are, not surprisingly, overwhelmingly young women who bear this phenotype: the nameless *maquiladora* whose corpse is discovered as the novel opens and whose voice narrates her own murder; Cecilia, the young *maquila* worker, who is murdered while pregnant with a child Ivon and her partner plan to adopt; and the corpses of the many young women Father Francis leads *rastreos* to recover. Contrastively, lighter skinned victims like Ivon's younger sister Irene are noted as lying outside of the norm. Compounding this exploitation of Indigenous labor is the United States' investment in the *maquilas* and their retrograde systems of gendered "labor hyperextraction": as Lisa Lowe points out, "Mexico's *maquiladora* sector...is dominated by U.S. corporations, which own at least 90 percent of the factories" and is "a source of billions of dollars per year in export earnings for Mexico" (2001, pp. 14–15).

Gaspar de Alba's novel provides a lucid portrayal and analysis of the exploitation of Mexican women in the *maquilas* and the related femicide; however, while color and class remain sublimated themes throughout the novel, *Desert Blood* never overtly addresses the bare fact that the *hijas del sur* who work the *maquilas* and who are the overwhelming targets of the Ciudad Juárez femicide are Indigenous women (or women who are phenotypically Indigenous, whether they identify as *India* or not). Newspaper accounts and other media all affirm that the pervasive "type" that is targeted for rape and murder along the border is short, dark, thin, and with straight hair; this description and the fact of these young women's origins in Southern Mexico, which is home to Purepecha, Mixtec, Zapotec, Chontal Maya, Yucatec Maya, Chol, Tzeltal, Mazahua, Tzotzil, Nahuatl, Huastec, Zoque, Amuzgo, Tlapanec, Trique, Tojolabal, and numerous other tribal nations, illustrate the unvoiced Indigeneity that is wrought throughout *Desert Blood*, in addition to the systemic violence and exploitation Gaspar de Alba seeks to portray. Further, these women's geographical location on the border underscores their identities as Indigenous women who suffer the imposition of arbitrary borders by a settler-colonial state.

Unvoiced Indigeneity in *Desert Blood* and the popular cultural narrative of the Juárez femicide operate as a textual code for unpacking the larger hemispheric significance of these young women's deaths. Even Ivon's sister, Irene, who eventually becomes a target of the femicide when she is drugged and abducted from a party at *La Colonia*, a housing development on the border that is overrun by drug trafficking and other illicit businesses, must become *figuratively Indigenous* and/or *la atravesado* by jumping in the river and proclaiming herself a "wetback." The fact that she is abducted shortly thereafter illustrates that while Irene is a Chican@ from El Paso, the very fact of her *mestizaje* and blood relation to the young *mestiza* women usually targeted by criminals along the border further inscribes the arbitrariness of the border and its imposition onto Indigenous peoples. In fact, the consumptive rapacity sparked by NAFTA now has expanded its target to declare "open season" on Chicanas, those women of Mexican descent living north of the border, and to make them figurative *hijas del sur*. As Ivon reflects, "all they [the kidnappers] saw was another thin, dark-skinned, dark-haired young Mexican woman, and didn't realize she was a Mexican with the privilege of U.S. citizenship. For all the perps cared, she was just another expendable penny" (Gaspar de Alba, 2005, p. 255).

Irene Mata has argued that Gaspar de Alba uses her queer protagonist, Ivon Villa, to engage "her position as a border crosser" and "to employ oppositional thinking to try to make sense of the violence in Juárez," a move that shows Gaspar de Alba's theoretical affinity for Chela Sandoval's *Methodology of the Oppressed* (Mata, 2010, p. 18). Further, Ivon's queer identity is an integral part of this oppositional intellectual praxis; if "what makes women more vulnerable laborers is not only their economic circumstance, but also their subordination in the patriarchal hierarchy of the state," who better to unpack and address that oppression than a lesbian Chican@, who is doubly erased within heteropatriarchy? (Mata, 2010, p. 20).[11] Thus, queer ways of being function as both a way of knowing and an oppositional intellectual practice that furthers the ends of the novelist in critiquing the distribution of capital and its relationship to cycles of violence.

Almanac of the Dead and *Desert Blood* in conversation: Toward a borderlands critique of the philosophy of separation

There are many Mexicos; there are also many Mexican borders, any one of which could fill its own book.

—LUIS ALBERTO URREA

While both *Almanac of the Dead* and *Desert Blood* conceive of Indigeneity and queerness differently, they provide a critique of the border and resource extraction economy that advances our understanding of settler colonialism and its associated economic structures. In fact, these novels together supply tools that may help us dismantle these predatory economies and envision new ones based on Indigenous principles of right relationship and responsibility to the natural world. For Silko's Indigenous characters, like Calabazas, and others, the U.S.-Mexico border is a false colonial imposition that does not fundamentally alter the people's way of being.

Aided by their deep knowledge of the desert, Yaquis and other Indians who are involved in trade across the border simply find ways to circumvent the border patrol. Reflecting on his trafficking business, Calabazas denies the validity of the border:

> We don't believe in boundaries. Borders. Nothing like that. We are here thousands of years before the first whites. We are here before maps or quit claims. We know where we belong on this earth. We have always moved freely. North-south. East-west. We pay no attention to what isn't real. Imaginary lines. Imaginary minutes and hours. Written law. We recognize none of that. And we carry a great many things back and forth...We have been here and this has continued thousands of years. (Silko, 1992, p. 216)

Thus, the movement of Indigenous peoples cannot be stopped by the colonial imaginary: Native peoples will always find ways to circumvent these separations.

Similarly, Gaspar de Alba imagines the border in the vein of previous borderlands theorists such as Gloria Anzaldúa. The border is a creative space that defines *mestiza* identity as liminal, illegal, and undefinable. For Gaspar de Alba, the border is a central part of Chican@/*mestiza* identity, while it is a space that confounds the success of criminal investigations into the deaths of Juárez women: the overlap of multiple judicial systems and the global north's exploitation of Mexican labor serves to render criminal investigation powerless, at best, and corrupted and complicit, at worst.

At heart, both novels critique the imposition of the border and the corruption it generates, and they articulate complex analyses of the resource-extraction economy and, by association, the philosophy of separation that informs it. Mines and precious metals play prominent roles in each novel, establishing how a capitalist economic system places value on rare metals and supports their mining, extraction, smelting, and refining to create something (coins) of agreed-upon exchange value. No consciousness is accorded to the impact upon environment that such mining endeavors have. That the uranium mines at Laguna Pueblo have produced a community with the highest cancer rates in the United States is rarely, if ever, discussed in any history of nuclear energy and warfare. That the ASARCO copper refinery at El Paso pollutes the air every day except the weekend of the Sunbowl similarly silences the physical poisoning of Chicanos, Mexicanos, and other Indigenous peoples on the border. In both cases, particular bodies do not count within a resource-extraction economy, or, as Gaspar de Alba describes it, they are as "expendable" as copper pennies.[12] There is also a spiritual price to be paid for this resource-extractive superstructure: Lecha and Zeta's father's spirit dries up like the silver repositories he seeks; he is left with nothing but a gigantic absence between his throat and his chest. J. W.'s character functions analogously, showcasing his spiritual bankruptcy through his continual association with raw capital and coins and his final terminus presumably in jail for his involvement in the pornography ring that preys upon Irene.

Returning now to the witchery narrative as articulated by Silko in *Ceremony* and *Storyteller*, there is a further critique of the resource extraction economy (or "extractivism," as Leanne Simpson terms it), owing to its entwinement with a philosophy of separation, a salient feature of EuroWestern epistemology that is antithetical to Indigenous ways of knowing. In the witchery narrative, the world is complete without white people until witches of all the tribes gather for a conference and decide that "this time it wasn't enough" (2012, p. 124). Here the horrific story that the unknown witch tells is inspired by a lack of satisfaction with what one already has; thus, the witchery itself is driven by consumption. As the witch intones, European peoples grow away from the earth and become afraid of it; they also grow away from the sun, the plants, and the animals until they no longer see them as alive, only as objects: "They see no life/When they look/they see only objects./The world is a dead thing for them" (2012, p. 126). Their divorce from the earth becomes so great that they eventually would destroy the entire globe by detonating nuclear bombs, as previously discussed. This devastation is immediately preceded by a genocidal attack on the original peoples ("entire tribes," "entire villages"), whom the Europeans are driven to kill by fear until those who survive "die anyway/at the destruction they see" (Silko, 2012, p. 127).

In *Almanac of the Dead*, Silko writes of this phenomenon as being entangled with language: Europeans become so fixated upon names that they forget the entity that is named itself.[13] This belief in separation is what makes warfare and genocide possible: when Europeans no longer believe in the life of plant, animal, or human, but only themselves, they are capable of perpetrating horrible crimes in the name of personal gain and wealth. Similarly, Gaspar de Alba highlights the various people, coyotes, corrupt officials, drug dealers, and pornographers, who are entirely willing to be complicit in or perpetrate crimes at the expense of those deemed "expendable." (Read: young, dark, Indigenous women.) Thus, both novelists not only provide incisive analyses of the settler economy's corruption, but they also point to the epistemological framework that undergirds its processes (viz., the false belief in separation: that things can be known outside of the whole of which they are composed, and that borders can be imposed upon people who are Indigenous to their territory). Further, both novels illustrate in their own specific ways how Indigenous peoples circumvent the border as colonial imposition, and in so doing, they establish that the border only survives based on the investment (literal) that those in power make into it, and maintain by its constant inscription and policing. The unempowered, Indigenous populations will always find their way around the confines of the border; yet, as Gaspar de Alba points out, there may be sacrifices made in that disavowal of the border. Nonetheless, the powerlessness of the border to enforce its own legitimacy is always present and acknowledged by the settler state's constant efforts to affirm its veracity and efficacy as a marker of something other than a rogue nation.

Conclusion

This analysis has sought to illustrate how two widely varying novels, *Almanac of the Dead* and *Desert Blood*, depict the problematic of the border and critique its complicity in a resource-extraction

economy. Both novels figure Indigeneity prominently, though in
Gaspar de Alba's case, the Indigeneity remains "unvoiced," making
its way into the novel's consciousness via encoding into the
narrative. Both novels depict the exploitation of Indigenous peoples
at the border as problematic, and both lay bare the connection
to a EuroWestern philosophy of separation that makes this
separation possible.[14] Silko's endeavor is an epistemic intervention
in the narrative of (the) América(s), one that reclaims and deploys
Laguna Pueblo narrative structures, tropes, and theory.[15] Because
the novel appears to self-consciously traffic in the European trope
of queers as toxic and liminal (by way of critiquing those very
claims), an additional effect of this epistemic deployment is a re-
pathologization of queers, if read through the EuroWestern frame
of abject sexuality. Nonetheless, while problematic, Silko's epic
illustrates the incredible messiness of decolonization in the present
(and in the future) post-contact era and may indeed suggest
alternative avenues for the consideration of others embarking on
similar projects. Both novels provide a critique of settler perceptions
of queerness as pathological, and both attempt to make gains from
these seemingly unsalvageable frameworks: for Gaspar de Alba,
this is borderlands theory of la atravesado, and for Silko, this is
illustrating the comparative health of seemingly toxic queers in
comparison to far more toxic colonialities. Arguably, Gaspar de
Alba's approach is more empowering, but not necessarily more
productive per se. Both novels critique resource extraction and the
exploitation of Indigenous peoples, looking in different directions
across the border and with varying effects.[16]

Notes

1   Throughout this chapter, I will use Chicana/o as a general term and
    with specific reference to Silko's work. When discussing Gaspar
    de Alba's *Desert Blood*, I will utilize Chican@, in order to reflect
    a politicized and gender-inclusive identity, as Sandra Soto does in
    Reading Chican@ Like a Queer.
2   In the essay, "Identification Pleas," Eric Gansworth (Onondaga)
    recounts an experience he had in 2002 when he crossed the border
    at Acuña, Mexico, and tried to re-enter the United States, using his
    Haudenosaunee tribal identification card: "National identification
    papers, it seems, are good enough documentation for the United

States from every other nation except those housed within its borders. Haudenosaunee law stipulates we are not citizens of the United States, regardless of any federal laws on Indian citizenship" (2003, p. 277).

It is noteworthy that Chicana/o political identity has been linked to a claiming of Aztec Indigenous roots, as opposed to other tribal nations. In part, this tribally specific claim arises out of the wealth of documentation and museum holdings from the Aztecs, in addition to the engineering achievement of Tenochtitlan. Chicano Studies scholar Wilson Neate has noted that within Chicana/o consciousness "worldview, values, traditions, culture and philosophy were considered recoupable in some pure form and applicable to the lived experience of the present" (p. 117).

Meanwhile, Gloria Anzaldúa critiques this aspect of Chicana/o identity formation as focusing overwhelmingly on the role of the male Aztec warrior and disavowing other tribal identities evidenced by the maligning of Malinche (Mayan, female, egalitarian). In fact, Anzaldua predicts that the Aztec predominance would have faded inevitably as a result of the growing prominence of non-Aztec women. See Domino Perez's "Words, Worlds in Our Heads: Reclaiming La Llorona's Aztecan Antecedents in Gloria Anzaldúa's 'My Black Angelos'" for a study of how Anzaldúa engages non-Aztec Indigenous tropes to circumvent the reductive Spanish father/Indigenous mother binary.

3   In *Across the Wire*, Luis Alberto Urrea makes the following observation about the police state at the border:

> Borderlands locals are so jaded by the sight of nightly people-hunting that it doesn't even register in their minds. But take a stranger to the border, and she will *see* the spectacle: monstrous Dodge trucks speeding into and out of the landscape; uniformed men patrolling with flashlights, guns, and dogs; spotlights; running figures; lines of people hurried onto buses by armed guards; and the endless clatter of the helicopters with their harsh beams. A Dutch woman once told me it seemed altogether "un-American." (p. 11)

4   See Paula Gunn Allen's *The Sacred Hoop: Recovering the Feminine in American Indian Traditions* for a fully developed exploration of the feminine principle.

5   Lindsey Smith refers to these tropes as "Laguna orientations" (p. 146).

6   Will Roscoe observes, "Gender was also acquired through initiations. Zuni men and women were not born; they were made or cooked. Gender was a social, not a natural, attribute" (p. 129).

7   Let me be clear that this essay is in no way an apologia for the
     reinscription of negative queer stereotypes in Silko's *Almanac of the
     Dead*. Instead, this essay aims to explore the cultural framework that
     informs Silko's teleology (i.e., witchcraft narrative), and while Silko
     is well aware of the Laguna Pueblo traditional embrace of third and
     fourth genders, her epistemic intervention in the settler narrative of
     the Americas necessarily traffics in the predominant stereotypes of
     that colonial culture.

8   In *Other Destinies*, Owens writes, "American Indian novelists—
     examples of Indians who have repudiated their assigned plots—are
     in their fiction rejecting the American gothic with its haunted, guilt-
     burdened wilderness and doomed Native and emphatically making
     the Indian the hero of other destinies, other plots" (p. 18). In *Indians,
     Environment, and Identity on the Borders of American Literature*,
     Lindsey Smith performs an insightful reading of Menardo's fate as
     representing one such "other destiny" (p. 156).

9   Note: As stated earlier, I will use Chican@ as a gender-inclusive
     and politically specific term in my discussion of *Desert Blood*. I
     use *mestiza* here to refer to women of Indigenous ancestry from
     Mesoamerica, who may or may not identify as Indigenous and who
     are, nonetheless, read as brown and Indigenous in the larger social
     fabric of North America.

10   As María Socorro Tabuenca Córdoba observes, the crime prevention
     campaigns in Ciudad Juárez portray potential perpetrators of
     sexual crime as fair-haired and light-skinned upper-class men and
     their victims as working-class women who inhabit dark spaces
     (pp. 100–105). These representations implicitly acknowledge the
     identity of the *maquiladora* workers as dark, Indigenous others, as
     does the title of Córdoba's essay, "Ghost Dance in Ciudad Juárez."

11   One might argue that Ivon is triply erased by her identity as a
     Chican@ by EuroAmericans north of the border as well.

12   This aspect of both novels speaks directly to Lisa Lowe's call to
     address "the need for a critique of citizenship defined as the right to
     property" and "rights-based mediation appeals" through "a more
     'radical' challenge to the system itself" (p. 13).

13   A number of Indigenous language speakers and teachers have noted
     how Native North American languages are rich in verbs (tenses,
     pronouns, polymorphism with adjectives) and relatively sparse in
     nouns in comparison to English and other European languages.
     This object fixation in English connects with Silko's critique of the
     philosophy of separation via the witchcraft narrative.

14   Lecha explains, "Indians had nothing to do with elections … the
     white man had always been trying to 'control' the border when

no such thing existed to control except in the white man's mind" (p. 592).

15   In fact, this notion of Laguna Pueblo epistemic intervention was explored at length in a 1999 work by David L. Moore, "Silko's Blood Sacrifice: The Circulating Witness in *Almanac of the Dead*." In this work, Moore provides a rich and adept reading of Silko's use of systemic violence and recurring blood tropes as an endeavor to redeploy the Arrowboy myth and its function of witnessing, in order to alter the viewer. He observes, Silko "leads her readers through the personal ritual of *Ceremony* to sacrifice their egos, their epistemologies, and their ideologies on the rebuilt altar of history in *Almanac*" (p. 151).

16   My heartfelt thanks go to Randi Lopez for reading this chapter in draft form and providing feedback from Chican@ Studies and Queer Studies perspectives.

References

Allen, P. G. (1992), *The Sacred Hoop: Recovering the Feminine in American Indian Traditions*. Boston: Beacon Press.

Anzaldúa, G. (1987), *Borderlands/La Frontera: The New Mestiza*, 2nd edition. San Francisco: Aunt Lute Books.

Archuleta, E. (2005), "Securing Our Nation's Roads and Borders or Re-Circling the Wagons? Leslie Marmon Silko's Destabilization of Borders." *Wicazo Sa Review*, 20:1, 113–137.

Berglund, J. (2006), *Cannibal Fictions: American Explorations of Colonialism, Race, Gender, and Sexuality*. Madison: University of Wisconsin Press.

Cherniavsky, E. (2006), *Incorporations: Race, Nation, and the Body Politics of Capital*. Minneapolis: University of Minnesota Press.

Córdoba, M. S. T. (2010), "Ghost Dance in Ciudad Juárez at the End/ Beginning of the Millennium," in A. Gaspar de Alba and G. Guzman (eds), *Making a Killing: Femicide, Free Trade, and La Frontera*, Austin: University of Texas Press, pp. 95–119.

Gansworth, E. (2003), "Identification Pleas," in M. Moore (ed.), *Genocide of the Mind: New Native American Writing*. New York: Nation Books, pp. 269–279.

Gaspar de Alba, A. (2005), *Desert Blood: The Juárez Murders*. Houston: Arté Publico Press.

Gaspar de Alba, A. and Guzman, G. (eds) (2010), *Making a Killing: Femicide, Free Trade, and La Frontera*. Austin: University of Texas Press.

Holm, S. (2008), "The 'Lie' of the Land: Native Sovereignty, Indian
    Literary Nationalism, and Early Indigenism in Leslie Marmon Silko's
    Ceremony." *American Indian Quarterly*, 32:3, 243–274.
Lowe, L. (2001), "Utopia and Modernity: Some Observations from the
    Border." *Rethinking Marxism*, 13:2, 10–18.
Mata, I. (2010), "Writing on the Walls: Deciphering Violence and
    Industrialization in Alicia Gaspar de Alba's *Desert Blood.*" *MELUS*,
    35:3, 15–40.
Moore, D. L. (1999), "Silko's Blood Sacrifice: the Circulating Witness
    in *Almanac of the Dead*," in L. K. Barnett and J. L. Thorson (eds),
    Leslie Marmon Silko: A Collection of Critical Essays. Albuquerque:
    University of New Mexico Press, pp. 149–183.
Neate, W. (1998), *Tolerating Ambiguity: Ethnicity and Community in
    Chicano/a Writing*. New York: Peter Lang.
Owens, L. (1992), *Other Destinies: Understanding the American Indian
    Novel*. Norman: University of Oklahoma Press.
Perez, D. (2003–4), "Words, Worlds in Our Heads: Reclaiming
    La Llorona's Aztecan Antecedents in Gloria Anzaldúa's 'My Black
    Angelos.' " *Studies in American Indian Literatures*, 15:3–4 (Fall 2003–
    Winter 2004): 51–63.
Roscoe, W. (1991), *The Zuni Man-Woman*. Albuquerque: University of
    New Mexico Press.
Silko, L. M. (1992), *Almanac of the Dead*. New York: Penguin.
Silko, L. M. (1996), *Yellow Woman and a Beauty of the Spirit*. New York:
    Touchstone.
Silko, L. M. (2006), *Ceremony*. New York: Penguin.
Silko, L. M. (2012), *Storyteller*. New York: Penguin.
Smith, L. C. (2008), *Indians, Environment, and Identity on the Borders
    of American Literature: From Faulkner and Morrison to Walker and
    Silko*. New York: Palgrave.
Soto, S. (2010), *Reading Chican@ Like a Queer*. Austin: University of
    Texas Press.
Urrea, L. A. (1993), *Across the Wire: Life and Hard Times on the
    Mexican Border*. New York: Anchor Books.

5

Silko, Freud, and the Voicing of Disavowed Histories in *Almanac of the Dead*

Deborah L. Madsen

While most critical analyses of *Almanac of the Dead* remark at some point on the novel's heteroglossic, multivocal qualities arising, in part, from Silko's multitudinous cast of characters, the character that most dominates every reading of the narrative has been relatively neglected: the narrator.[1] Indeed, I want to suggest that a way of interpreting Silko's claim that in the novel she was "trying to give history a character" is to think of the anonymous third-person narrator as precisely that character: a sustained, and sometimes disruptive, presence in the novel that translates the voice and historical vision of the ancestors (Neimann, 2000, p. 108). This work of translation is much more than semantic conversion or decoding between languages (though this is part of Lecha's work with the ancient notebooks); translation in this context is the kind of postcolonial philosophical exchange described by Arnold Krupat's elegant term, "anti-imperial translation" (p. 170). Krupat formulates this phrase in the context of his discussion of the anticolonial dynamic that characterizes "tensions and differences from 'the imperial center'" (Krupat) in contemporary Native American literature, as these texts engage in the complex process of translating Indigenous world views into the language of English literary convention. Translation, in this sense, references for

Krupat "the ways in which any particular Native American literary text interpellates any of a number of Indigenous perspectives and language usages in such a way as to make the text's 'Indian' language constitute a translation, one in which the 'English' on the page does indeed 'foreground the tension,' and 'emphasize the differences' between 'Indian' and 'English' " (p. 173).

Compelling as it is, Krupat's insight can be pushed further to encompass the distinctive stylistic dimensions of Silko's epic historical narrative and, specifically, the work of her narrator. I want to argue that in *Almanac* Silko is engaged in a process of "anti-imperial translation" that deconstructs the exceptionalist settler-colonial history of the Americas while simultaneously testifying to the disavowed history of Indigenous peoples. The narrator translates the voice of the ancestors in a dialectical process that at once exposes the hegemonic narratives of "discovery," "contact," and "expansion through progress" as the repressed primal history of violence in the Americas while, at the same time, witnessing "the 500 year war that never ended" and the beginning of the fulfillment of a history encoded in the ancient almanacs. More than the revision of received interpretations of historical events, more than the simple decoding of prophecy, this process requires the performative translation of historical meanings across fundamentally antagonistic epistemologies—not just European versus Native, settler versus Indigenous, white versus red, brown, and black identity binaries—but the ways of knowing characteristic of Silko's destroyers versus all who would oppose them. I use the word "performative" advisedly because in his discussion of epistemological or cross-cultural "anti-imperial translation," Krupat makes a valuable distinction between meaning as a function of "narrative or song language" and meaning that arises from the "dramatic and performative nature of oral literature" (pp. 167, 178 n.20). It is in this performative sense that Silko's narrator translates: by telling the stories of the characters, by mediating the characters' stories, by passing on the stories from the ancient almanac, by transmitting the stories encoded in a vast array of different kinds of texts from Sterling's pulp magazines to Clinton's college notes on Black history. In order to translate the voice of the ancestors, the narrative voice must be at once transcendent and embodied; trans-American, transglobal, and transhistorical, and yet particular. Thus, the narrator performatively tells the stories that the characters are either telling or being told in the diegesis and, through them, voices the disavowed history of the past five hundred years in the Americas while prophesying the changes that have started and those that are yet to come.

Of course, Silko's narrator is not a conventional character that acts in the fictional, diegetic world of the novel; however, the narrator does mediate every detail of that world. The stylistic vehicle of this mediation is a form of free indirect style that Silko sustains throughout the novel. The effects of this stylistic choice are multiple, arising from the ability granted to the narrator to function on several discursive levels simultaneously. Free indirect style creates a multiperspectival narrative voice, one that is at once both immanent and transcendent, by combining the first-person interiority of the diegetic characters with the exteriority of the omniscient narrator's third-person voice. The fusing of the extradiegetic perspective of the narrator with the intradiegetic focalization of the characters produces a complex doubling or multiplying of narrative voice(s). In this way, the narrator not only communicates the specific stories, experiences, values, and perceptions (in short, the reality) of the characters but also functions as the voice of Indigenous history, performing as the main character of the novel.

But the narrator does more than just figure the vision and voice of the ancestors. The performativity of the narrative voice creates a relationship with the reader that, for Silko, is fundamental to her project. In the interview with Linda Neimann referenced above, Silko explains the power of the stories that are necessary to ensure the continuance of the People: "These stories work on unconscious levels that we don't have control of and access to by direct everyday means. When I was working with these narratives, I wanted them to have an after-effect in the unconscious" (pp. 107–108). Both the content of the narrator's work (the stories that are told) and the way in which the narrative work is done (how those stories are told) are designed to shape the reader's reception of the novel on the deepest levels of cognition. Silko's words echo those of Freud in *Group Psychology and the Analysis of the Ego* (1922), where he describes how

Our conscious acts are the outcome of an unconscious substratum created in the mind mainly by hereditary influences. This substratum consists of the innumerable common characteristics handed down from generation to generation, which constitute the genius of race. Behind the avowed causes of our acts there undoubtedly lie secret causes that we do not avow, but behind these secret causes there are many others more secret still, of which we ourselves are ignorant. The greater part of our daily actions are the result of hidden motives which escape our observation. (p. 74)

Though Freud has a marginal European philosophical presence in the novel in comparison to Marx, his account of the traumatic legacy of a disavowed primal history of violence, communicated through stories and neurotic individual and cultural behaviors, illuminates aspects of Silko's narrative practice.

Silko, Freud, and the primal scene of violence

In her work on the novel, Deborah Horvitz explores the role of unconscious communication in relation to Freud's theory of traumatic repetition, reminding us how "*Almanac* suggests that the textual process of decoding its narrative parallels that of untangling the disguised content of the unconscious, for the actual manifestation of each code is the same. That is, both appear through dreams, symbols, stories, and repetitive, frequently surreal, imagery" (1998, p. 49). Indeed, the work of one of the narrative's more important inscribed readers is explicitly likened by the narrator to psychoanalysis: "Lecha proceeded with the woman [the TV producer's vengeful girlfriend] in ways that closely resembled the work of a psychoanalyst or counselor" (p. 143).[2] Lecha records all the woman's memories of her former lover, searching for patterns in the details; later, Seese recalls Lecha asking, "Had Seese heard about Freudian theory? ... Freud had interpreted fragments—images from hallucinations, fantasies, and dreams—in terms patients could understand. The images were messages from the patient to herself or himself" (p. 173). In the course of the narrative, Lecha and Seese interpret the fragments that are Yoeme's notebooks on the ancient almanacs. Through Lecha the narrator invokes Freud's distinction between the "manifest" or obvious meaning and the "latent" or unconscious meaning of imagistic messages. The narrative presents us with repeated clusters of images that represent potential patterns of meaning; these repeated images exist not in relations of sameness but coexist as part of a pattern that, in the fictional world, may expose the unconscious anxieties of the characters and, in the dimension of the narrator's telling of the story, speak to a deep legacy of trauma.

This is not to claim that Silko and Freud think identically about the symbolic significance of repetition, and Horvitz makes this clear: "Undoubtedly and emphatically, Silko is calling attention to...the enormous power residing within the retelling and the repetition of the stories" (p. 50). In contrast, in *Beyond the Pleasure Principle* (1920) Freud describes the compulsion to repeat as a defense mechanism, a form of avoidance that, as Freud explains, substitutes the delusory "sovereignty of the inner psychical reality" for "the reality of the outer world" and then "the way to insanity is open" (p. 123). *Almanac* insists that the stories are alive; that the people will survive so long as the stories are kept alive through repeated tellings. Horvitz argues that repetition without stories or the history they create is symptomatic of the behavior of the destroyers, citing Serlo's reflection on the repetition of violence perpetrated by the Israeli descendants of Holocaust survivors on Palestinians (p. 546). We might also recall Mosca's claim that "[e]ach time a Palestinian child was shot by Israeli soldiers, Hitler smiled" (p. 212) or Calabazas' assertion that "Hitler got all he knew from the Spanish and Portuguese invaders" (p. 216), or Lecha's memory of the images that Yoeme had shown when she and Zeta were children, "woodblock prints of churchmen...breaking Jews on the wheel" (p. 717). In the similarity of these repeated thoughts expressed by distinct characters, we are presented by the narrator with a genealogy of violence that reaches back five hundred years.

The legacy of violence extends even further back in chronological time. Sterling remembers the stories told by Aunt Marie of the Inquisition and also of Montezuma, "the biggest sorcerer of them all"; he reflects, "No wonder Cortés and Montezuma had hit it off so well together when they met; both had been members of the same secret clan" (p. 761). Tacho concludes his explanation to Menardo of sorcerers and their misuse of the power of blood with his observation that "God the Father himself had accepted only Jesus as a worthy sacrifice" (p. 337), and Mosca evokes the bloodshed of the Crusades to explain the alienation of Christians and Muslims from God (p. 611). The community of destroyers includes European Christians who, Tacho remarks in terms that will be echoed by Yoeme's description of the Christian Church as "a cannibal monster" (718), eat Jesus' "flesh and blood again and again" at Mass (p. 475), and the destroyers also include the Indigenous priest described in the old notebooks making a human sacrifice, blood congealing on the altar like "the rind of a fragrant fruit" (p. 593). The metaphor of fruit is evocative of the repeated image of "strange fruit" that recurs throughout the narrative, again linking the destroyers' acts of violence into a sustained historical legacy. The image "strange fruit" is repeated in the description of one of Max Blue's assassination victims (p. 355) and Judge Arne's "taste for strange fruits" (p. 645), which have been contextualized by Yoeme's earlier explanation of her order to cut down all of her husband's beloved cottonwood trees because of the use made of them to lynch Native people (p. 129).

It seems to me that the problem with destroyers such as Beaufrey, Serlo, Judge Arne, Max Blue, and others is not that they are isolated from their ancestors and "have absolutely no link with their pasts" (Horvitz, p. 51) but that they are very much connected to ancestors who themselves were/are destroyers. This is one of the profound ironies that emerge from the narrator's multiplied perspective. The narrative repeatedly identifies grandfather figures with the phrase "the old man": Root's grandfather who wants to pass as white is "old man Gorgon" (p. 221); Serlo's grandfather who teaches him eugenics is "the old man" (p. 546), as is Judge Arne's grandfather who teaches him bestiality (p. 650); and Zeta thinks of "Grandpa Guzman" as "the old white man" (p. 131). While these grandfathers may all be aligned with the destroyers, Menardo's tribal grandfather is referred to as "the old man" and so too is the "old man" whose stories are repeated by Menardo's grandfather (pp. 256–259). Menardo rejects his tribal ancestry in favor of passing as white, like "old man Gorgon," and so this fusion and confusion around the recursive phrase, "the old man," suggests that two related patterns of inheritance are at work in the world of the novel and that characters, such as Root the "throwback," according to Calabazas (p. 221), can choose whether to become one of the destroyers.

Clearly, repetition is very important to the narrative project of *Almanac* but something else is going on as well. Lecha's memory of Yoeme's image of the Church as "a cannibal monster" suggests something of this. Lecha begins her recollection by describing Yoeme's action; she then uses free direct speech to report (but not quote) Yoeme's words—"Yoeme said the mask had slipped at that time, and all over Europe, ordinary people had understood in their hearts the 'Mother Church' was a cannibal monster" (pp. 717–718)—but as Yoeme's sentence ends and the next begins, it is impossible to determine whether the speaker remains Leche reporting Yoeme or the narrator assuming again control of the narration. Here, as so often in *Almanac*, free indirect style works to put into irresolvable question the "ownership" of words, thus attributing a powerful multivocality to those words. And the words that follow are very significant: "Since the Europeans had no other gods or beliefs left, they had to continue the Church rituals and worship; but they knew the truth" (p. 718). The narrator, perhaps through Lecha reporting Yoeme's words, is suggesting that the motive for the ongoing power of the "cannibal monster" is the unconscious process of disavowal. Like obsessive repetition, disavowal is a mechanism of avoidance: refusing traumatic knowledge, behaving as if it were not true, even though its repressed truth is unconsciously acknowledged.

In my reading, disavowal is central to Silko's narrative project in *Almanac* as she charts the disavowed history of settler-colonial genocide in the Americas. In this respect, the most relevant of Freud's writings on disavowal is his final work, *Moses and Monotheism*, begun in 1934 and completed after he fled Nazi-occupied Vienna in 1938. This radically discontinuous, sometimes contradictory, text resonates with Silko's novel through Freud's reflections on exile (his reluctant move to London), murderous racial hatred (anti-Semitism), and the transmission of guilt as the motive for cultural practices such as organized religion and Judaism in particular. His theorizing is based on the fundamental analogy he proposes between the neurotic behavior of the individual and that of communities, the idea that "mankind as a whole also passed through the conflicts of a sexual-aggressive nature, which left permanent traces but which were for the most part warded off and forgotten; later, after a long period of latency, they came to life again and created phenomena similar in structure and tendency to the neurotic symptoms" (p. 129). There are several points to note here: specifically, the structural importance of primal acts of violence, the disavowal of this violence, and the "permanent traces" that will not remain repressed but return in the form of neurotic symptoms.

In his metapsychological history of monotheism, these "traces" are the imperfectly repressed, disavowed, memories of the primal parricide that are transmitted intergenerationally to individuals and communities through inherited traditions. Freud proposes that underlying the emergence of the Judaic or Mosaic religion are the repressed collective memories of the original killing of Moses, and the guilt arising from these memories endures in the "memory-traces in our archaic inheritance." Repressed guilt then motivates religious practices that symbolically or latently acknowledge but manifestly avoid knowledge of the primal parricide; Freud interprets the sacrifice of Jesus in these terms, as symbolic restitution for or expiation of what becomes the Christian notion of "original sin." Indeed, the Christianity founded by Paul of Tarsus is, in Freud's account, structured around the symbolic repetition of the murder of Moses; "the supposed judicial murder of Christ" (p. 162) was an event of sufficient power to awaken the memory trace, to cause its shift from the unconscious to consciousness though in an altered form.

Turning to Silko's novel, of course there is no single primal act of violence represented in the narrative that is comparable to the killing of Moses. Rather, there are many scenes and images that evoke a long history of violence in the Americas, a history disavowed by narratives of "discovery" and manifest destiny in which Christianity is deeply complicit: Lecha links the sacrifice of Jesus to the Jewish Holocaust (p. 174); Menardo's grandfather links the biblical story of exile from Eden to the settlers' "abandonment of the land where they had been born" (p. 258); in the context of the anticolonial struggle to take back the land, Tacho echoes Yoeme's image of the cannibalistic Church by reflecting, "Typical of sorcerers or Destroyers, the Christians had denied they were cannibals and sacrificers" (p. 475)—a phrase that anticipates the Notebook's allusion to Aztec human sacrifice (p. 594) and Beaufrey's fascination with the cannibal Albert Fish, a descendant of *Mayflower* settlers (p. 533). Mosca links the betrayal realized in the crucifixion to the ongoing betrayal of "Jesus' creed of forgiveness and brotherly love" symbolized by the Church's display of wealth and later asks, "What did the Church want? Was it different from what the generals wanted, or from what the rich wanted from the poor and the Indians?" (p. 623); and, late in the narrative, Lecha explains how she overcame her resistance to Yoeme's view of the Catholic Church as "a dead thing, even before the Spanish ships had arrived in the Americas" (p. 717) by understanding the deep psychic motives of settlers who substitute the compensatory act of killing for acknowledgment of "the loss [of] their connection with the earth" (p. 718). The link between the violence of colonial settlement, the long history of the destroyers' cannibalistic pleasure in death and destruction, and five hundred years of Indigenous resistance to genocide in the Americas constitutes a history that is disavowed by settler narratives in what Silko has called "one of the tragedies of the United States—a sort of collective amnesia about the past, sort of like the Germans during the Jewish Holocaust" (Perry, p. 321).[3] This disavowal, and the bloody history that it attempts to repress, is witnessed by the omniscient narrator of *Almanac* and the manifold stories to which the narrative testifies.

Narrative voice: Structure and style

Toward the end of *Moses and Monotheism*, Freud reflects on his growing confidence that the symptoms originating in a history of repressed violence have as their latent meaning the "historical truth" of that disavowed violence (p. 94). But this raises the question: how is this archaic inheritance transmitted from generation to generation and what forms do these symptoms take? Freud's answer is formulated as "memory traces," memories that undergo repression and so become disconnected from other intellectual processes and "inaccessible to consciousness" (p. 152). These traumatic memories cannot be simply told in manifest terms because consciousness would have (and has already) refused them. Only by speaking to the language of the unconscious—in dreams, "slips," visions—can the memory traces of traumatic events be revealed and the disavowed history exposed by these traces be mapped out.

It is this activity in which Silko's omniscient third-person narrator is engaged and out of which, I argue, the narrative voice assumes the dimensions of a character that is intratextual while remaining extradiegetic. That is, the narrator is not an agent in the novel's story world but is the dominating presence of the narrative as it is told.[4] In important respects, the structure consists of the narrator telling the stories that characters are telling about stories and the organization of these stories is captured self-consciously by the narrative's repeated image of the red-tailed hawk. While thinking about the stories he has heard about the Apaches of Arizona, Calabazas recalls one story told by Mahawala and the old ones that "did not run in a line for the horizon but circled and spiraled instead like a red-tailed hawk" (p. 224). This image captures the recursive sequential structure of *Almanac* but when it is applied to Lecha's work with Yoeme's notebooks, it suggests more of the novel's free associational and subjective quality. Reaching for the old manuscript, Lecha likens the feeling she has after taking her medication to "feeling as thin as an air current a hawk might ride ... she could imagine the gliding and soaring of the red-tailed hawks that often flew near the ranch house" (p. 245). If the parts, books, chapters, and words on the page circle and spiral, then the flow of symbolic latent meaning that Lecha is engaged in transcribing from the eponymous almanac is like an air current, buoyant yet unpredictable.

It is from the interplay of these dimensions of *Almanac*—the manifest organizational form and the latent conceptual structure—that the character of the narrator develops. David Moore has argued that the structure of the novel remains "open to the historical moment," through the juxtaposition of chapters and the refusal to close narrative gaps or ultimately to resolve the plot (2001, p. 164). While this is undoubtedly true, I would add that these are features of Silko's strategy aimed at constructing an active narrative voice that develops the figure of the narrator into a character in the text. The distinct quality of this narrator is suggested by Brewster Fitz who, in his account of Silko's characteristic creation of the "writing storyteller," in the figure of an anonymous third-person narrator of free indirect style, recalls that "[i]n interviews ... Silko has implicitly linked this third-person narrator with a spiritual narrator and with the voices of many spirits for whom she is the scribe" (2004, p. 8). In his earlier essay, "Coyote Loops," Fitz offers an extended description of Silko's style and resulting suspension of the distinction between subjective and objective perspectives in her fiction. Objective and rational descriptions of perceptions and experiences do not permit access to repressed and disavowed knowledge: the priority of Silko's narrator in *Almanac*. However, on the level of specific narrative incidents, this free indirect style generates profound ambiguity by refusing explicitly to attribute "ownership" of words and thoughts to an objective speaking or thinking agent. Sometimes this ambiguity allows the narrator to express a self-conscious irony: for example, when reporting Awa Gee's obsession with secrecy (p. 684) while telling all his secrets. Not only does the narrator acquire qualities associated with a novelistic character (a capacity for self-irony), but also such moments locate the narrator in the discursive space of the ancestors, a space that is embedded in the particularities of the fictional world while transcending that world.

The trans/historical location of the narrator is underlined by rare but dramatic narrative ellipses in which the thematic linkages that usually bridge chapters are notably absent. A relatively simple example that highlights the contribution of this technique to the characterization of the narrator occurs in Part Five, Book One. Mosca's thoughts about treachery and betrayal (p. 611) bring to an end the chapter "Tucson, City of Thieves" and the series of four chapters focalized through him; in the following chapter the narrative moves abruptly to Seese's cab ride to Miracle Mile (p. 612) where she plans to sell her kilo of cocaine to Tiny. In a linear, sequential reading, this shift of focus between chapters is rudely abrupt. The link between them, however, is apparent in a second or retroactive reading that aligns the reader with the knowledge of the narrative's future events—events that are already known to the narrator. Seese is going to be set up and betrayed by Tiny; Jamey will fall victim to the treachery of his police colleagues. What this ellipsis does is to emphasize the omniscience of the narrator as a storyteller for whom time in the diegetic world is experienced in the manner described by the ancestors. For the narrator, there is no past and future, only a present that encompasses all time.

Narrating the language of the ancestors

It is from the historical perspective of the ancestors that the narrator presents the symbolic language of the unconscious. The narrative's complex system of images, repeated in the discourse of distinct characters, converges in the voice of the narrator. The privilege attached to this narrative voice derives from its work of translating the voice of the ancestor spirits. Mosca, reflecting that the spirit voice lodged in his shoulder does not say much, concludes that the spirits have the power to "put the idea in your head out of the blue" (p. 627). This is precisely what the translating narrative voice does: through the cumulative pattern of images, the narrator is able to put into the reader's head—seemingly "out of the blue"— an idea that has, in fact, been contextualized by earlier repetitions. These images connect to form networks of meaning that exceed the capacities of individual characters, exposing the disavowed history of violence that is their latent meaning. The recursive flower imagery, for example, is grounded in the fragment from the ancient notebook that reads: "The land of the dead is a land of flowers" (p. 572). Just some of the instances that link flowers with death include Menardo's perception of the purple blossoms climbing the mortuary walls as resembling nothing so much as human intestines (p. 334), which recalls Seese's misrecognition of the photographs of Eric's corpse "nearly buried in blossoms of bright reds and purples" (p. 106); Seese's nightmare of yellow roses (p. 52) during her drugged sleep following the abortion resonates later with the image of yellow blossoming trees on Serlo's *finca* (p. 550) to locate transhistorically the space occupied by Serlo and Beaufrey as a place of death akin to the almanac's "land of the dead."

If the novel's flower imagery works, in part, to look back to the past to relate the destroyers Serlo and Beaufrey to a long legacy of violence, the network of images associated with fountains and pools of water enables the narrator to predict the future. In Seese's first encounter with Lecha, she watches her television performance as Lecha recounts the dead babies and children found each day in Mexico City, "not counting the ones found floating facedown among the water lilies in fountains outside the presidential palace" (p. 47), a performance that causes Seese to dream that "she finds Monte's corpse in a fountain at a shopping mall" (p. 47). Later, from Lecha's perspective, the free associative process of identifying, sifting, and organizing clues is dramatized in the television appearance, where she predicts that the severed heads of the U.S. ambassador to Mexico and his chief aide will be found floating among the water lilies on the canals of Xochimilco (p. 164); it is in the very different context of one of El Grupo's social meetings that Menardo is worried by the news that "more severed human heads had been found floating among the flowers of Xochimilco" (p. 329). The same image of water lilies characterizes the fountain Calabazas passes as he makes his way to the monsignor's apartment where he discovers his adulterous wife (p. 243) and Menardo, who, following the death of Iliana, is left with his marble mansion, "his pool of water lily blossoms" (p. 472), and his adulterous second wife. The pools filled with water lilies are associated with betrayal and violent death, but at the end of the narrative, Leah Blue looks over the desert and in her imagination recreates the landscape as an image of her future real estate development: "sleek, low villas of pale marble with red bougainvilleas and even water lilies for the floating gardens in the canals" (p. 750). Her vision of Venice, Arizona incorporates multiple images of death, and, to heighten the irony, the narrator reports Leah's perception of the changing colors of the sunset reflected off the clouds—"silvers and golds becoming chrome-yellow, fire-orange, fire-red, fire-purple" (p. 752)—colors reminiscent of the reds and purples that characterize David's photographs of Eric's corpse; colors that evoke the power of the fire macaws. Leah reassures herself that her vision of the future will make her rich, and the manifest meaning of the scene she conjures suggests that she is correct, but the latent meaning of the narrator's discourse allows a glimpse into a future of betrayal, chaos, and violent death for Leah Blue.

Interconnections among the images that inflect Leah's vision with such profound irony are presented cross-textually and converge in the narrator's perspective which, again, is at once immanent and transcendent. At significant points in *Almanac*, the narrative highlights the importance of this perspective by combining the power of imagistic repetition with narrative ellipsis. The problem that initially dominates the novel is Seese's search for her missing son, which is postponed by Lecha's promise that when the transcription of Yoeme's notebooks is complete, she will find Seese's son. The disturbing effects of working with Lecha on the almanac fragments, in the chapter "Shallow Graves," focus on the traumatic stories Seese witnesses as she sorts Lecha's mail, but after reading "a dozen or so plea letters," she encounters something that gives both her and the narrator pause: "she read the letter that stopped her. Without a greeting, a date, a return address, a big manila envelope had come registered and certified first class" (p. 173). The narrator does not reveal the contents of the envelope and the ellipsis is sustained until the end of Part Four, when Serlo hands David "an eight-by-ten manila envelope" (p. 563) containing photographs of Monte's autopsied body. The latent meaning of the envelopes is reinforced by the resistance of both Seese and David to identify the images in the photographs as Monte. The parallel is underlined by the passage from the notebooks that Seese has just transcribed, in which the description of human sacrifice by disembowelment is suggestive of an autopsy and so alludes to Monte's fate at Beaufrey's hands. Lecha has found Monte not by locating his body but by teaching Seese how to read the language of dreams through her work with the ancient almanac.

The most dramatic intersection of ellipsis and recursive imagery concerns Sterling, the character described by Silko as the "moral center" of the narrative (Perry, p. 330). The circular form of *Almanac* starts and ends with Sterling, who is the subject of the narrative frame controlled by the narrator. Very early in the novel the narrator claims that Sterling is "in training for a special assignment" (p. 20), but the nature of that assignment is not clarified until the very end. His tasks as gardener on the ranch include cleaning the swimming pool and running errands with Seese in Tucson, but these hardly require "training." Like Seese, his special assignment is to learn to read, to hear the voices of the ancestors and, ultimately, to learn the true meaning of the sacred stone snake's return to Laguna: he "had not believed the old prophecy ... , but he had seen what was happening in Tucson with his own eyes" (p. 755). From an avid reader of pulp magazines, Sterling comes to know that the images in his magazines never existed except as simulacra (p. 757), as he develops into the novel's central reader of spirit messages. Back at Laguna, Sterling thinks about the slow return of the buffalo, and, as he watches the ants, he knows the ants as spiritual messengers (p. 758). He remembers the old story about the destroyers differently now because, as the narrator claims, "Tucson had changed Sterling" (p. 762). And, although he tries to forget "everything Lecha had told him," to disavow his experience and believe that "Tucson had only been a bad dream" (p. 762), finally his perspective is that of the stone snake: "he knew what the snake's message was to the people" (p. 763).

Conclusion: The dynamics of disavowal

Throughout *Almanac*, the repetition of narrative images produces a transcendent narratorial ontology, which is the vehicle for the latent spirit of the stories. Performatively, the narrator translates the imagistic language of the ancestors speaking through the almanac, through dream imagery that contextualizes and extends the almanac's fragments. "The ancestors' spirits speak in dreams," Angelita tells the people (p. 518), and here to underline the accuracy of her words, the narrator refrains from paraphrase, quoting Angelita's exact phrasing. The reality of this dream language is emphasized by Freud; in his 1922 essay "Dreams and Telepathy," he insists that "[t]he psychoanalytic interpretation of dreams... does away with [the] difference between the dream and event, and gives both the same content" (p. 206). In *Almanac*, the reality of the ancestors' dream speech, the identity of dream and event, converges in the narrator's repetition of phrases and images that belong to the verbal and experiential registers of distinct characters. Thus, repetition adds a transcendent dimension to these images, generalizing their significance beyond the subjective and individual, through the work of the translating narrator.

"The malaise in *Almanac* represents (in terms of psychoanalysis) a return of the North American repressed: the reality of violent conquest," Ann Stanford notes (p. 28). Her emphasis on the disavowal of colonial violence is echoed in the suppressed tribal histories of the Americas and Africa that are reinstated by characters like Angelita and Clinton. Angelita ensures that Bartolomeo is tried for crimes against tribal history; Clinton, knowing that "[i]gnorance of the people's history had been the white man's best weapon" (p. 742), broadcasts that history in his radio transmissions, noting ironically that while the "white man" had control of the radio, "he didn't have nothing alive left to say" (p. 416). What is important, as Clinton and other characters acknowledge, is what is not said: the disavowed history of genocide and Indigenous resistance. However, access to this history is obscured by the "carefully constructed historical narratives" referenced by Stanford that must be unlearned before we can be tutored in the repressed meanings of inherited stories.

As part of the effort to render visible these historical connections, *Almanac* incorporates, in addition to fragments from the ancient almanac and notebooks, Angelita's chronology of Indigenous rebellion (p. 527–530), Wilson Weasel Tail's list of legal injustices (p. 714–715), and Clinton's history of the people's resistance (p. 742–746). While these documents manifestly expose the disavowed reality that the U.S. empire rests on stolen land and stolen lives (p. 714), factual lists such as Angelita's and Clinton's are nuanced by the narrator's continual return to the latent meanings voiced by the ancestors. Through the filter of Mosca's thoughts, for example, the narrator advises, "ancestor spirits had the answers, but you had to be able to interpret messages sent in the language of the spirits" (p. 603). As Kimberly Wieser explains, "[f]or American Indians ... visual thinking is part of the holistic thinking equation. Personal vision is always conjoined with the knowledge of the People, handed down by one's elders, and it is more than a 'mental' phenomenon—things can be 'known' not only with the mind but also with the heart, body, and spirit" (2007, p. 535). Factual lists speak to the mind; but the heart, body, and spirit are addressed by the ancestors in the poetry that Weasel Tail practices, which "would speak to the dreams and to the spirits, and the people would understand what they must do" (p. 713). Through repetition, the narrator insists that dreams will instruct the people how to take back the land and repeatedly the narrator emphasizes the unconscious motives that will cause the people to walk north. The Barefoot Hopi writes to prisoners about the latent, spiritual meanings of their dreams and, according to Mosca, "the Hopi had already infiltrated their dreams with the help of the spirit world" (p. 620); Awa Gee's words draw on the recursive imagery of blood as he explains how "[w]hen the time came, the people would sense it; they would feel it in their blood without recognizing what they were about to begin" (p. 688). It is Angelita who, reporting at the Holistic Healers Convention on behalf of El Feo and Wacah/Tacho, underlines the importance of interpreting, hearing, and knowing the latent spiritual meanings of the ancestor's messages. She reports to the convention that "Wacah believed that one night the people would all dream the same dream, a dream sent by the spirits of the continent. The dream could not be sent until the people were ready to awaken with new hearts" (p. 712).

Located in the transhistorical, transtextual discursive position that is akin to that of "the spirits of the continent," the narrator works constantly to translate the characters' stories into this form of knowing from the heart, body, and spirit. Working with each character through free indirect style, the narrator creates and exploits the doubleness of the novel's language to perform discursively the "psychic chasm" (Stanford, p. 28) that separates histories of disavowal from the reality of conquest. Thus, the narrator shares Zeta's laughter at Greenlee's racist joke—she "laughed out loud because everything essential to the world the white man saw was there in one dirty joke" (p. 704)—but does not explain explicitly why the joke is funny. Indeed, it is Greenlee who is ridiculously funny, not his joke; the real joke is his blindness to the sacrilege he commits by comparing a snake to a human penis and his naïve ignorance of the consequences of mocking the spirits. A more subtle form of ironic humor arises from the narrator's exploitation of the gap between settler-colonial and Indigenous epistemologies, when the narrator ventriloquizes Serlo's fear that "[b]rown people would inherit the earth like cockroaches" (p. 561). Because when the land is returned, the people will indeed have inherited the earth.

In an interview with Kathleen Kelleher for the *Los Angeles Times*, Silko explains her project in *Almanac*: "This whole novel is about reasserting claims for ideas and the truth that all people in America—African, Mexican, Native and Anglo Americans—forget." Silko says,

It is not just about reasserting claims for the artifacts, pottery and land, but ideals. These ideas and ideals were destroyed 500 years ago when the Europeans burned old Mayan and Aztec almanacs...Freud talked about forgetting, and it happens to people collectively and as a nation. And so, in America today, whether it's personal or collective, (history) needs to be articulated and remembered. Painful as it might be.... (Kelleher, 1992, n.p.)

Almanac draws on Freud's theory of the disavowed collective memory of a primal act of violence to expose the state-sponsored repression or disavowal of the anticolonial race war that has been waged in the Americas since 1492. Such a narrative requires that both the falsely avowed and the disavowed perspectives on history be told in a double-voicing of the manifest and latent meanings of the historical record. The "inherited unconscious substratum created in the mind by hereditary influences," described by Freud in *Group Psychology and the Analysis of the Ego* (p. 74), as the latent origin of our manifest behaviors is, in *Almanac*, narrated through the performative translation of the voices of the ancestors that transcend distinctions among past, present, and future and address us all. Concluding her reading of Freud's *Moses and Monotheism*, Cathy Caruth observes that "history, like trauma, is never simply one's own, that history is precisely the way we are implicated in each other's trauma" (1996, p. 24). The way we are implicated in each other's histories Silko dramatizes in *Almanac of the Dead*, a novel "in which every story or single character is somehow connected with the other" (Silko quoted Stanford, p. 39 n.7).

Notes

1   On heteroglossia, see in particular Moore (1994).
2   In a 1992 interview with Linda Niemann, Silko describes how she overcame a writing block by setting aside her manuscript of *Almanac* to read Sigmund Freud. She likens the writing process to psychoanalysis—"It's like do-it-yourself psychoanalysis. It's sort of dangerous to be a novelist. I really learned it with this one—you're working with language and all kinds of things can escape with the words of a narrative"—then moves abruptly from the issue of the generative power of language to evoke the figure of Freud: "…About two-thirds of the way through, I just finally had to stop and read Freud, and I read all eighteen volumes, one right after the other" (Neimann, p. 109).
3   "Acting-out" and the allied concept of "working-through" are explained in Freud, 1914 and 1917.
4   However, as Porter Abbott explains, interior monologue is direct and works as the vehicle for stream of consciousness; Silko uses a free *in*direct style that sustains the grammatical third person (p. 78).

References

Abbott, A. P. (2008), *The Cambridge Introduction to Narrative*, Second edition. New York: Cambridge University Press.
Caruth, C. (1996), *Unclaimed Experience: Trauma, Narrative, and History*. Baltimore: Johns Hopkins University Press.

Fitz, B. E. (2002), "Coyote Loops: Leslie Marmon Silko Holds a Full House in Her Hand." *MELUS*, 27:3, 75–91.

Fitz, B. E. (2004), *Silko: Writing Storyteller and Medicine Woman.* Norman: University of Oklahoma Press.

Freud, S. (1922), *Dreams and Telepathy*, in *The Standard Edition of the Complete Psychological Works of Sigmund Freud*, trans. James Strachey with Anna Freud, Alix Strachey, and Alan Tyson, Vol. XVIII. London: Hogarth Press and the Institute of Psycho-Analysis, 1975, pp. 195–220.

Freud, S. (1939), *Moses and Monotheism*, trans. Katherine Jones. London: Hogarth Press.

Freud, S. (1975a), *Beyond the Pleasure Principle* (1920), *The Standard Edition of the Complete Psychological Works of Sigmund Freud*, trans. James Strachey with Anna Freud, Alix Strachey, and Alan Tyson, Vol. XVIII. London: Hogarth Press and the Institute of Psycho-Analysis, pp. 1–64.

Freud, S. (1975b), *Group Psychology and the Analysis of the Ego* (1922), *The Standard Edition of the Complete Psychological Works of Sigmund Freud*, trans. James Strachey with Anna Freud, Alix Strachey, and Alan Tyson. Vol. XVIII, London: Hogarth Press and the Institute of Psycho-Analysis, pp. 65–143.

Horvitz, D. (1998), "Freud, Marx and Chiapas in Leslie Marmon Silko's *Almanac of the Dead*." *Studies in American Indian Literature*, 10:3, 47–64.

Kelleher, K. (1992), "Predicting a revolt to reclaim the Americas." Interview with L. M. Silko, *Los Angeles Times*, January 13, n.p. [Online] http://articles.latimes.com/1992-01-13/news/vw-184_1_american-indian-literature

Krupat, A. (1994), "Postcoloniality and Native American Literature." *The Yale Journal of Criticism*, 7:1, 163–180.

Moore, D. L. (1994), "Decolonizing Criticism: Reading Dialectics and Dialogics in Native American Literature." *Studies in American Indian Literatures*, 6:4, 7–33.

Moore, D. L. (2001), "Silko's Blood Sacrifice: The Circulating Witness in *Almanac of the Dead*," in Louise K. Barnett and James L. Thorson (eds), *Leslie Marmon Silko: A Collection of Critical Essays.* Albuquerque: University of New Mexico Press, pp. 149–183.

Neimann, L. (2000), "Narratives of Survival." Interview with L. M. Silko in E. L. Arnold (ed.), *Conversations with Leslie Marmon Silko.* Jackson: University Press of Mississippi, pp. 107–112.

Perry, D. (1997), "Leslie Marmon Silko," in Donna Perry (ed.), *Backtalk: Women Writers Speak Out: Interviews by Donna Perry.* New Brunswick: Rutgers University Press, pp. 313–348.

Silko, L. M. (1991), *Almanac of the Dead*. New York: Viking Penguin.

Stanford, A. F. (1997), "'Human Debris': Border Politics, Body Parts, and the Reclamation of the Americas in Leslie Marmon Silko's *Almanac of the Dead*." *Literature and Medicine*, 16:1, 23–42.

Wieser, K. G. (2007), "Vision, Voice, and Intertribal Metanarrative: The American Indian Visual-Rhetorical Tradition and Leslie Marmon Silko's *Almanac of the Dead*." *American Indian Quarterly*, 31:4, 534–558.

6

Seeing Double: Twins and Time in Silko's *Almanac of the Dead*

Beth H. Piatote

*Linear time was created by colonialists to put "distance"
between colonials and their unspeakable crimes against
indigenous people; capitalism, twin of colonialism, uses
linear time to make a commodity of human life so
it can be bought and sold.*

(LESLIE MARMON SILKO, IN A LETTER TO MICHAEL KORDA)

In the opening scene of *Almanac of the Dead*, an old woman, Zeta, is boiling a dark mixture at the stove, while her twin sister, Lecha, waits in a wheelchair for a shot of painkillers. Zeta stares at the pot and glances "through the rising veil" of steam at a younger woman, Seese. Lecha stares steadily at Seese, her "nurse," who counts pills at the table and fills a syringe. Ferro and Paulie, two more figures in the kitchen, clean guns while Ferro looks at Lecha, his mother. Zeta's dark mixture is dye; she lifts a sleeve of her clothes from the pot to reveal a shade Lecha calls "the color of dried blood. Old blood." Ferro, with contempt for Lecha, repeats her words: "The old blood, old dried-up blood [...] the old, and the new blood." Zeta does not respond, as she "has never cared what Lecha or anyone else thought. Lecha is just the same" (p. 19). These eerie opening paragraphs present twin images that are "just the same" and yet critically different: dye is not blood; a "nurse" may be something else; twins are similar but not the same; and the name "Seese," despite its reference to sight, evokes a dark opposite: cease. The dominant objects in the scene—the simmering pot, the drugs, the guns—represent things that are controlled by humans yet have an agency or force of their own. The boiling pot transforms its contents; the drugs seep through the body; the guns can destroy whatever lies in their path. From the start of the narrative, all things have similarities to be seen and discerned; the agentive force of "things" demands a careful eye. The mixing of "old blood" and "new blood" hints at a theme that emerges more fully through the book: time (as past/old and present/new) gains materiality in the body. The embodiment of time and the agency of "things" reflect a world that is unstable, in which there is no fixed point of orientation, either temporally or materially. While the activities of the characters differ—mixing, cleaning, and counting—all of the characters are visually tracking each other, pointing to the dominant interpretive practice of the book: seeing. To make meaning of this world, one must see its elements in relation to each other, one must discern fine differences, one must distinguish between twins. The novel is filled with twins, both biological and metaphorical, and it is incumbent upon the reader to recognize and discern them, including the most terrifying twins of all: capitalism and colonialism.[1]

Twins and time resemble each other in *Almanac*, and this is only logical. An almanac, after all, is a compendium of days in which correspondences of time are assumed. Based on past occurrences and patterns, an almanac predicts when a certain set of forces are expected to converge again and produce a new day that is very much like a previous one, predicting which days are auspicious for various activities. As Lecha explains of old almanacs, they "don't just tell you when to plant or harvest, they tell you about the days yet to come—drought or flood, plague, civil war or invasion" (p. 137). Silko's novel, structured as a narrative almanac, offers episodic entries of past and present events that anticipate and predict future possibilities. There is no single linear plot or central protagonist to follow, rather a cast of more than thirty characters who circulate through the book, engaging in various forms of warfare. Objects, too, express animate life and desires: "Knives, guns, even automobiles, possessed 'energies' that craved blood from time to time" (p. 512). The *Almanac* presents a world in motion, a world in which "revolution" is both an ideological call and geophysical fact. The turning of time, or the act of revolution, explicitly contests the vitiating effects of colonization. The central techniques of colonization involve the colonizers taking over a place by dominating its Indigenous peoples, controlling its resources, and severing the memories and functions of an autonomous, uncolonized past. Colonization strives to "fix" the past, to stop time for the colonized, to bring the previous life and times to an end. For the colonizers, the Indian wars are over; conquest is complete. But this premise is explicitly challenged in the *Almanac*, which declares on its frontispiece: "the Indian wars have never ended in the Americas" (p. 15). The story is not over. This extension of the temporal frame, positing an ongoing struggle, a present and future of the Indian wars in the Americas, is a critical aspect of the *Almanac*'s politics, which flatly rejects the notion that the Conquest is or ever will be complete.

In putting time in motion, the novel "unfixes" time and creates a relational experience of nonlinear movement, thus countering the progressive narrative of time upon which colonization depends. The novel rejects basic temporal orientations that separate events by chronology; thus the past is never left behind, but is always possibly present or soon to be manifest again. As a book of days, the *Almanac* calls upon the reader to recognize *time* as it circulates unbound through the work. But time is not an unaccompanied being; the present time is ever paired with its twin from the past, or possibly the future. The key to reading the *Almanac* is to see and recognize the enormous cast of characters as embodiments of time and to follow their movements through the text as they converge or diverge to produce different and similar days. In this chapter, I propose a method of reading the *Almanac* that understands all of its elements in motion, that watches as these elements assemble to create days, and that relies upon the apprehension of pairs, twins, and foils as "embodied time" that illuminates the double trajectories of creation and destruction, connection or alienation. Conceptualizing and seeing/reading "embodied time" and animate "things" as relational defies colonial modes of progressive time and capitalist practices of objectification and commodification. As Silko has written of her novels, "I want to help the reader break away from the fiction of linear time to experience Time as it really is. No matter what else my novels might appear to be about, at their very core they are about Time—non-linear time, and they try to give the reader the experience of the world free from linear time" (Papers; Letter to Korda). A world free of linear time is a world of time unbound, a world of revolution.

The novel's insistence on the present state of the Indian Wars accounts for its graphic violence. It is not a pleasant place to be, as the opening images of blood, guns, and drugs suggest. The *Almanac* is a war novel, as Lidia Yuknavitch argues, that focuses not only upon one war (the Conquest) but also sheds light upon a range of "invisible, economically determined wars…such as drug wars, race wars, sex wars, wars on crime, wars on poverty, wars on homelessness, even psychic warfare" (p. 100). As such, the novel's pages are saturated with violence, cruelty, torture, exploitation, and alienation—the forms of violence unleashed by capitalism's modes of objectification and exploitation. As Shari Huhndorf has argued, at the heart of the struggle against colonialism is the contest over land and ongoing calls for Indigenous resistance. In revealing ongoing states of war, the novel likewise reveals ongoing states of revolution; with its focus on the retaking of Indigenous territory, its interlinking of slavery, colonization, environmental destruction and class-based oppression, the *Almanac* "presents the Americas as a singular entity with a shared colonial past and revolutionary future" (p. 143). The counterforce to this drive is the repositioning and the reconceptualization of land, resources, and humans and animate things in relation to each other. To this end, the novel's work of storytelling—its offering of mythical, symbolic, historical, and narrative events—connects the characters by revealing their patterns of connection or alienation. As a method of reading the *Almanac*, one can begin with sets of similar pairs (biological twins, blood and dye, poison and medicine, the past and the present) and trace their divergent movements to reveal the novel's vision of survival/revolution or death.

Seeing time

The *Almanac* demands that readers decode its complex, interwoven plots by learning to recognize signs and characteristics of the "days" that circulate through the book. Knowledge and recollection of the past are necessary preconditions for seeing into the future, and seeing into nonmaterial realms (through dreams or psychic communication, for example) can illuminate the true nature of what is transpiring in the present moment. Silko employs a Mayan notion of time that is cyclical and repetitive, in which days and times recur (Reineke, p. 66). These days and times maintain distinct, recognizable identities, as Silko writes in her essay collection, *Yellow Woman and a Beauty of the Spirit*:

> Since the days eventually returned, the Maya believed it was possible to know the future, if one understood the identities, or souls of the days from their last appearance among humans. Certain people in touch with the spirits knew the days, weeks, months, and years intimately and could say exactly whether the days to come were peaceful, full of plenty, or menacing and on the brink of disaster. (p. 136)

In *Almanac*, the "souls" of days move freely: "The days, months, and years were living beings who roamed the starry universe until they came around again" (p. 313). From this temporal frame, being able to see into the future does not come from the ability to imagine or conjure the unknown, but rather from the recognition of that which is already known. According to the *Almanac*, "A human being was born into the days she or he must live with until eventually the days themselves would travel on. All anyone could do was recognize the traits, the spirits of the days, and take precautions" (p. 251). The ability to adjust oneself to "spirits" of the days depends upon acts of seeing, of recognition.

The expansive cast of characters, as some critics have pointed out, is not a set of fully drawn humans but more a collection of allegorical figures, with exaggerated characteristics. This makes sense when the characters and their actions are viewed as the "souls" of days, as the embodiments or bearers of particular times. The overdrawn portraits bring forth the essence of the days more clearly, so that correspondences and analogues are more easily seen. The characters and events in the book that are parallel can be conceptualized as the same "day." Two similar events, such as when the figures of the "little grandparents" are stolen from the Laguna people to be put on museum display and when a movie crew films the sacred stone snake eighty years later, may be understood as the same day, because a similar ethos or character ruled the day. The same "month" or "reign" may be revealed whenever the plentiful cast of destroyers (those who seek and take pleasure in destruction for its own sake) including Beaufrey, Serlo, Trigg, Cortez, de Guzman, and others, clamor after blood, sex, and power. To say "the same day" is not to imply "the identical" day, but rather it is to recognize that the same forces are moving and forming to create a particular time. In *Almanac*, embodied time expresses its own consciousness, or the soul of a day. Embodied time arrives and departs, showing its character through the actions and desires of humans and animate objects.

In order to understand the analogues of the past/future to present time, one must be familiar with the past; one must know history. A number of characters recite history as orators. Angelita de Escapía, the revolutionary Marxist, testifies against Bartolomeo (himself an echo of Bartolomé de las Casas, the sixteenth-century friar) for his "crimes against tribal histories" (pp. 525–532). Clinton, a Vietnam vet, interprets the legacy of slavery through a "liberation radio broadcast" as part of his effort to organize a resistance army, believing that "if the people knew their history, they would realize they must rise up" (p. 431). But the recitation of history is not its only form of accounting; bodies themselves are texts that bear stories, histories, and/or ghosts. In the *Almanac*, fragments of the ancient Mayan almanacs are borne on the bellies and backs of children. The ancient almanacs have their own sense of embodiedness, as Virginia E. Bell suggests, "this manuscript is conceived of as corporeal, stained with blood and held between horse gut parchment, a material description of text that challenges the opposition between writing as technology and orality as an act of the natural body" (p. 24). The relationship between books of days and the bodies that carry and/or produce them are intimate or even coextensive. In the same way that the book has a body, so too bodies and their desires display the characteristics of time or days. The character Mosca, for example, has a body that expands as he takes on the "weight of ghosts" and carries history. In the *Almanac*, engagement with history is shown as an active process, and the rejection of history is also a conscious process. The decision by other characters, such as Menardo, to suppress history is portrayed as a conscious choice and a rigorous practice. Menardo, like Mosca, puts on weight, but the weight he chooses leads not to revolution but to destruction.

Seeing twins

The centrality of seeing—both discerning sameness and difference—is represented in multiple ways in *Almanac*. Understanding time as embodied means that changes in time are registered through changes in the body, and these changes can be most clearly apprehended through seeing pairs, or twins. In this chapter, I propose reading Mosca and Menardo as twins who bear significant similarities but respond differently to history. Physical changes such as putting on weight provide the visual representation of changes in time. In the novel, both stories and ghosts have physical weight that is borne or rejected by the various characters, and thus the act of putting on weight—whether putting on extra fat and flesh or putting on another type of weight, such as armor—conveys particular meanings. Bringing together the practices of reading twins and recognizing time, it is possible to see the bodies of the characters as temporal maps, as embodiments of particular forces that illuminate trajectories toward survival or destruction. The ability to carry ghosts, to move with history, is a way to participate in the changing of time, or revolution. Taking on spirits, histories, and ghosts reflects an acceptance of the animate force of the world, and represents one of the forces of resistance in the ongoing Indian Wars; as David L. Moore suggests, "when Native storytellers depict an animate universe, they elude death and redefine the history of suffering as sacred…Conquest requires reductive judgments. Yet those who tell the stories of a land alive with spirits, of an animistic world, are able to declare the white man 'impotent' against that different reality" (p. 85). The act of reading time as embodied requires the reader to apprehend not only the characteristics or desires of days, but also tracking the changes that those temporal bodies make, and how those changes participate in or resist revolution. In this novel, the spirits that give animation to things and movement to time take on a readable materiality in the bodies of characters.

Menardo and Mosca are not biological twins in a book replete with such pairings. Yet they bear significant similarities: they are of Indigenous heritage, positioned mirror-like on opposite sides of the U.S.-Mexico border; they each have special abilities to see, and they each "put on weight" in an effort to prepare for impending political unrest. Menardo's weight, a white bulletproof vest, is literally "dead weight" that leads to his unanticipated death, while Mosca's weight, some flab and a creak in his body, is pleasure-giving, prophetic, and life-giving. Menardo's and Mosca's respective constriction and expansion of the body relate to their abilities to take on history.

Both Menardo and Mosca have special abilities to see, both in the material world and realms beyond, which are related to their Indigenous heritage. Menardo is one of the few characters granted an "I" (that is, a first-person narration) in the massive text; the "I" suggests its homonym, the "eye." Menardo is one who sees. When his character is introduced, he speaks in his own voice, describing "the old man," his grandfather:

> Full of beer he used to get very serious, and when I was a young child, I felt frightened. It was then he bragged the ancestors had seen "it" all coming, and one time I interrupted to ask what "it" was, and he waved his hands all around the shady spot where we were sitting and he said, "The time called Death-Eye Dog." There was no one in the area who could talk the way the old man did. (p. 257)

In this passage, Menardo's grandfather exhibits a form of knowledge that exists in relation to and across time. The grandfather can see or recognize time, and in this instance he names the period of colonialism as the era of the Death-Eye Dog. In this moment when Menardo speaks in his own voice and reveals his grandfather's knowledge, he expresses a link to the past that, in terms of the novel's main themes, is the primary hope for moving into the future. Speaking in his own voice, Menardo contests the fracture of memory by articulating an historical consciousness, which challenges both colonization and the economic forces of capitalism that drive it. That is to say, Menardo's sense of an embodied and relational position to time and to others resists the colonial practice of distancing oneself from the past under a new order, and the capitalist impulse to objectify other humans or resources.

Menardo's brief narration (a mere three paragraphs) goes on to describe the old man's fascination with European thought. Framing colonization from an Indigenous standpoint—as a pathology produced by improper kinship relations—the passage names Europeans as "the orphan people" who, like "orphans taken in by selfish or coldhearted clanspeople," found it difficult to remain whole and "failed to recognize the earth was their mother." Like their progenitors Adam and Eve, the Europeans were destined to wander aimlessly "because the insane God who had sired them had abandoned them" (p. 258). This passage names the alienation of humans from their "mother" as a distinct process of separation between the parent God and the European children. In the absence of a relational connection to their "mother" it became possible for colonialism and capitalism to arise, as these forces of exploitation depend upon the separation of time and the objectification of others. Even as Menardo describes this process of spiritual alienation, he is taking part in it; as the narrative continues, he effectively orphans himself from his lineage and attempts to re-create himself through the active suppression of his Indigenous heritage and knowledge.

Menardo's transformation is represented in the text through a shift away from first-person perspective; he loses his voice. Immediately following the discussion of the "orphan people," the narrative moves to third person:

> Menardo has loved the stories his grandfather told him about the old man who drank stinking beer and talked about and sometimes talked with the ancestors. Menardo had loved the stories right up until the sixth grade when one of the teaching Brothers had given them a long lecture about pagan people and pagan stories. (p. 258)

It is at the moment that colonization takes hold, here in the form of colonial narratives about Native peoples, that Menardo loses his first-person voice. Subsequently, a set of decisions on Menardo's part reveal that he is moving toward a rejection of his own body, family, and histories in order to embrace the power available to him through the colonial political power structure. This drive, as it turns out, is a death drive for Menardo, as it ultimately leads to his destruction. By shifting here from the intimacy of first-person voice to the more remote third-person voice, the novel gives insight into Menardo's internal shift of subjectivity and, on another level, the separation of his voice from his body.

At the same time that Menardo finds his cultural identity under attack, he encounters racialization: classmates make fun of his fat body and "flat nose," the latter taunt serving as slang for "Indian." Once his body explicitly and painfully signifies Indianness, and thus a constructed inferiority, Menardo begins in earnest his quest to transcend his identity. By the end of this chapter, Menardo invents a new narrative to explain his flat nose. He describes it not as a family trait (he is, after all, in the process of orphaning himself), but borrowing a line from a famous boxer from Chiapas (presumably Indigenous), Menardo says that his flat nose is the result of an injury inflicted by an opponent.

Mosca, too, is introduced as a character who can see, and whose capacities for seeing difference expand as the novel unfolds. When Mosca first appears, the text notes that his given name is Carlos and "Mosca" is a nickname given by Calabazas. Root calls Mosca by the English translation, "The Fly," and his visage fits the name: a wiry figure who wears large sunglasses that exaggerate his eyes. The name thus evokes a creature with a multifaceted lens for sight, someone with an excess capacity for seeing. One of Mosca's gifts is his ability to see witches, to discern different types of energy moving through the world. A critical characteristic of Mosca's visual power is his ability to see differences and sets of relationships. In an early scene in the book, Root and Mosca are the reluctant students of Calabazas, who marches them through the desert at night to teach them a lesson: "Those who can't learn to appreciate the world's differences won't make it. They'll die" (p. 203). The ability to see differences is a basic tool of survival, both personal and political. In terms of seeing time, one must not only be able to distinguish the characteristics of various days but also be able to locate their movement. Time is ever in motion, either moving toward the present or receding from it.

Body armor/Body amour

One of the ways to recognize the characteristics of time is through seeing desire as expressed by the characters, whether they hunger for power or justice. Menardo's path from adolescence is a desperate attempt to attain whiteness through imitation and association. He marries above himself, creating a union with the well-heeled Iliana, a descendant of one of the original Spanish colonists of the area, and he establishes his own company called Universal Insurance. In selling his product to potential clients, Menardo stakes a colonialist position: "He was there, he told them, because the 'new world' could belong to them just as the old one had" (p. 261). He socializes with the general, the governor, the judge, and the police chief, all representatives of colonial power, and he has an affair with, then marries, the young architect, Alegria, a descendant of conquistadors. His location near the border, which "leaked rabble-rousers and thieves like a sewage pipe" (p. 261), evokes not the possibility of solidarity with other Indians, but rather presents him with a unique business opportunity: a new insurance product to guarantee protection against Indigenous political unrest. All of these acts together contribute to a process of alienation that leads, ultimately, to Menardo's end as he puts on the white bulletproof vest, symbolically "vesting" himself in the cultural and material capital of whiteness.

As the narrative continues, Menardo climbs the social and economic ladder in Mexico through the expansion of Universal Insurance, and his suppression of his own Indigenous heritage and history takes the form of willful blindness. He becomes desperately blind about a number of things: Alegria's infidelities, his status among the elite political and military figures he socializes and conducts business with, and the death warnings that come to him through dreams. Menardo's greatest blindness can be seen in his view of himself; he fools himself into believing he has attained whiteness in the eyes of others. His self-absorption exists in inverse proportion to his self-awareness, a basic blindness that leads him into orchestrating his own mortal drama.

Menardo actively suppresses the prophetic visions available to him through dreams. For a while he confides the ominous content of his nightmares to his Indigenous servant, Tacho, whose people are known to interpret dreams. Tacho prompts, and Menardo readily invents, the most innocuous interpretations of the visions that are disturbing Menardo. Unable to deny completely the truth of his dreams, he awakens at night in a sweat and develops a stomach condition. The tool that eventually provides relief for Menardo is the gift of the bulletproof vest from the underworld criminal Sonny Blue. Menardo becomes deeply attached to the vest, wearing it at all hours; he wears it to bed to keep his nightmares away. In this way, the vest, which is designed to protect Menardo from external harm, propels him toward death as it blocks internal wisdom and vision instead. From Menardo's first appearance in the text, his trajectory moves from embodiment and seeing toward blindness and death, from "sees" to "cease."

While Menardo aspires to whiteness, Mosca rejects it for himself and abhors it in others. Mosca's relationship with his ancestors runs an opposite course from Menardo's: "Mosca had not always believed all the notions of the old tribal people, but he had seen for himself over the years that the old people had told the truth" (p. 605). Whereas Menardo once loved the old people and their stories but comes to reject them, Mosca's early skepticism transforms over time into belief. Mosca keeps the stories of the people close and his body serves as a conduit for messages from the spirit world. He believes that he has "a higher calling than ordinary men" (p. 606) and is not afraid to die because of his understanding that the dead continue to participate in the struggles of the living.

Both Menardo and Mosca see a revolution coming; times are changing. In response to the political and social unrest moving northward from Chiapas, both Menardo and Mosca "put on weight" as a measure of protection. For Menardo, the weight is the white bulletproof vest. For Mosca, it is a layer of fat. It would seem that there is less protection in the latter than the former, but in fact the fat prepares Mosca to survive, while the vest prepares Menardo to die. As embodiments of time, Menardo's and Mosca's bodies operate as temporal maps, showing both the weight of the past and the prospect of the future. Menardo's weight constricts as he suppresses the past, while Mosca's weight of ghosts, of history, expands. Again, the key is to see both the similarity and the difference in how these two figures put on weight, and how that weight functions in relation to their bodies and the characteristics of time.

In Menardo's case, the vest is an unyielding and undynamic presence on his body. The vest is literally white, and thus it expresses his desire to clothe himself in cultural and material whiteness. Yet, more significant than the proclaimed protection that it offers from outside forces, it blunts his inner life forces, including his expression of sexuality. When he dances at the governor's house with Alegria, she twists away from him, complaining that the vest is crushing her. While their sexual relationship continues to disintegrate (she quits sleeping with him when he starts wearing the vest to bed), his affection for the vest is described in provocative terms: Alegria teases him about "fondling" his vest, and it is said that he touches the vest "tenderly" and "wanted to be alone" with it (pp. 324–325). The vest is elevated beyond other inanimate objects, but this comes only from Menardo's projections onto it and the faith Menardo places in it. Rather than performing its stated duty of protecting Menardo from outside forces, the vest suppresses his internal knowledge and sexual vitality, robbing him of self-preserving instincts such as caution and wisdom. It deadens him from the inside out.

The image of dying from the inside out is one that receives multiple iterations through the text and is linked to the prophetic "disappearance of all things European" note that appears on the *Almanac*'s frontispiece map. This form of dying is marked by weightlessness, as in the early sections that describe Lecha and Zeta's father, a geologist who "had been stricken with the sensation of a gaping emptiness between his throat and his heart" (p. 121) and had dried up and died like a cactus in a drought. The process of his death was "as if he had consumed himself" (p. 123). Weightlessness, in this example and others, is the consuming spiritual vacuum that characterizes the destroyers, the agents of colonization and exploitation. A similar image appears in one of Silko's chapters in *Yellow Woman*: "You see that, after a thing is dead, it dries up. It might take weeks or years, but eventually, if you touch the thing, it crumbles under your fingers. It goes back to dust. The soul of the thing has long since departed" (p. 25). In *Almanac*, the destroyers are characterized by internal spiritual deadness, or movement toward that deadness. Tacho offers the prophesy that "whiteness" would consume itself: "The white man would someday disappear all by himself. The disappearance had already begun on the spiritual level…All ideas and beliefs of the Europeans would gradually wither and drop away" (p. 511).

Conversely, the novel associates weight with the capacity to bear the burdens of history, to carry the spirits of the dead, and to bear such weight is a necessary precondition for revolution. In the past and present Indian Wars, neither the living nor the dead have given up fighting for control of the continent. In "The Weight of Ghosts," Calabazas tells a story about a man riding his mule, trying to pass through an area where many Yaqui people had been slaughtered by Mexican troops. But the ghosts in the area are restless and begin to pile onto the mule for a ride, which exhausts the animal. The man is told that it is not the mule's fault—it is the weight of ghosts, which weigh two or three times what they weighed in life: "The body carries the weight of the soul all the life, but with the body gone, there's nothing to hold the weight anymore" (p. 191). Extrapolating from Calabazas's story, it is possible to see weight as the presence of disquieted spirits from the past who are attempting to move across landscapes of place and time. This weight, the weight of ghosts, is not separate from the history that created it; to carry ghosts is to carry the stories of the massacre.

Such weight is represented through Mosca's physical changes: he gains weight and takes on a creak in his shoulder, representing both past and future knowledge. His new weight signals the arrival and embodiment of history: "Mosca felt a burden, not his alone—ancient losses, perhaps to war and famine long ago" (p. 607). At the same time, the creaky voice in Mosca's shoulder offers guidance, not unlike Tacho's twin who carries a spirit macaw on his shoulder. Mosca knits history and prophesy together as a discourse of embodied knowledge: "Because talk was not necessary so long as you remembered everything you knew about your ancestors. Because ancestor spirits had the answers, but you have to be able to interpret messages sent in the language of spirits" (p. 604).

In the novel, changes in the body signify changes in time. Weight is a sign of time on the body. Both Menardo and Mosca respond to the growing Indigenous unrest and political revolt by putting on weight, but these forms of weight differ in form and purpose. Menardo's weight is but a shell and functions as a barrier to his ancestral knowledge, deadening him from the inside out. Mosca's weight, in contrast, is integral to his body and prepares him for the dangers ahead. Mosca even seeks out a fat reader, a person who has the ability to see the future by reading the contours of the body. In the chapter in which Mosca visits the fat reader, fat is described as a life-giving force, one related to sexual pleasure and physical survival. Fat readers have the ability to communicate with fat, even to massage messages into the body to enhance sexual pleasure, a detail that contrasts strongly with the sexually deadening effects of Menardo's vest. The fat reader explains the relationship between pleasure and survival: "Thin ones tended not to be well attached to life. Without capacity for pleasure, thin ones preferred the sensation of denial or pain. Injury and illness could easily carry off a thin woman or man. Skinny ones burned up in fires and blew away in big winds" (p. 608). These images again reference weightlessness as a consuming and destructive state. Recognizing that Mosca has only recently put on weight, the fat reader links his weight to the future: "fat that had been with a person all of his life related to the past;

fat that had appeared suddenly was related to events in the future" (p. 608). She interprets Mosca's fat as a warning of hardships to come and instructs him to fatten up more. She also warns against suppressing bodily knowledge: "She was still amazed, she said, at today's people and their fear of body fat. The human body grew to the size necessary for its survival" (p. 608).

What is most significant about Mosca and Menardo and their relationships to weight is the trajectories their different weights chart in relationship to the ongoing Indian Wars. Menardo is born fat, bearing ancestral memory, but he rejects the weight of his past and takes on a different kind of weight—a faith in a power structure represented by the white bulletproof vest. He positions himself against his own people in the ongoing Indian Wars. He does everything he can to deaden his senses against his Indigenous identity—rejecting the old stories, his physical attributes, his family, his prophetic dreams, his social situation. In joining the destroyers, he not accidentally turns his destructiveness upon himself. Mosca takes a path toward revolution and survival. He accepts hard lessons from Calabazas as he learns to "see" and to replace his skepticism with acceptance of the old stories. As he grows older, he takes on the burden of history, the weight of ghosts; he opens his body to the knowledge of spirits. In recognizing the movement of time and the animation of things, he takes part in the revolution. He embraces the present state of the Indian wars, and prepares for the hardships to come.

Linear time, as Silko suggests, is a tool of capitalism because it severs the present moment from the past; it leaves "behind" the atrocities of colonization, enslavement, and occupation that is the history of the Americas. Linear time produces temporal distance that allows human life to be objectified and thus commoditized and put to use in a capitalist system. The *Almanac* creates a world, in Silko's words, "free of linear time" by refusing the notion that the past is ever left behind. Indeed, all aspects of time (past, present, and future) are constantly in motion and constantly in relation to each other. Times travel together, converge and diverge, and create and re-create conditions of existence. The world of the *Almanac* refuses to be "fixed" within a colonial, capitalist order, thus underscoring the novel's argument that the Indian wars are not over. By representing time as embodied, mutable, and in motion—as the conceptual twins Menardo and Mosca put on different kinds of weight and move in different trajectories—the novel gives time a distinct subjectivity and agency that resists objectification. These embodied times are not *things* but *beings*, and in the novel even things (knives, guns, cars) are not things but agentive forces capable of desire and movement. Movement toward revolution is dependent upon an historical consciousness, as represented by Mosca's weight of the past that will help him survive into the future. To read the *Almanac*, time must be understood as embodied, relational, and in motion, and understanding embodied time as always multiple or twinned with a corresponding time is key to experiencing the decolonial vision of the *Almanac*.

Note

1   Portions of this chapter appeared in *Paradoxa: Studies in World Literary Genres*, 15 (2001), 198–210.

References

Bell, V. E. (2000), "Counter-chronicling and Alternative Mapping in *Memoria del Fuego* and *Almanac of the Dead*." MELUS, 25:3/4, 5–30.

Huhndorf, S. M. (2009), *Mapping the Americas: The Transnational Politics of Contemporary Native Culture*. Ithaca: Cornell University Press.

Moore, D. L. (2013), *That Dream Shall Have a Name: Native Americans Rewriting America*. Lincoln: University of Nebraska Press.

Reineke, Y. (1998), "Overturning the (New World) Order: Of Space, Time, Writing, and Prophesy in Leslie Marmon Silko's *Almanac of the Dead*." SAIL: Studies in American Indian Literatures, 10:3, 65–83.

Silko, L. M. (n.d.), Leslie Marmon Silko Papers, 1977–2004. Yale Collection of American Literature. Beinecke Rare Book and Manuscript Library.

Silko, L. M. (1991), *Almanac of the Dead: A Novel*. New York: Simon and Schuster.

Silko, L. M. (1996), *Yellow Woman and a Beauty of the Spirit: Essays on Native American Life Today*. New York: Simon and Schuster.

Yuknavitch, L. (2001), *Allegories of Violence: Tracing the Writing of War in Late Twentieth-Century Fiction*. New York: Routledge.

Part Three:
Gardens in the Dunes

"Old Snake's Beautiful Daughter": Introduction to Part Three

David L. Moore

Perhaps because of her spirit of experimentation, or because of the different spirits of different days and eras, certainly because of her discursive gifts, each of Silko's books is unique and strikingly distinct, even divergent, from her others in tone, style, and structure. Yet a rhythm is evident. She has explained that she is not interested in meeting publishers' demands for quick literary production, and she is content with a pattern of approximately one novel per decade, as each story's own integrity requires her attention and devotion, her witness and testimony. Further, she attends to a larger calendar: "Time is one of my interests and obsessions, and nonlinear time is more the kind of time that old-time pueblo people experienced" (Banti, 2010). After balancing the global witchery of *Ceremony* (1977) and the oceanic surge of *Almanac of the Dead* (1991), Silko swam back upstream to quieter headwaters in her photographic work, *Sacred Water* (1993), and then let those waters flow into *Gardens in the Dunes* (1999). In the interim between the second and third novels, she also published her works in *Yellow Woman and a Beauty of the Spirit* (1996).

While all of her works share a fundamental affirmation of Native survivance and a critique of colonialism, each novel takes a different approach, with crucial overlaps and interconnections. If *Ceremony* is mythic, *Almanac* is epic, and *Gardens* is lyric. If the first tends toward the spiritual, the second tends toward the historical, and the third toward the psychological—while all three weave all of these dimensions. *Almanac* directly examines vast social and historical forces, with characterizations merely as brief lenses into those forces, while both *Ceremony* and *Gardens* explore such history through a more focused lens on individual lives. While *Ceremony* heals things into balance "for now," the cacophony of global mixtures in *Almanac* finds some incomplete harmony in *Gardens*. All of Silko's work is indeed mythic, and in her mythopoetics various opposite qualities interpenetrate, blend, and blur on the larger ground. Thus, the parlor novel that is *Gardens* takes place in the vast edifice that is *Almanac*, and we read the historical witchery in both of these from *Ceremony*'s ledge of witness. *Gardens*' orchids grow out of *Almanac*'s blood-soaked soil, healed by the *Ceremony* of the four directions.[1]

Because *Gardens* circles thematically round the Ghost Dance, it is a nonlinear answer to a fundamental, tough question implicit in *Ceremony* and explicit in *Almanac*, where it is posed by the poet-lawyer Wilson Weasel Tail at the International Holistic Healers Convention in Tucson: "Today I wish to address the question as to whether the spirits of the ancestors in some way failed our people when the prophets called them to the Ghost Dance" (p. 722). He both rouses the audience and renders them silent as he explains how the anthropologists and historians misunderstood the Ghost Dance and its seeming defeat at Wounded Knee in 1890:

> The truth is the Ghost Dance did not end with the murder of Big Foot and one hundred and forty-four Ghost Dance worshipers at Wounded Knee. The Ghost Dance has never ended, it has continued, and the people have never stopped dancing; they may call it by other names, but when they dance, their hearts are reunited with the spirits of the beloved ancestors and the loved ones recently lost in the struggle. Throughout the Americas, from Chile to Canada, the people have never stopped dancing; as the living dance, they are joined again with all our ancestors before

them, who cry out, who demand justice, and who call the people to take back the Americas! (p. 724)

Whether dancing in public in powwows, or in classrooms, or in courtrooms, or secretly in kivas or other sacred ceremonies across Indian Country, Silko here affirms an ongoing revolution, a powerful circle. As Weasel Tail clearly explains, along with numerous other references in *Almanac*, this is a nonviolent revolution: "...the battle would be won or lost in the realm of dreams, not with airplanes or weapons" (1991, p. 475). All things European will disappear by their own injustice. "Give back what you have stolen or else as a people you will continue your self-destruction" (p. 725).

Gardens in the Dunes is Silko's further exploration of that nonviolent revolution. Thus the flowers, the orchids. Thus the gardens, the seeds. Both the Indigenous girl, Indigo, and her EuroAmerican guardian, Hattie, find their ways back to their various roots in the American Southwestern desert or in the ancient rocks of Europe. "The farther east they traveled, the closer they came to the place the Messiah and his family and followers traveled when they left the mountains beyond Paiute country" (1999, pp. 320–321). When they join the Ghost Dance, they align themselves with irresistible, mythic forces of history. "The Spirits of the Night and the Spirits of the Day would take care of the people" (1991, p. 523).

If *Almanac* is perplexing to many readers for its vast and dark vision, a focus on *Ceremony*'s Arrowboy as witness sets that epic vision into mythic context: the Keres oral tradition of witness in Estoyemuut, as we discussed in the introduction to this volume. When readers recognize how Silko draws them into Arrowboy's and her own act of witnessing, the vast novel comes more into focus. Yet its challenge of facing the brutalities of history remains daunting. *Gardens* is perplexing to many readers for opposite reasons, for its seeming lightness and gentleness, in the midst of its political critique of colonialism. Due largely to Silko's choice of a juvenile narrator's predominating point of view, among various colonial voices returning to their roots, some readers have felt that *Gardens* is not a radical enough response to her *Almanac*. Yet, as also discussed in the introduction to this book, the delicate orchid of this vision has the fiber of a mythic understanding of history to strengthen it. Again, the youthful voice that carries much of *Gardens* is a mark of Indigenous cultural respect for children, which is tied to the larger democratic principle of noninterference, built on respect and reciprocity. Thus, the fresh flowers are faces of future generations gazing from the ground.

The intertangled roots of these novels are specific. Again, just as *Almanac* had roots in *Ceremony* via affirmations of Arrowboy, *Gardens* has roots in *Almanac* via affirmations of the Ghost Dance. *Gardens* challenges readers to think in global, cross-cultural ways that *Almanac* prophesied. The spirit of Native continuity that the Barefoot Hopi affirms in *Almanac* is enacted precisely, carefully, and cross-culturally in *Gardens*. "Calabazas took the words of the Hopi to heart. He believed the change was in motion and was a process that had never stopped; it would all continue with or without him" (1991, p. 739). As Wilson Weasel Tail raises the question near the end of *Almanac* about the Ghost Dance and failure, he sets up the key challenge for the characters of *Gardens in the Dunes*. And Weasel Tail's response also measures the frame of *Gardens*: "...the Ghost Dance was to reunite living people with the spirits of beloved ancestors lost in the five-hundred years war" (p. 722). *Gardens in the Dunes* builds on that effort to reunite with beloved spirits by enacting the Ghost Dance, across continents on a global scale.

In "World of Water, World of Sand: Teaching Silko's *Gardens in the Dunes* and Sullivan's *Star Waka*," Becca Gercken takes a fresh theoretical approach, applying a transnational and comparative lens to Silko's novel and to Sullivan's Maori poem cycle. She argues that these two texts, when read together, are particularly well suited for helping students grasp concepts of both diversity and unanimity in transnational expression. Such diverse cultures remain "together (yet) *distinct*," quoting Chadwick Allen, on a global scale. She emphasizes the ways in which the novel and the poems compel us to reconsider long-established perceptions of Indigenous literatures and cultures in settler-colonial countries. Both Silko and Sullivan offer definitions of Indigeneity that are simultaneously free of geographical boundaries and tied to key markers of tribal identity. As a result, while there is a strong notion of "home" and place in Silko's novel and Sullivan's poetry, the notion of Indigeneity as transportable is key in both texts. Gercken makes a striking point that Indigo is "the strongest of all of Silko's characters" by conveying this theme of freedom in transnational and transcultural Indigeneity.

As a mobile sense of "home" is indeed key to the parallel narrative strands of *Gardens*, Gercken's analysis both contextualizes and illuminates the dynamics of Silko's text.

Resonating with the themes of *Gardens*, it is significant also that Gercken emphasizes this recent shift in theoretical perspective, where she answers the call in *The Journal of Transnational American Studies* special issue on Transnational Native American Studies to move the focus from "the exchanges and contact between Indigenous people and mainstream settlers" to "Indigenous experiences and realities" (Huang et al., 2012, p. 3). Gercken thus affirms, "The definitions of Indigenous identity offered by Silko and Sullivan offer students a new way to understand and to separate Indigenous identities from the confining characteristics of the imperial enterprise, its colonial nostalgia, and its historicizing impulse."

This radical shift in perspective makes a temporal about-face in Lincoln Faller's chapter, "EuroAmerica, Europe, and the Indigenous: The Complex (and Complicating) Dialectics of Silko's Jamesian Turn." Faller discusses what may be a version of the transnational in different terms in a different era, where Silko's *Gardens in the Dunes* maps cross-Atlantic ties both similar and quite different from those in the work of Henry James. Pointing out that another major contemporary Native American author, James Welch, in his novel *The Heartsong of Charging Elk* (2000), also "marked the turn of this century by sending Native characters across the Atlantic to extended stays in Europe" (and like *Gardens*, *Heartsong* is set near the turn of the earlier twentieth century), Faller follows Silko's lead in her published assertion that she owes a considerable debt to Henry James. Digging beneath what he sees as the relatively flat characterizations of *Gardens* in their emblematic ideological positions of the novel, Faller finds fascination in fundamental structures of the narrative. The Indigenous presence, which is Silko's primary concern, complicates and triangulates James' standard dialectic of EuroAmerican and European—complicated further by crucial gender dynamics in Silko's novel. Yet Silko finds Indigeneity in Europe as well. Thus, Faller maps dialectical questions in the novel with profoundly gendered dimensions, questions about both the past and the future of Indigeneity across continents. And Faller is content, as is the text, to let those questions resonate: "In their complication and lack, finally, of any ultimate resolution, these dialectics, I'll argue, ought to keep readers from coming to settled conclusions, which is all to the good..." The questions remain open to a future.

Finally, Rebecca Tillett brings the discussion back around to the beginning with "'Sand Lizard warned her children to share': Philosophies of Gardening and Exchange in Silko's *Gardens in the Dunes*." Tillett gives us an original analysis of primary structures of thought and culture in the novel. Within a larger context of what she describes as "a renewed international interest in the philosophies of gardens and gardening, and...the cultural and political histories these philosophies expose and enable," Tillett follows "the related growth in international interest in traditional Indigenous gardening practices and philosophies," especially as global awareness of climate change has fostered "a greater need for sustainability." Thus, in contrast, Tillett points out, "By the early nineteenth century," gardens had "become a standard symbol of colonial conquest."

Her chapter establishes another vital scholarly, cross-cultural context. Tillett reexamines *Gardens in the Dunes* through "a range of studies" that have emerged or been reissued in recent years, including Gregory Cajete's *Native Science: Natural Laws of Interdependence* (2000), alongside foundational research such as Gilbert Wilson's *Buffalo Bird Woman's Garden: The Classic Account of Hidatsa American Indian Gardening Techniques* (1917), Carol Buchanan's *Brother Crow, Sister Corn: Traditional American Indian Gardening* (1997), and Michael Caduto and Joseph Bruchac's *Native American Gardening: Stories, Projects and Recipes for Families* (1996). Tillett also draws on recent studies of European gardening, especially Peter Linnebaugh's *Stop, Thief!: The Commons, Enclosures, and Resistance* (2014), and Robert Pogue Harrison's *Gardens: A Meditation on the Human Condition* (2008). She explains that Silko sets a variety of gardening traditions and philosophies into dialogue within her novel via the Indigenous child narrator Indigo, so Tillett's analysis attempts to facilitate a greater dialogue between Cajete's discussion of Indigenous science, Wilson's, Buchanan's, and Caduto and Bruchac's commentaries on the relationships between Indigenous gardening techniques and spiritual and political philosophies, Harrison's assessment of classical European philosophies about the earth, and Linnebaugh's political reading of capitalism's engagement with the natural world. As Tillett traces the intersections of these critical texts with the topics that Silko raises within *Gardens in the Dunes*, the reader may unearth deeper insight into differences between principles of historical capitalism and "an awareness of exchange, sharing and reciprocity as a biological principle," where, quoting Harrison, "life exists where giving exceeds taking." Tillett outlines an ethos of reciprocity in the novel to contrast with that exploitative history.

Together these three chapters clarify both the complexity and the simplicity of this quietly captivating novel. The transnational nature of Indigeneity comes clear across oceans and centuries, perhaps heading toward a new garden.

Note

1   For this introduction to *Gardens in the Dunes*, I draw from my article "Ghost Dancing through History in Silko's *Gardens in the Dunes* and *Almanac of the Dead*" (2007). It is relevant to note further how that article gathered ideas as a sequel to "Silko's Blood Sacrifice: The Circulating Witness in *Almanac of the Dead*" (1999).

References

Banti, K. (2010), "A Conversation with Leslie Marmon Silko on *The Turquoise Ledge*." *Seattle Times*. [Online] http://seattlest .com/2010/10/19/interview_leslie_marmon_silko_on_th.php [Accessed: October 19, 2010].

Huang, H., Deloria P., Furlan, L., and Gamber, J. (2012), "Charting Transnational Native American Studies." *The Journal of Transnational American Studies*, 4:1, 1–15.

Moore, D. L. (2007), "Ghost Dancing through History in Silko's *Gardens in the Dunes* and *Almanac of the Dead*," in Laura Coltelli (ed.), *Reading Leslie Marmon Silko: Critical Perspectives through* Gardens in the Dunes. Pisa, Italy: Pisa University Press (Association of American University Presses). Lincoln: University of Nebraska Press (2008), pp. 91–118.

Silko, L. M. (1991), *Almanac of the Dead*. New York: Penguin.

Silko, L. M. (1999), *Gardens in the Dunes: A Novel*. New York: Simon and Schuster.

7

World of Water, World of Sand: Teaching Silko's *Gardens in the Dunes* and Sullivan's *Star Waka*

Becca Gercken

The reservation space and the returning-home plot as key signifiers of Indigenous identity have long been foci for American Indian literature scholars.[1] These themes continue, and novels set on reservations or concentrated on the return home continue to appear in significant numbers, but the changing locus of Indigenous populations, who are now largely urban rather than rural, and shifts in the critical conversation toward a trans-Indigenous approach, lead us to new questions.[2] Much of Leslie Marmon Silko's work lends itself to what has been this dominant critical conversation; one need look no further than her first novel *Ceremony* and Tayo's complex return to his reservation to understand these threads. *Ceremony* is still widely taught as many consider it one of the two central books in the early canon of the American Indian Literary Renaissance, with N. Scott Momaday's 1968 novel *House Made of Dawn* being the other. And while it is useful for our students to understand why the plot lines of stories such as *House Made of Dawn* and *Ceremony* are so central to the American Indian literary canon, it is also imperative that we help our students embrace the dynamic possibilities of criticism that considers Indigenous identity beyond the reservation and even beyond North America. Hsinya Huang et al. write in the introduction to their special forum "Charting Transnational Native American Studies" in *The Journal of Transnational American Studies* that scholars "need to create aggregates that rest on a platform broader and more robustly empirical than the relatively arbitrary and demonstrably ephemeral borders of the nation" (2012, p. 10). In his introduction to *Trans-Indigenous: Methodologies for Global Native Literary Studies*, Chad Allen frames a question that helps us build that platform: "In the abstract, 'together equal' sounds like a noble goal...Within a context of ongoing (post)colonial relations, shouldn't the objective of a global Indigenous literary studies in English run more along the lines of 'together (yet) *distinct*'?" (2012, p. *xiii*, emphasis in original). In the close readings of *Gardens in the Dunes* and *Star Waka* that follow, I argue that these two 1999 texts, when read together, are particularly well suited for helping our students grasp the concept of "together (yet) distinct" through readings that emphasize the ways in which the novel and the poems compel us to reconsider long-established perceptions of the Indigenous literatures of settler-colonial countries. This analysis is not meant to be an exhaustive reading of the scholarly conversation, rather an effort to join that conversation by engaging with new materials and an expansive notion of Indigeneity.

Both Silko and Robert Sullivan offer definitions of Indigeneity that are simultaneously free of geographical boundaries and tied to key markers of tribal identity. As a result, while there is a strong notion of "home" and place in Silko's novel and Sullivan's poetry, the notion of Indigeneity as transportable is key in both texts. For Silko's protagonist Indigo and for Sullivan's multiple personas, Indigenous identity and a sense of home can be found just as easily in objects tied to that identity as they can be found in the physical bodies or places of Indigenous peoples. It makes no matter if the object is originally from that culture, as with Sullivan's wakas, or if it is outside the culture, as with Indigo's seeds; what matters is that the Indigenous people in contact with the objects understand them as being part of their culture. The objects are made to be, or be understood as, Indigenous through the characters' and personas' epistemologies and life ways. Indigo escapes a residential boarding school only to be taken in by a white family who bring her on a trip through Europe where she collects seeds to bring home to the

Sand Lizard people's gardens in the dunes. For Indigo, these seeds, and the lessons they invoke from her grandmother about a proper relationship with the earth, keep her tied to home and to Sand Lizard life ways even as she travels the globe. For Sullivan's personas, who range from an autobiographical contemporary Maori man to the gods of Maori cosmology, the waka, or ocean-going canoe, not only explains but also signifies the Maori presence in New Zealand and proves itself to be—like the Maori people—remarkably adaptable. The wakas are not only transportable; they are themselves a form of transport. Both Silko and Sullivan have chosen objects that signify movement and the ability to start over in a new location to represent the adaptability and tenacity of Indigenous peoples and their cultures.

Two Indigenous authors from opposite sides of the world—one from a world of water, one from a world of sand—both suggest that Indigenous identity can be understood beyond body and place. Yet both authors do more than that, as their texts teach us that signifiers of Indigenous identity, objects understood by the Sand Lizard or Maori people as part of their culture, can themselves transform any space, creating a new realm of Indigeneity not limited by reservation boundaries, Indigenous plants, or traditional materials. Thus, Indigo's seeds, whether they are from South America or Europe, represent not only home but also her ability to make a Sand Lizard home, whether or not that home is in the Dunes. Similarly, Sullivan's Honda vehicle is his own personal waka, reminding him of how his people came to be in New Zealand or Aotearoa, the Land of the Long White Cloud. Silko's seeds and Sullivan's wakas create useful tension between the notions of place and movement that suggests an alternative to the oft-repeated historical and critical narrative that movement in the face of colonialism must signify a disruption of Indigenous lifeways. Here movement—of both Indigenous people and objects—and the places they occupy are associated with adaptation that ensures the survival of lifeways. A. LaVonne Brown Ruoff invokes Mary Louise Pratt's notion of contact zones in her analysis of *Gardens in the Dunes*, noting that by "locating the action of her novel on two continents and addressing Indigenous characters' interactions with Europeans and Euro-Americans" Silko "expands the range of Native American Literature" (2007, p. 17); an analogous argument could be made in relation to *Star Waka*.[3] And while the idea of contact zones can be helpful, I think it is

more useful at this juncture in Indigenous studies to answer the call
in *The Journal of Transnational American Studies* special issue on
Transnational Native American Studies to move the focus from "the
exchanges and contact between Indigenous people and mainstream
settlers" to "Indigenous experiences and realities" (Huang et al.,
2012, p. 3). The definitions of Indigenous identity presented by
Silko and Sullivan offer students a new way to understand and to
separate Indigenous identities from the confining characteristics of
the imperial enterprise, its colonial nostalgia, and its historicizing
impulse.

Trans-Indigenous gardens

Silko's title, *Gardens in the Dunes*, immediately suggests that the
novel is about Indigenous place, and indeed much of the early
information we get about the protagonist Indigo is her relationship
with and response to the land around her. Indigo responds to new
environments as much as if not more than she does to new people.
The novel opens by situating Indigo in her beloved dunes:

> The rain smelled heavenly. All over the sand dunes, datura
> blossoms round and white as moons breathed their fragrance
> of magic. Indigo came up from the pit house into the heat; the
> ground under her bare feet was still warm, but the rain in the
> breeze felt cool—so cool—and refreshing on her face. She took
> a deep breath and ran up the dune, where Sister Salt was naked
> in the rain…She took handfuls of sand and poured them over
> her legs and over her stomach and shoulders—the raindrops
> were cold now and the warmth of the sand felt delicious. (1999,
> p. 13)

With her opening paragraph, Silko establishes that Indigo is not just
on the land, she is of the land, as is her sister who enjoys the rain
with her. Silko continues this pattern with each new space Indigo
enters. Of particular note is her response to the orange groves
around the Sherman Institute from which she escapes, and Edward
and Hattie's house, where she finds shelter. The first time Indigo
runs away from the boarding school, she heads into the desert, a
space she recognizes and can negotiate. But the boarding school

employees "easily tracked her and caught her within a few hours" (1999, p. 69). She realizes that the "orange trees would hide her better than the low desert brush" (1999, p. 69) and enters the massive commercial groves that surround the school. She does not reject the space because of its associations with Western consumerism and the boarding school but instead focuses on its value to her: it will keep her safe from trackers.

Yet, Indigo does more than inhabit the space, she indigenizes it. Silko writes that in the orchard, "the only sound was the bees, a soothing sound that reminded her of the bees that hovered at the spring above the old gardens. When Indigo was little, Grandma Fleet used to tease that the bees sang a lullaby for Indigo's nap so she must not disappoint them" (1999, p. 69). Through her memory and her association of creatures in the orchard with creatures in the dune gardens, Indigo finds peace and a connection not only to the land, but also to her family: "Wherever they were, Sister Salt and Mama must have thought about her at that moment because suddenly she was thinking about them too. She felt their concern for her and their love; tears filled her eyes" (1999, p. 69). The relationship between land and family is strengthened when Indigo remembers that "Grandma Fleet still loved them and prayed for them from Cliff Town, where the dead went to stay" (1999, p. 69). The orchard provides physical protection from the men searching for her, but just as important is the emotional protection Indigo gains through her willingness to bridge the gap between the dune gardens and the commercial orchards of California. This early sequence signals to readers that Silko is invoking place in a more complex way than a homing plot. Indigo wants to get back to the dunes, but she does not need to be in the dunes to be in an Indigenous place.

This pattern continues when Indigo seeks refuge in the Palmers' gardens. A lilac bush is her initial hiding place, but once the monkey Linnaeus and Hattie spot her, she knows she needs to relocate as soon as night falls. While the garden's style and its plants are largely unfamiliar to her, Indigo again indigenizes the space through her actions and her familial memories. She notes the red roses and immediately connects them to her grandmother: "What a fragrance they had! Grandma Fleet used to talk about the flowers the Mormon ladies grew, but never had she nor anyone ever talked about flowers so fragrant and big as these" (1999, p. 82). She then alters the space when "the sensation of the rich damp soil under her feet made [her] want to dance" (1999, p. 82). These actions indeed indigenize the garden space, transforming it into a Sand Lizard landscape once Indigo removes the obstacle of her school uniform. Rather than discarding it, Indigo again chooses adaptation, recognizing that "the school dress with its long sleeves and long skirt would serve as a blanket as well as a pack to carry any food she might find around here" (1999, p. 83).

Indigo's willingness to adapt—which Silko clearly and repeatedly defines as adopting Western practices into Sand Lizard culture rather than abandoning Sand Lizard traditions—is her hallmark, and it travels with her as she moves to gardens ever more distant from her Gardens in the Dunes home. While at Hattie's parents' house, she continues the schooling in gardens begun by Grandma Fleet, but through the Western texts of books and illustrated plates. Hattie watches as Indigo "lingered over books with pictures of gardens with water splashing from fountains and statues and even a long stone wall covered with spouts of gushing water" (1999, p. 178). Indigo is especially interested in the images that will help her be able to understand the new plants in relation to what her grandmother has taught her: "Hattie showed her diagrams of a lily bulb and a gladiolus corm. Indigo's expression went from concentration to delight. These bulbs were giants compared to the bulbs of little plants she and Sister Salt used to dig from the sand to eat raw" (1999, p. 178). The elaborate gardens of Hattie's extended family are another sort of textbook as Indigo is "delighted in examining the late tulips and the gladiolus and the lilies until her hands, face, and even the front of her dress were streaked with bright yellow-and-orange pollen" (1999, p. 178). Hattie, while pleased with Indigo's interest and relieved to be holding up her end of the bargain with the Sherman Institute to educate Indigo while she is in her care, does not seem to understand the connections that Indigo is making between her Sand Lizard home and people and the new plants she encounters.

Ironically, the first Western person to note connections between European and Western plants confuses and embarrasses Indigo when she does so. Aunt Bronwyn tells Indigo that "your people...the American Indians, gave the world so many vegetables, fruits, and flowers—corn, tomatoes, potatoes, chilies, peanuts, coffee, chocolate, pineapple, bananas, and of course, tobacco" (1999,

p. 244). Rather than feeling comforted by this information, "Indigo felt suddenly embarrassed. Sand Lizard people barely were able to grow corn, and they had no tomatoes, peanuts, or bananas" (1999, p. 244). Amidst the scientific minutiae that Bronwyn (and Edward, and the other Western gardeners) notes about plants, America's Indigenous people, Northern and Southern, are lumped together. While Silko spends considerable time emphasizing the ideas of transplantation and hybridization, the vastness of the continent, its different climates, and its different people are ignored or glossed over by her American and European characters, who instead make distinctions among hue, shade, color, size, and other characteristics of thousands of plants.

But the Sand Lizard girl makes no such mistake and continues to take in new lessons and new seeds. As Indigo, Hattie, and Edward prepare to leave England, Aunt Bronwyn presents Indigo with a gift:

> a small, silk-bound notebook where Aunt Bronwyn hand-printed the names (in English and Latin) of medicinal plants and the best conditions and methods to grow them. All the other pages in the green silk notebook were blank, ready for Indigo to draw or write anything she wanted. Bundled on top of the notebook with white ribbons were dozens of waxed paper packets of seeds wrapped in white tissue paper. (1999, p. 267)

Indigo's interest in the plants stems not from an awareness that she can find flora that interest her outside of her dunes, but rather from her determination to bring them *back* to the dunes. She is not drawn to the visual drama and scientific achievement of Edward's sister's blue garden, nor Aunt Bronwyn's, nor even Edward's transplanted plants and hybrids. Instead, she is drawn to the embodiment in these plants of the lessons her Grandma Fleet taught her, a continuation of Sand Lizard tradition of growing stronger through adaptation. It is not surprising, then, that her first concern, when Italian Customs return her luggage after Edward's illegal scheme to harvest citron cuttings, is her own seeds and notes on how to care for her new plants. Silko writes that "Indigo was worried about the envelopes and tiny boxes of flower and vegetable seeds she had been saving for the gardens in the dunes" (1999, pp. 328–329). The seeds are not only about her past and her memories of the time spent in the gardens with Grandma Fleet, Sister Salt, and her mother; they are also her assurance that she is a Sand Lizard even in Europe and of the promise of her future in the garden.

Silko reinforces this interpretation of the seeds and their role in Sand Lizard survival through the subplot of Sister Salt and her baby with Big Candy. Although Big Candy is an African American, Sister Salt knows that the seed he has planted in her will create a Sand Lizard baby:

> Sand Lizard mothers gave birth to Sand Lizard babies no matter which man they lay with; the Sand Lizard mother's body changed everything to Sand Lizard inside her. Little Sand Lizards had different markings, and some were lighter or darker, but they were Sand Lizards. (1999, p. 202)

Sister Salt goes on to describe mixed race children in much the same manner that the novel's botanists discuss hybrid plants. She argues that among the Sand Lizards, "sex with strangers was valued for alliances and friendships that might be made" (1999, p. 202). Once again, *Gardens in the Dunes* teaches us that bringing in the new strengthens rather than weakens Sand Lizard culture and ties Indigo's interactions with new flora to a larger world view that includes all living things. It is this Sand Lizard epistemology that causes Indigo to note with delight that "seeds must be among the greatest travelers of all!" (1999, p. 291).

Thus, a key lesson we learn from *Gardens in the Dunes* is that Indigo can thrive in these new spaces and that by adapting she will ensure the Sand Lizard people's ability to survive. Through Silko's focus on plants and their mobility, she expands readers' understanding of Indigeneity from its narrow meaning in a settler-colonial American context. As plants from South America thrive in New England and plants from Asia thrive in England, readers grasp the constructed nature of Indigeneity and realize how much context is necessary for us to understand what and where is Indigenous. This framework puts Sand Lizard people on equal footing with settler colonials while also elevating Indigo, whose ability to maintain her cultural heritage and to learn and adapt quickly in both worlds signifies that she is the strongest of all of Silko's characters.

Trans-Indigenous waka

Like Silko, Robert Sullivan focuses on adaptation and uses objects to represent that change. However, while Silko focuses on seeds and an expansive definition of Indigeneity, Sullivan focuses on an object from the heart of his Maori culture, the waka. And while *Gardens in the Dunes* highlights cultural interaction as the site of adaptation, *Star Waka* (1999) focuses on technological transformation as the site of adaptation. Thus, the ocean-going waka represents both Maori origins and ongoing lifeways.

In two poems, "Honda Waka" and "*waka rorohiko*," Sullivan emphasizes the Maori people's ability to bridge the gap between their origins and their contemporary lives in Aotearoa. In "Honda Waka," Sullivan eulogizes his Honda automobile, sold to a "wrecker in Penrose for $30" (1999, l. 3). Sullivan focuses his description of the modern waka around his whakapapa, his family: "That car took me to Uncle Pat's tangi [funeral] in Bluff" (1999, l. 9). He goes on to note that when his daughter Temuera was born, "A friend followed us in it on the way" (1999, l. 12) and that he "went to Otako, and Wellington,/ in the Honda to visit family" (1999, ll. 15–16) and "Drove Granddad across the creek in the Honda/ at night after the family reunion bash" (1999, ll. 19–20). By describing his vehicle as a waka and connecting its use to familial ties, Sullivan reminds readers that Maori culture is not static and that using modern means of transportation makes the Maori no less traditional than their ancestors. Indeed, the emphasis on strong family ties serves to underscore their connection to their ancestors. Sullivan goes on to link the Honda waka to his achievements, writing that "The Honda took me to Library School" (1999, l. 78) and the "Honda has seen a high percentage/ of my poetry" (1999, ll. 22–23). These images link Sullivan's achievements to the vessel that made his existence in New Zealand possible and associates them with the fearlessness of his ancestors. Without the word waka, this poem simply describes a man's rust bucket car, family ties, and work; with the word waka, Sullivan places his whakapapa and his work as a librarian and poet in the context of a Maori presence a thousand years old. Moreover, through his emphasis on transformative moments—births, deaths, graduate school—he reminds readers that his people are part of an adapting, living culture.

Sullivan marks a similar connection in *"waka rorohiko"* although with an ambivalence not present in "Honda Waka." In this poem, the persona describes hearing the phrase "computer waka" at a community organization: "I heard it Awataha Marae/ in te reo—waka rorohiko–/ 'computer waka', about a database/ containing whakapapa" (1999, ll. 1–4). He gives readers the phrase in Maori—te reo—first, before writing it in English, placing his traditional language in the primary position and thus emphasizing its importance. But the blending of tradition with new technology is not cause for celebration here as it is in "Honda Waka"; instead the persona is concerned that tapu, or sacred information, is being made available for publication. The desire to protect sacred elements of Maori culture conflicts with the autobiographical persona's librarian training, which calls for "access for all, no matter who, how,/ why" (1999, ll. 7–8). This poem captures the dilemma Indigenous people face in regard to adaptation. After years of fighting, the dominant culture's notion that one must assimilate rather than adapt and the perception that "real Maori," like "real Indians," only existed centuries ago, how do Indigenous people explain to non-Indigenous people that some aspects of a culture should not adapt to contemporary technology? The poem tells readers that there are no easy answers to that question.

While *"waka rorohiko"* reveals uncertainty, most of the poems in *Star Waka* accentuate the longevity and adaptability of Maori culture. In the poem "Some definitions and a note on orthography" (italics in original), Sullivan comments on the inadequacy of the English language in characterizing the waka:

in English the waka
is a canoe
but the ancestral waka
were as large
as the European barks
of the eighteenth century explorers. (1999, ll. 1–6)

He goes on to explain that the problem is not the size of the ship implied in the English word but rather that the English word's connotations reveal the colonizing impulse to diminish the achievements of the Maori people. Thus, Sullivan writes, "size isn't

the key factor here/ it is the quality of the crews" (1999, ll. 7–8).
He also makes clear that the English language does not properly
convey the communal nature of the waka and warns readers that
the colonizing impulses of language are still found in the failure of
editors to "pluralise/ Maori loan words although most have/ ceased
italicizing them/ to give a sense of inclusion" (1999, ll. 16–19). The
persona notes that although the lack of italics can create a sense
of inclusion, of Maori and Euro-New Zealand unity, it can also be
read as "pacification" (1999, ll. 22). While the poem ends on the
dark note of "pacification," the poem itself and indeed the entire
collection work to resist colonial efforts to dominate Maori culture
and to control its representation.

   In "Formats (1)" (1999, ll. 1), Sullivan offers a similar strategy of
adaptation that again pairs the waka with technology. The poem is
a brief twelve lines:

   sepia
   paint
   text
   video
   dat
   email
   html
   doc files
   water
   cd rom
   cd photo
        waka

The poem offers a list of words, almost all of which are methods
to capture and convey communication or forge a connection.
Only one word, sepia, invokes the past with notions of sepia-
toned pictures, while the majority of the words reflect modern
computer technology. The notable exceptions are water, in line 9,
and waka, in line 12. The reference to water amidst the computer
terminology reminds readers that water is still a crucial means
of communication for the water-bound land of the long white
cloud. Even more important is the word waka and its placement
on the page—it is pushed to the right of the rest of poem's lines,
standing alone. This location suggests not only that the word waka

contains—or perhaps even subsumes—the words above it, but also that the waka is what is moving forward, going on into the future, not the words signifying technology, which contemporary readers understand as always on the brink of obsolescence. It is the waka that prevails.

Throughout *Star Waka*, the waka marks adaptation. As change occurs within the Maori community, whether that change is from the colonizer's efforts to assimilate the Maori or from the advancements of the computer age, the waka remains a cultural constant. The waka, through its constancy as a representation of Maori identity, history, and culture, becomes the signifier of adaptation. And thus Maori identity, while connected to the land, is about movement to and within the space of New Zealand rather than a fixed location or particular body.

What happens if we keep reading canonical texts the same way? What happens if we read new texts using existing methodologies rather than seeing how the texts might shape a new methodology or pedagogical approach? What happens if we create narrow parameters for the category of "Indigenous literature," which precludes reading across texts to see the experience of American Indians alongside the experience of the Maori? What might be lost—or missed entirely? With this reading of *Gardens in the Dunes* and *Star Waka*, I hope to have demonstrated that by making room for new texts and by approaching familiar texts in new ways, we stimulate not only new readings, but also new pedagogical strategies and perhaps even new methodologies. As Shari M. Huhndorf writes in *Mapping the Americas: The Transnational Politics of Contemporary Native Culture*, focusing on the connections between Indigenous communities "challenges us to rethink critical assumptions that remain rooted in the literature of earlier decades" (2009, p. 2). We spend much of our time as teachers reminding our students that Indigenous peoples and their cultures are neither static nor fixed in the past. We must remind ourselves of these facts and create dynamic rather than static reading lists and conversations with our students.

In *Trans-Indigenous*, Allen asks "How do we harness this diversity [of Indigenous identities] for our own rather than others' intellectual and political purposes? How do we control the discourses of an Indigenous-centered scholarship rather than allow rigid or fundamentalist versions of those discourses to control us?"

(2012, p. *xxxiii*). I suggest that if we expand the canon to include narratives too often overlooked in Indigenous studies, such as those found in Silko's *Gardens in the Dunes* and Sullivan's *Star Waka*, we can help our students develop a more complex and nuanced understanding of trans-Indigenous literatures and the peoples whose cultures they represent. Silko and Sullivan challenge both the settler-colonial narratives of Indigeneity and the critical canon of Indigenous literature and its criticism in their refusal to be contained by static and corporeal definitions of Indigenous peoples. Allen reminds us that it is not a matter of "which writers and texts" we choose "but rather how to train ourselves—and how to train the generation behind us—for the Indigenous scholarship of the future" (2012, p. *xxxiii*). And while I agree that much of the answer to the question of "what should be our critical approach" lies in the methodologies we adopt, there are primary texts that can help us shape new narratives of trans-Indigenous literature, and Silko's and Sullivan's are among them.

Notes

1   William Bevis notes that

> in marked contrast [to Euro-American novel's "leaving" plots], most Native American novels are not "eccentric," centrifugal, diverging, expanding, but "incentric," centripetal, converging, contracting. The hero comes home. "Contracting" has negative overtones to us, "expanding" a positive ring. These are the cultural choices we are considering. In Native American novels, coming home, staying put, contracting, even what we call "regressing" to a place, a past where one has been before, is not only the primary story, it is a primary mode of knowledge and a primary good. (1987, p. 582)

2   Louis Owens' *Dark River* and Stephen Graham Jones' *Ledfeather* are but two examples of reservation-set Native American novels that do not fall into the homing plot, while Sherman Alexie's *Indian Killer* is an example of a novel that resists easy categorization in terms of the plot and the protagonist's Indian identity.

3   *Reading Leslie Marmon Silko: Critical Perspectives through Gardens in the Dunes*, edited by Laura Coltelli, provides scholars and teachers with a range of interpretations of the novel as well as cultural and historical context.

References

Allen, C. (2012), *Trans-Indigenous: Methodologies for Global Native Literary Studies*. Minneapolis: University of Minnesota Press.

Bevis, W. (1987), "Native American Novels: Homing In," in B. Swann and A. Krupat (eds), *Recovering the Word: Essays on Native American Literature*. Berkeley: University of California Press, pp. 580–620.

Huang, H., Deloria P., Furlan, L., and Gamber, J. (2012), "Charting Transnational Native American Studies." *The Journal of Transnational American Studies*, 4:1, 1–15.

Huhndorf, S. M. (2009), *Mapping the Americas: The Transnational Politics of Contemporary Native Culture*. Ithaca, NY: Cornell University Press.

Ruoff, A. L. B. (2007), "Leslie Marmon Silko's *Gardens in the Dunes*: Contact Zones and Cross Currents," in L. Coltelli (ed.), *Reading Leslie Marmon Silko: Critical Perspectives through Gardens in the Dunes*. Pisa: Pisa University Press, pp. 7–20.

Silko, L. M. (1999), *Gardens in the Dunes*. New York: Simon and Schuster.

Sullivan, R. (1999), *Star Waka*. Auckland, New Zealand: Auckland University Press.

8

EuroAmerica, Europe, and the Indigenous: The Complex (and Complicating) Dialectics of Silko's Jamesian Turn

Lincoln Faller

A kind of dialectical relationship exists between the gardens in the dunes and the gardens at Oyster Bay and between Indigo and her older sister and the wealthy white women.

(SILKO, "AN APPRECIATION OF HENRY JAMES," 2012, p. 211)

Juxtaposition is much ... especially ... in foreign countries.

(HENRY JAMES, "ADINA" 1999, 1:916)

In a highly interesting development, two leading Native American novelists marked the turn of this century by sending Native characters across the Atlantic to extended stays in Europe. I speak of course of Leslie Marmon Silko's *Gardens in the Dunes* (1999) and James Welch's *Heartsong of Charging Elk* (2000), both extraordinary novels and both deserving more attention from readers and critics than they so far have achieved. Both novels, clearly, make claims for the capacity and scope of their authors, breaking out as they do from the usual boundaries of "native-themed" Native fiction, giving significant attention to non-Native characters and locating a significant part, if not most, of their action (Europe!) on quintessentially non-Native turf.

Of the two novels, however, *Gardens in the Dunes* may well seem, from any narrow view of the usual (if not mandated) business of Native American fiction, the more transgressive. Where Welch's novel focuses on a single Lakota protagonist and his struggle to survive in an environment even more alien to him than the United States—another Black Elk if you will, had Black Elk never managed to return from France—the stories of Silko's Sand Lizard sisters, Indigo and Salt, are only intermittently the main business of her novel. The novel's most developed character, in any usual sense of that term, is Hattie, a privileged daughter of the (white, to be sure!) upper classes who is faced by, must deal with, and eventually seeks to escape the frustrations, the oppressions, indeed the violence of, as Silko calls it, "puritanical patriarchy" by leaving her previous life behind (Silko, 2012, pp. 210, 211). Getting lesser attention, but still a good deal, is Hattie's plant-hunting, feckless, and ultimately doomed husband, Edward Palmer, whose trajectory, in contrast to hers, tends ever downward toward bankruptcy, disgrace, increasing self-deception, and death. Even Wylie, the white American manager of a massive irrigation project, and Big Candy, his indispensable African-American sidekick, are of considerable interest to the novel, especially the latter, as it unfolds, in a major subplot, the story of Indigo's sister Salt. And if this were not enough, where Welch would seem beholden to *Black Elk Speaks* (1932) to some extent for inspiration, Silko, by her own confession, was far more deeply indebted to a source of a very different kind.

"Without the stories and novels of Henry James," she declares in "an appreciation" of that writer, "I quite likely would not have written *Gardens in the Dunes.*" Silko is speaking here of the particular use she made of James in finding the "confidence" to imagine Hattie and Edward and their set, particularly in the episodes set in Oyster Bay. Not, however, "the least concerned about…writing about wealthy white Americans in Boston, London, or Rome," as per James, indeed she did not (Silko, 2012, pp. 206, 209). Her European travelers never encounter towns larger than Bristol or Genoa, focusing mostly on their experiences in and around Bath, Lucca, and rural Corsica, and even in these places they don't see much of European society or its usual cultural monuments. Silko's "Jamesian turn," then, for all the comparisons and contrasts it evokes in its juxtaposition of America and Europe, takes very much its own peculiar path.

In writing *Gardens in the Dunes*, Silko had in mind that some reviewers of her previous novel, *Almanac of the Dead*, faulted it for being "political" and "angry" (Silko, 2012, p. 207; Arnold, 2000, p. 163). Whatever one may think of the artistry or craft of that novel—it does have its faults—it certainly presents a scathing and, for most readers, a deeply discomfiting indictment of the rapacious brutality inflicted on Indigenous peoples in the Americas by the dominant, and dominating, culture—or, to pick no bones, white people. Apparently, wanting to strike a different note, and feeling that "gardens and flowers are happy peaceful subjects," Silko thought, "why not write a novel full of gardens with a myriad of flowers, even orchids, and blossoming shrubs and great trees?" (2012, p. 207). *Gardens in the Dunes* is not angry, but as she herself came to realize, gardens are indeed "political" (Arnold, 2000, p. 164). Commentators on the novel have certainly agreed. Its gardens, the characters who move through them, their relationship to those gardens as well as to each other have all provided a rich basis for exegeses on the novel's critique of colonialism, imperialism, patriarchal privilege and misogyny, capitalism, and the disregard for, indeed the devastation of, the natural world that all these entail. In these readings there is a tendency to see the novel's characters as agents or objects of these tendencies, as emblems, that is, despite Silko's effort to make them seem "more realistic" than the "extreme and emblematic" characters in *Almanac of the Dead*, who are not like "living people or characters" (Perkins, 1999, p. 113).

Henry James contended that before all else, novels are obliged to be "interesting" (1986, p. 170). But how "interesting" can a novel be if it is to be taken primarily as an expression of an ideological position however meritorious (and I myself do find it so), especially as its author has in so many interviews—and these are frequently cited in "political" readings of the novel—so clearly expressed her dim view of EuroWestern (can I even say?) "civilization"? I ask this question because I find the novel very interesting indeed, and in ways that far exceed its ideas or ideology. And this, too, I must add in all honesty, as the characters in and of themselves or in their interactions with each other do not seem to me quite as interesting as where they go and what they see there, or do not see, and where they finally end up. The novel's characters may be more than simply emblems but then, too, it seems not especially concerned with character or character development.

Indigo, to be sure, does get a great deal of attention and is arguably the center of the novel, though not quite the "central consciousness" so characteristic of Jamesean narrative. The novel in any case begins and ends with her happily ensconced in the gardens that give it its name. A prodigiously sensitive and autonomous child, she participates in a Ghost Dance and sees the Messiah, is carried off to a BIA boarding school, escapes, gets taken up by a rich and sophisticated white woman who clothes, educates, and considers adopting her, travels back and forth across the United States, crosses and recrosses the Atlantic, visits England, Italy, and France, returns to endure the poverty and degradation of an American Indian reservation, and then, together with her sister, comes home to those gardens once again without ever undergoing any radical challenges to or changes of heart, mind, or character. For all her new experiences, Indigo remains unfazed by what she's seen and learned of the white world, having (aside from her connection with Hattie) no attachment to or continuing interest in it. Her story, it's been suggested, is worth considering as a captivity narrative (Morisco, 2010, p. 141). If so, she returns as exalted and, too, as impervious from her experience of subjection to an alien culture as Mary Rowlandson does from hers. What might be called her "lack of character development" over the course of the novel represents and constitutes an unyielding resistance to the assimilation that the disciplines of schooling, the kindness of a sympathetic and well-placed white woman, even the luxury of fancy clothing (which she easily discards once back in Arizona) each in their different and various ways aims to effect.[1]

Hattie is more what one would expect of the central character in a novel interested in tracing the course of a character's trajectory over time. Her sense of self and her outlook on the world undergo radical change; indeed, beginning with the strange light she sees in Aunt Bronwyn's garden and culminating with her near encounter at the second Ghost Dance with the Messiah, she undergoes a conversion experience. Turning away from the Church toward a spirituality that (though it includes Jesus) is essentially pagan, she abandons what she had thought to be her life's defining work, the reincorporation of a feminist perspective into the foundational texts of Christianity, abandons, too, her disappointment of a husband and then, again, his corpse, becomes assertive enough for the first time in her life to strike back at male sexual violence by burning down half the town of Needles, and, leaving parents behind, departs the United States to live in Europe. Though she is certainly an attractive and sympathetic character, she is not possessed of anything like a nuanced and intricate psychology. Her timidity—which makes the sexual insults of Hyslop and Dr. Gates so powerfully traumatic—is conventionally female, as are her increasingly maternal feelings toward Indigo. But how to find a basis in her upbringing or education for her feminism and heretical tendencies, those elements that Silko says were inspired by the real-life Margaret Fuller? (Silko, 2012, p. 210; Arnold, 2000, p. 179). These seem simply givens, not outgrowths of experiences described or even adverted to by the text. How, for instance, has she developed into the person she is, given the very opposite tendencies of the mother and father who raised her? There is, as Deborah A. Miranda has shown, more to be understood about Edward's character along these lines than hers.[2]

What most impels the novel, it seems to me, is not an engagement with its characters, but something much more difficult to define. It puts into play a complex set of dialectics along a number of intersecting and multidimensional axes. These involve distinctions between men and women, male and female, of course. Thus, Hattie's scholarly career, her marriage, the brutal assault she endures, all speak to female oppression and patriarchal privilege, while gardening, in all its varieties, is almost exclusively female. More interesting, however, particularly given Silko's avowed debt to James, are the dialectics that emerge not just from setting (Euro) America and Europe in juxtaposition, as he so frequently does, but also the Indigenous to each and to both.[3] Nor is the Indigenous only American, for there are traces still of it in Europe, too. In their complication and lack, finally, of any ultimate resolution, these dialectics, I'll argue, ought to keep readers from coming to settled conclusions, which is all to the good. Novels that allow such conclusions tend to get displaced by them, reduced to a set of propositions.

James and Silko,
America and Europe

The most obvious Jamesean element in *Gardens in the Dunes* is its sending off three of its leading characters to confront, and be confronted by, what James in "The Siege of London" (1883) could call the "novelty" of "European civilisation" (1999, 2: 566). Among the particular works of his that Silko singles out in her "appreciation," there is that story and also "Adina" (1874), "The Last of the Valerii" (1874), "Madame de Mauves" (1874), *Daisy Miller* (1878), "The Pension Beaurepas" (1881), "The Lady Barbarina" (1884), *The Aspern Papers* (1888), and, indirectly, *The American* (1877) and *The Portrait of a Lady* (1881).[4] This can seem an odd and somewhat miscellaneous collection of pieces, omitting as it does so many of the major novels and including some relatively minor works, but a good number include gardens, and, Silko indicates, there was in that fact enough to interest her as she imagined the gardens that would feature in her novel.

In this congerie of narratives, however, it is also possible to see certain particular points of connection and influence, of relation and departure, of reversal and revision as Silko, playing off James, develops her own "international theme." There may be a personal element, too, in Silko's singling out some of these stories. As she mentions more than once in her "appreciation," she dislikes cowboys, and both Littlemore in "The Siege of London" and Longstraw in "Lady Barbarina" are singled out by her for being once such, before they went off to live in Europe (2012, pp. 206, 211, 212). "The Siege of London" would otherwise appear to have no bearing at all on *Gardens in the Dunes*, except, possibly, for its focus on an unconventional, somewhat scandalous upstart of a woman (it's not for nothing she's called Mrs. Headway) who manages, by sheer dint of effort and the careful study of manners originally quite alien to her, to break into and ultimately be celebrated by the social elite of a nation not her own. Need I add that she hails from New Mexico? Silko mentions "Lady Barbarina" primarily for its inclusion of another parvenu and interloper feted by London society, the egregious Longstraw. He, too, acquires a celebrity that more polished and presumably more socially acceptable Americans do not. Among his alluring qualities,

James indicates, is the "legend" that surrounds him: "a trapper, a miner, a pioneer," he "had been everything that one could be in the desperate parts of America." "He had shot bears in the Rockies and buffaloes on the plains; and it was even believed that he had brought down animals of a still more dangerous kind among the haunts of men" (1999, 2:789). Apparently the point here, as in "The Siege of London," is that the English prefer their Americans brash and somewhat wild, to conform, that is, to their notions of the type. And this, despite the best efforts of highly refined Americans such as Littlemore and Waterville in "The Siege of London" or Jackson Lemon in "Lady Barbarina" seem worthy of far greater acceptance and respect. For Silko, though, who quotes these details about Longstraw's past at greater length than I have, his "legend" is not just an opportunity to make a mildly ironic point at the expense of the English. As perhaps only a Native reader would be so quick to see so clearly, Longstreet is no mere joke. That last little detail about him in James's description "is a reference to the hunting and killing of Indians, which continued well into the twentieth century in the West" (Silko, 2012, p. 206). Silko turns James's point back toward America, where it reflects badly on EuroAmericans and their (for Indigenous people, certainly) disastrous history. Such redirection, such reflection are pervasive characteristics of the Jamesean turn she takes in *Gardens in the Dunes*.

Something of a comparable reversal or redirection of a Jamesean trope might be seen in the small carved stones excavated at Bath that become, for Hattie, powerfully influential talismans as, drifting increasingly further from the Church, she develops what might (though not entirely properly) be called a pagan spirituality. The light she sees in them anticipates the light she sees at the Ghost Dance, which turns out to be the light of the Messiah. In the power Hattie feels in her excavated objects, and in their effect on her, she travels a path not unlike that of the Count Valero in "The Last of the Valerii." But where the Count's growing inclination toward paganism, marked by his increasing enthrallment to the statue dug out of his garden, is (at least for the American narrator and his niece, the Count's wife) dangerous and threatening and must be stopped, Hattie's rejection of Christianity is liberating and positive. The buried classical sculpture excavated to such dismaying effect in "The Last of the Valerii" has its echoes, too, in the sculptures both excavated and left in the ground in Laura's garden in Lucca, where they, too, exercise a mysterious though beneficial power, and also, possibly, in the masses of sculpture carted away from Susan's once Italian garden in Oyster Bay. The latter, though, are just so much dead stone without any power at all, not even as aesthetic objects (as none of these other objects just simply is). In "The Last of the Valerii" and also in "Adina," where the excavated artifact is an exquisite Roman brooch, possibly once belonging to an emperor, artifacts erupting out of Europe's pre-Christian past produce trouble and need to be relegated back whence they came. In "The Last of the Valerii," the statue is reburied, and in "Adina," the brooch is thrown into the Tiber. In both cases, the disturbance these artifacts produce is felt most keenly by Americans, the narrator and his niece in the former, Sam Scrope in the latter, and in both cases it is these Americans who are responsible for the relegation. Americans, too, have their preconceptions about Europe and how Europeans should be, and, for reasons possibly worth speculating on, apparently they want nothing "pagan" to intrude on these. Consider, for instance, how much Longmore in "Madame de Mauves" disdains the Count for his "pagan" qualities while valuing his American wife, and presumably himself, as "Christian" (1999, 1: 853). All these stories were written while there were still ongoing "Indian wars." Is it somehow important to them that Europe not be "pagan" because Americans—very much inclined to value the "superior" culture of the lands from which they'd come—had been so long engaged with obliterating or, at the very least, suppressing and Christianizing, all that was "pagan" (which is to say Native or Indigenous) in their own, new country?

Americans in Europe is James's great theme, his effort to clarify "whatever an American is," to quote Aunt Bronwyn in conversation with Hattie and Indigo (p. 244). He works at this theme by juxtaposing American sensibilities, manners, and habits of thought to those of Europeans. As many critics have observed, James's Europe does not suit Americans, and so it seems especially from the works that Silko mentions. This is not just true of characters wholly untouched by Europe and somewhat of an embarrassment to those of their countrymen who encounter them there, like the Ruck family in "The Pension Beaurepas," for whom Europe is just one big shopping trip far from the source of their soon-to-be-lost wealth, or Tom Tristram in *The American*, whose long sojourn in Paris has been something of a bore and left him a bore. Christopher

Newman's infatuation with Claire de Cintre in that novel comes a cropper and ends disastrously for her because he has no idea of the impression he is making on her or her family, whose outlook on the world is so different from his. None of James's Americans in Europe fares so badly, of course, as Daisy Miller, who dies there. Others are merely stunted or weak in a variety of ways, imaginatively, morally, or emotionally, even at their most sympathetic deracinated and lost, emotionally undeveloped, weak at seizing the day. The worst are Gilbert Osmond and Madame Merle in *The Portrait of a Lady*, the most Europeanized Americans in the novel and the most corrupt. And though, in the same novel, Ralph Touchett is quite sympathetic and indeed the real love of Isabel Archer's life, and she his, semi-invalid that he is, he is too diffident and ineffectual for their relationship to develop as it might have.

Perhaps the most pathetic character in the works Silko cites is Aurora Church in "The Pension Beaurepas." Brought to Europe as a child and raised there in a series of temporary lodgings, she dreams of going back to the United States, but, as both she and the narrator of the story know, she occupies a "false position." "I want to be an American girl, and I am not," she says before disappearing with her perfectly awful mother (1999, 2: 436). Then there is Winterbourne in *Daisy Miller*, who "felt he had lived in Geneva so long that he had lost a good deal…had become dishabituated to the American tone" and "lost his instinct" for reading American character (1999, 2: 246–247). Though he feels attracted to the delightful but doomed Daisy, he is kept at a disapproving and ineffectual distance by his debilitating inhibition and a taint of Swiss prudery. As the narrator of *The Aspern Papers* observes, Americans living in Europe are "liable to take up" "strange ways" and lose "in their long exile all national quality" (1999, 3: 256, 228). Where James apparently thought this a regrettable tendency, Silko, judging from her sympathetic presentation of Aunt Bronwyn and her final disposition of Hattie, clearly does not.

If there is thesis and antithesis in the dialectics of James's juxtaposition of Americans to Europe, there is generally no viable synthesis. If Europeanized Americans such as Gilbert Osmond and Madame Merle seem to represent such a synthesis, it is not something readers ought to value or appreciate. "One may be very American and yet arrange it with one's conscience to live in Europe," claims Madame de Mauves who'd utterly misjudged the Frenchman she married, but, hardly engaging with him or the France around her, she actually lives in "a little country of my own" (1999, 1: 848). At the bleakest, thesis and antithesis cancel each other out. Asked if she's an American, Miss Tita tells the narrator of *The Aspern Papers*, "we used to be ... we are nothing" (1999, 3: 239). Americans who choose Europe over their home country—or have it chosen for them—do not fare well in James's fiction. However enriching (or not) their experience of Europe might have been, return to America is essential to "what one might call the Jamesian myth of America as place of return and redemption" (Oltean, 2010, p. 46). But not so with Silko's *Gardens in the Dunes*. Indigo, to be sure, is restored to her status quo ante, with the addition of a monkey, a parrot, and a collection of new seeds that provide her, most notably, with a crop of edible gladiolas. But never having taken up "strange ways" and never at risk of losing her particular "national quality," she is in no need of redemption. Edward, who in his own way also remains essentially untouched by his experience in Europe, comes home in disgrace and, looking now to cash in on meteorites instead of botanicals, craters. How interesting, then—and how unlike James's disposition of Isabel Archer—is the conclusion Silko appends to her own "portrait of a lady," along with how she gets to it. Isabel Archer is not improved but diminished by Europe, and her choosing to stay there in an oppressive marriage is quite regrettable and, at best, morally and emotionally ambiguous. But Hattie's turning away from America—where, though she nearly gets to see the Messiah, she is also raped, beaten, and left for dead—to live in Europe marks a liberation and redemption, an opening not a closing down of self. In her aunt's gardens and in her projected visit to the professora's gardens in Italy, she will not only find refuge from the unhappiness she's experienced in her home country but also experience an unprecedented felicity. As a positive example of a Europeanized American, Hattie may seem that thing that Jamesean juxtaposition could never reach, a viable synthesis of the American and European, the result of a fully worked out dialectic. Actually though, and fortunately for its "interestingness," nothing is quite so neatly cut and dried in *Gardens in the Dunes*.

Where the relatively simple dualism of James's juxtaposition of Europe and America allows author and readers to see their ways to conclusions—characters and our interest in them over the course of his narratives move in one direction or the other, to a resolution of

sorts—nothing so clearly occurs to give overall shape or closure to
Gardens in the Dunes.[5] For one thing, there is so much more to it
than just the stories of Indigo, Hattie, and Edward—thus the Ghost
Dance episodes and the whole story of the Colorado River project,
which includes the story of Sister Salt and concludes (!) with the
chaos of the Mexican dog show, Delena's theft of the money Wylie
and Candy have hidden away, Candy's near fatal pursuit of Delena
into the desert, her escape, and his unwittingly setting off to Mexico
with a cargo of the rifles she's bought with the stolen money. More
important to the rich and ultimately somewhat baffling complexity
of Silko's novel, to repeat a previous point, is that its dialectics set
not just EuroAmerica and Europe in juxtaposition, but also Native
America. This juxtapositioning is done not so much in the Jamesean
way, via the consideration of characters and their fates, as through
the consideration of gardens and gardening, horticulture, as so
many critics have pointed out, standing as a metonym for culture.
The old gardens in the dunes (Native American) are positioned
against the EuroWestern, the latter including the EuroAmerican (the
Oyster Bay gardens of Susan James) and the European (the gardens
of Aunt Bronwyn and the professora), which themselves differ
significantly from each other, which means the Native American
stands, dialectically, in a somewhat different relation to each.

Instead of just the one dyad so central to Native American fiction,
the Native versus the EuroWestern, here the EuroWestern is broken
into two parts. There are thus four dialectics, the Native American
versus the EuroWestern, plus three others: Native American versus
EuroAmerican, EuroAmerican versus European, and Native
American versus European. And this is to speak only at the largest,
most general level, for there are different and contrasting tendencies
to be detected within these large categories, for instance, between the
dunes gardens and the gardens on the reservation at Parker, between
Susan James's examples of conspicuous consumption at Oyster Bay
and the gardens of Hattie's father, which aim (however inanely) to
improve the living conditions of the urban poor, and even between
Edward's father's citrus groves and his mother's greenhouse. As it is,
the European is represented by the two rather different gardens of
Aunt Bronwyn and the professora. The prospect of tracing out the
vectors and valences of comparisons and contrasts in and among all
these juxtapositions, along all their intersecting axes, thinking them
through and drawing out their implications, trying to fit them into

some overall, global pattern, is mind boggling. What we have here is "a sphere of intersecting polarities, each a dialectic interacting dialogically with all the others." It is a situation, certainly, that prevents investment in any of the simple dualisms that inhabit and inhibit, as David Moore argues, the ways we read and respond to Native American literature (Moore, 1994, p. 19 et passim). Here, given limitations of space, we'll limit ourselves to the rich and intriguing implications of just two of the most prominent of these dialectics: that between the EuroAmerican and the European, and that between the Native American and the EuroWestern.

The EuroAmerican versus the European

The dialectic between Susan James's gardens at Oyster Bay and the gardens in Europe, where Hattie finds refuge and, presumably, some degree of happiness, is a lot easier to sort out and understand than the dialectic between either (or both together) and the gardens in the dunes. The Oyster Bay gardens are an alien, inauthentic, arrogant, and egocentric imposition of dubious taste and no practical good on land taken from Native people who, though still present (the Matinecocks) are forgotten and displaced to the very edge of the sea. As such, those gardens can stand for all that is and has been wrong with settler colonialism. Though on a much smaller scale and despite all their aesthetic pretensions, they are not at all different in impulse and effect from the Colorado River project, being just as disruptive and disregardful of the natural world and the Indigenous peoples who gain their sustenance from it (thus the Matinecocks of Long Island as well as the Chemehuevi at Parker), with this one difference: the diversion of the river will have some utility for some people, at least; it is not just an example of conspicuous consumption. Susan James wrecks her "Italian" gardens and replaces them with "English" gardens because she wants something more "natural," but her project represents the height of artifice and so, by definition, cannot be what she wants it to be. Indeed, when she wants to get "natural" (shall we say) with her gardener and lover, they do it not in her newly "natural" gardens but retreat to the forest beyond them. It is only there that they can shed, along with their clothing, the social and cultural conventions that inhibit what Indigo certainly sees, observing them, as natural and wholly normal impulses

The gardens in Europe—really English and really Italian—admit their artificiality. They are manifestly created by human hands over a very long period of time, developed out of the interactions of diverse peoples and their cultures with each other and the land over millennia, carrying in them the strata and overlays of invasion and conquest, of accommodation and assimilation, of persistence and resistance. Bath and Aunt Bronwyn's gardens there retain traces of Celtic Indigeneity, Roman invasion and settlement, the Saxon era, and the Norman conquest, along with the arrival of Christianity, which does not entirely suppress and displace the old paganisms, and, with the ruins of the old cloister, the displacement of one form of Christianity by another. The professora's gardens in Lucca hark back to an even older Europe, to a time of goddesses and gynocentrism that precedes the classical antiquity of Rome and Greece, a time before the institution of patriarchy and where, as the sculptural remains in her gardens indicate, the human and animal were not seen as separate and disjunctive categories, their forms combinable into objects of worship and awe.

Both gardens are situated in lands that, occupied and settled by foreign powers, have experienced immense cultural change. The Romans came to Lucca as well as to England but—as the joint shrine to Sulis and Minerva uncovered in the diggings at Bath and the persistence of still more ancient artifacts and traditions in England and Italy indicate (note the professora's story of the snake that so interests Indigo, probably pre-Roman in its origins)—they were far more accommodating and respectful of the Indigenous, or at the least far less interested in extirpating it, than anything in the American experience. And nothing that followed—not even Christianity—could suppress the ancient spiritualities that inhered with the people and the land, as Hattie discovers when she awakes on the stone in her aunt's garden and sees that mysterious, life-transforming light. It is difficult to imagine anything like these gardens being possible in EuroAmerica. That would have required the invaders not only to have taken cognizance of the histories and cultures of the peoples who preceded them, but also to respect them and to have assimilated to some extent to their values and views of the world and the place of humans in it. Silko speaks of the "dialectic" relationship between the pueblo peoples and the Europeans who colonized their lands, but, to be sure, the dialectic was felt more on one side than on the other (2012, p. 208). Perhaps the novel is so sympathetic to Mormons—certainly a curious fact—because their beliefs do attribute a long history of relationship between the Indigenous peoples of America, the Messiah, and those who came to settle it from across the sea. To Mormons, the "new" world is a very old world indeed.[6]

In any case, taken as tropes not just for national histories but also for ways of being in and relating to the world, the gardens in England and Italy that come to mean so much to Hattie stand in sharp and astounding contrast to the pseudo-Italian and pseudo-English gardens in Oyster Bay. Those gardens—with their erasure of the past, their suppression of the Indigenous, their adoption of adventitious modes utterly alien to the place they occupy, their wish to remake the world into products of their own limited imaginings, their lack of respect for all else around them—represent not just the brief and perverse nature of EuroAmerican landscaping but also of EuroAmerican history and experience at large. Hattie flees from that experience, understandably enough. But what should we make of that flight, of the seeming resolution of this particular dialectic between the EuroAmerican and the European? For some readers, this may seem a "happy" ending (thus Magoulick, 2007, p. 26; Van Dyke, 2007, p. 182). It surprises me, however, that none of the critics I've read on the novel express any disappointment that Hattie buries her manuscript, opting out of any struggle against the oppressive forces that in one way or another would diminish and degrade her and other women. What are these writers, so many of whom are women who clearly value the speaking of truth to power, but creators and publishers of manuscripts, like Silko herself? Not every budding feminist can be another Margaret Fuller, and it would be quite unfair to compare Hattie to Delena, a fierce and uncompromising revolutionary intent on upending the social and political order that oppresses not just her but also her whole community. But how "happy" can it seem that Hattie, going off to Europe, will not even *cultiver son propre jardin* but live in gardens not her own? Nor are these gardens entirely the refuge she might want. Though Silko herself has said that the European gardens "represent a kind of synthesis in which the pagan earth goddesses are imaginable again," that "kind of" seems to me tellingly ambivalent

(2012, p. 211). There are large earthmoving projects in the hills above Bath, reminiscent of the Colorado River project and all it signifies, ancient elements of the landscape are perpetually under threat of erasure or destruction, and a great war is impending in the not so distant future. For James, it would seem that America is the only right place for Americans. For Silko, "American" is a much more complicated category, including Indigenous peoples as well as those who have displaced and subjugated them; still, she is not necessarily suggesting that EuroAmericans ought best go back to Europe.[7]

The Native American versus the EuroWestern

At a low point in her life, Edward dead and swindled out of her fortune, the Church seeming "remote and strange" to her and "human life...woefully short," Hattie as is her wont unpacks and arranges the carved gemstones excavated at Bath that have become her talismans. "How she envied," we read, "the timeless space they occupied while mortals stumbled along in disgrace" (pp. 427, 439, 453). The transcendence Hattie yearns for here is not likely to be found on her return to Europe any more than in America. It is in America, though, that she gets closest to it, waking on the morning of the third day of the Ghost Dance to "the lemon yellow light" of dawn. This light has "the same color" as one of her now lost talismans and, as that light becomes "brighter and more luminous," she recognizes it as "the same light" she so momentously saw in her aunt's garden in England, that she dreamed of aboard ship coming back across the ocean, and presumably, though it's not specifically mentioned, that she saw on that miraculous wall in Corsica. Hattie feels "a thrill sweep over her" and, momentarily achieving the transcendence she had enviously attributed to her talismans, loses "all sense of time" (pp. 470–471). This light, she is told by Sister Salt, has been sent to comfort her and is a harbinger of the Messiah and his family, who will appear the next day. But on that morning, soldiers and Indian police break up the ceremony and the Messiah never appears. The reason the ceremony is disrupted, it turns out, is that she is there, and, from the point of view of her parents and other whites, needing to be rescued. Hattie's very presence at the Ghost Dance makes it and what she so yearns for—and what its Native participants so desperately need—impossible.

The beginning of the novel is structured in a way that allows readers to see and fully appreciate the desperation and despair that the Ghost Dance seeks to overcome and replace. We see Indigo and Salt awaiting the return of their grandmother in the "old gardens," where they've fled after the breakup of the first Ghost Dance when the Messiah did appear. Then the narrative moves back in time to tell how they, along with their grandmother and mother, wound up in Needles and to describe the misery and degradation of their lives there. Anger at all that "had been done to the Earth and all the animals and people" prompts the pan-Indian phenomenon of the Ghost Dance, the aim of which is to make "the Earth reborn" and "whole again" (pp. 25, 26). The dance itself is then described, and its disruption by the authorities. Because we encounter all this after our introduction to the old gardens, we feel even more than we otherwise might the crisis Needles represents not just for the Sand Lizard family but all Native people similarly situated, and their need, through this new ceremony, to transcend that situation. The Ghost Dance is a product of and a response to the misery, the alienation, the subjugation, and the hopelessness that Native people feel under the settler-colonial regime. Their wish for transcendence comes from despair at not being able to be in the world as one would want to be. They dance so as not, for that moment at least, to "stumble along in disgrace."

Compared to Needles or, indeed, any other locale in the novel including the gardens in Europe, the old gardens can seem Edenic or even, given the first adjective to appear in the novel, describing the smell of falling rain, "heavenly." But on reflection, neither term really fits. The sisters cavort naked in the rain, to be sure, without any self-consciousness or inhibition, as if they lived in a prelapsarian world. But there is here no presiding creator God the Father (the gardens were planted by Sand Lizard, whose nephew Grandfather Snake invited her people there), no Adam, that embodiment of masculine primariness and primacy (indeed no masculine presence at all except for Grandfather Snake), no human dominion over flora and fauna (which is to say no privileging division, as in Eden, between the human and the natural), no Satan (Grandfather Snake is a benign and helpful presence), and no original sin to taint and be passed on generation to generation (despite the free sexuality of Sand Lizard women). As for heavenliness, the concept hardly if at all applies. There is no need to conceive of a better world after or beyond this one because, in a very important sense, there is no death here, either. "Don't worry," says Grandma Fleet to Indigo, when the body dies "some hungry animal will eat what's left of you and off you'll go again, alive as ever, now part of the creature who ate you" (p. 53). Life continues in one form or another. Departed spirits persist too, those of the "beloved ancestors" returning as rain to nourish the earth (p. 17).

Human beings are just one of the many kinds of beings that inhabit the old gardens, all of whom stand symbiotically in mutual relationship, none superior in status to the others. The coyote, the eagle, and even the pack rat help humans in one way or another find sustenance, but humans must consider their needs as well, leaving them enough to survive, too, or else they won't be willing or able to cooperate. Even before we readers are instructed in these particular matters, we come—only a few hundred words into the novel—to a far more surprising claim. Plants, too, are sentient beings, requiring to be cared for "as if [they] were babies," to be greeted "respectfully" with concern for their "feelings." They become the particular responsibility of their human caregivers, who endow them with "pet names" like "Bushy, Fatty, Skinny, Shorty, Mother, and Baby" (pp. 16, 18). All this is very far from EuroWestern epistemologies or ethics (though the animism of Aunt Bronwyn and her guru, Gustav Flechner, come close), but beautifully so. The world of the gardens is a world where humans—how can we even say it?—take part and share in the being of all the world. "Don't be greedy," Grandma Fleet tells her granddaughters repeating what Sand Lizard herself told the people who settled in her gardens:

> The first ripe fruit of each harvest belongs to the spirits of our beloved ancestors, who come to us as rain; the second ripe fruit should go to the birds and wild animals, in gratitude for their restraint in sparing the seeds and sprouts earlier in the season. Give the third ripe fruit to the bees, ants, mantises, and others who cared for the plants. (p. 17)

Because, beyond these gestures of respect and gratitude, the Sand Lizard people also leave some of the harvest "to shrivel dry and return to the earth," "next season, after the arrival of the rain," even without any effort on their part to reseed, "beans, squash, and pumpkins [sprout] up between the dry stalks and leaves of the previous year" (p. 17).

According to Grandma Fleet, the old gardens were found "already growing" by "the old-time people"; they "had always been there" and will always continue to be, even—and this marks a great difference from the EuroWestern gardens in Oyster Bay and Europe—without the agency of humans (p. 16). The gardens keep recurring, as do the forms of being that live within them. Even vandals can't destroy them, as we discover when, at the end of the novel, a new snake at the spring replaces the old one that was killed, the chopped down apricot trees send up new shoots through the sand, and the Sand Lizard sisters and their Chemehuevi friends feast on gladiolas. Grandma Fleet, dead and buried at the base of those apricot trees, becomes them; those continuing to live in the gardens will eat their fruit and then themselves be consumed by something animal or vegetative. Her body dissolved, her spirit joins those others long dead in the form of lifegiving rain. The dead are always present by other means, and not just as fruit or rain; thus the "little grandfather" who reappears as Sister Salt's child. The old gardens are not "timeless" in any usual sense, not a place of transcendence, but a place of being-in-the-world that is hard to define in EuroWestern terms. What is the opposite of transcendence? What is the opposite of the dejection or abjection that makes us seek transcendence? Hattie seeks "timelessness" as an escape from her burdensome awareness of "mortality," and the people ghost dancing at Needles do so because they feel a still greater burden; the world they've known and cherished is dead or dying. But for the Sand Lizard people, as Grandma Fleet explains, there is no such burden. Death is just another way of continuing to live in other forms. In their old gardens, the Sand Lizard people live deep in the fullness of the moment in a stream of recurring moments, being in the world as all things around them are in it, as much themselves products of the earth and a part of nature as animals and plants. The old gardens are hardly gardens at all in the EuroWestern sense, not "a place where Nature is subdued, ordered, selected and enclosed" (Cirlot, 1971, p. 115), but something that challenges EuroWestern comprehension. Reading the novel's deeply engaging description of them, in English and so necessarily from a

EuroWestern perspective, we may think differently. But the gardens so described are like Indigo's name. As we eventually realize more than one hundred pages into the text, her name is not Indigo but something English speakers cannot pronounce (p. 113). Indigo is the name that English gives to the plant for which she is named; it is as close as English can get to what her name really is.[8]

If the old gardens are in any sense Edenic, it is because they represent a paradise lost—lost not just to Natives in America but to the invaders as well. They are a last, small remnant of the land that impressed the first arriving Europeans as "so delightful, and desirable; so pleasant and plentiful," as Robert Beverley wrote in 1705, "that Paradice it self seem'd to be there, in its first Native Lustre" (Beverley, 2013, p. 13). But, as readers can't help knowing, those gardens and what they represent are doomed soon to be lost, "wiped out and gone forever…completely obliterated," with all the little that remains of the Sand Lizard people and their culture (Arnold, 2000, p. 172). For just these reasons—their powerful attractiveness, the loss of all they represent across the whole vast continent, and then their own impending and inevitable disappearance—the old gardens in the dunes preside powerfully over all that follows in the novel they inaugurate. All gardens in this novel, as gardens typically do, represent something of a refuge from the larger world. Aunt Bronwyn's garden is a retreat not just from the hustle bustle of Bath but also from the spiritual emptiness of modern rationality, while the professora's garden connects her with a realm far removed from her errant, imperialist (and a failed one at that), unfaithful and deeply disappointing husband. Whatever else we may think of them, Susan James's gardens are also an effort to enclose herself in a space where she can have pleasures and a power otherwise denied late nineteenth-century women; there, defying sexual convention, she presides over her male gardener. Like the old gardens in the dunes, these EuroWestern gardens are, too, places of female freedom from "puritanical patriarchy"; they are spaces in which and over which women have authority, apart from a larger world where they do not. But there is, more importantly, a significant and powerful difference between these gardens and the old gardens in the dunes. They, like the Ghost Dance, are efforts to escape from what the world has become—a world fallen from what Christians might call a state of grace though not, certainly, through any female agency. Here the original sin, or at least its equivalent, is imperialism both narrowly and broadly defined, that is, as the subjugation of any one category of people by another, of the earth and its creatures by human beings. This is a sin, by the way, that taints even the quite lovely gardens of Aunt Bronwyn and the professora, with their collections of plants gathered by colonizing forces from all around the globe.[9] These gardens may represent the best that EuroWestern civilization, operating on its own ground, can do to produce an appropriate and sustaining environment for humans otherwise at odds with their world, but they simply do not measure up to the old gardens in the dunes.

Unlike readers of the novel, Hattie never sees those gardens, nor indeed does she even know they, or the kind of being in the world they sustain, exist. But that may well be in some ways a happy ignorance. The old gardens could never be a place for her; the mere fact of her being in them, like her presence at the Ghost Dance, would hasten their destruction. (And could she, in any case, *be* in them, given the sexual freedom of Sand Lizard females and, since she seems never to come to terms with her own sexuality, the limitations of her escape from "puritanical patriarchy"?) Whatever readers may imagine of the freedom, the enhancement of being, that Hattie may experience at the end of the novel, surrounded by the gardens of her aunt and the professora, it will not measure up to the standard established at the beginning of the novel by their encounter with the Sand Lizard girls in the gardens in the dunes. Here, too, the dialectic remains unresolved, though to a far greater degree than that between the EuroAmerican and the European. As so many commentators on the novel have shown, the gardens in Oyster Bay and in England and Italy are (as per Lévi-Strauss) "things to think with." Those in Oyster Bay get us to thinking about what is odd and lacking for all its dynamism, or just simply catastrophically wrong, in the ordering energies and aspirations of EuroAmerican culture—and this especially insofar as EuroAmerican culture differs not only from the Indigeneity it seeks to displace, supplant, and erase (and which, very importantly, is not at all patriarchal or puritan but gynocentric and freely sexual), but also from what is culturally (and certainly horticulturally) possible in its place of origins across the sea. Still, those European gardens are nowhere near so attractive as the gardens in the dunes, nor at all so challenging to our minds and imaginations. We have been in gardens like those in Europe and Oyster Bay, or, if not, at least can readily imagine having been so. We can register and parse their qualities, and, having done so, handle them as symbols or metaphors. But how to "think with" the old gardens in the dunes, standing as they do so far beyond not only EuroWestern experience and epistemology but also, in all their difference from Eden and all the other paradisical gardens of EuroWestern imaginings, beyond EuroWestern mythology and iconography, too? How to engage, to say nothing of attempting to resolve, a dialectic where one of the terms is—to EuroWestern readers, at least—if not unknowable, so strange and alien to apprehension that it is at best only barely imaginable?

Writing primarily for an American audience and typically publishing his work first in middle-brow magazines, James addressed readers who for the most part would never have the means to visit Europe, and certainly not in the ways his characters do. For all the cultural superiority of Europe, they could take comfort in thinking, America was *the* place for (white, to be sure) Americans. (Of course this is not what James himself thought, at least with respect to himself.) Silko's readers are allowed no such comfort in this novel or her others. Both *Ceremony* and *Almanac of the Dead* offer vehement indictments of the violence and greed, the cruel indifference of EuroAmericans in dealing with Native peoples. Although *Ceremony* offers white readers an out, ultimately making the problems of Natives native-engendered—"we invented white people," Betonie says, "it was Indian witchery" (p. 122)—*Almanac of the Dead* does no such thing. There is not a single sympathetic or redeemable white character in that novel (with the possible exception of the pathetic and clueless Seese), and, as the fate of Bartolomeo, the "European" Cuban "outsider" and the only white would-be revolutionary to figure in the novel suggests (he is hanged at the instigation of Angelita) that there is little or no conceivable role for whites to play in the coming revolution (pp. 315, 292). Both *Ceremony* and *Almanac of the Dead* are each in its own way so indigenocentric as to exclude EuroAmericans from any significant role in reimagining the world as a better place. In its critique of EuroAmerican culture, *Gardens in the Dunes* is far more accommodating, far more concerned with the problems non-Natives face in the America EuroAmericans have made, and far more sympathetic. Consider, for instance, how much more greatly Hattie and Edward suffer over the course of the novel than either of the Sand Lizard sisters. Indigo, as already noted, returns home unfazed and undamaged, and Salt, even more amazingly, is not at all degraded by her life as a teenage prostitute in a roustabout construction camp.[10] Edward may be a bad example, but he is no villain, rather the victim of villains who, except for Dr. Gates, remain faceless.[11] Learning of his death, Indigo thinks "he wasn't a bad man" (p. 441).

It is easy enough to decry imperialism and all its subcategories, colonialism, racism, sexism, the ruthless exploitation of the earth and its creatures. *Gardens in the Dunes* is as much against these evils as Silko's other two novels. But more than her other novels, it seems to me, it invites readers, especially its EuroAmerican readers, to take up the challenge of thinking how things might be different. If the vast preponderance of EuroAmericans are not to return to Europe or otherwise disappear—one of the great animating hopes and fantasies of the Ghost Dance—but remain on this continent, as of course they will, how shall they do so, in what relation to the land and all those (not just human beings) who occupied it before them, and all those who still do? The gardens in the dunes no longer exist but the way of living they represent was never available to any but their original, Indigenous inhabitants. We—and for me and most of the readers of the novel that is a more honest pronoun when speaking of EuroAmericans—cannot take those gardens as a model for our aspirations. Nor can we Ghost Dance with Native people—though, at least in Silko's novel, some of us once could—in order to remake and restore the earth; that moment is past. What, then, to do?[12]

The novel provides us with no program, nor need it. The question is far more engaging and interesting in its openness, and far more challenging, too, than even the most carefully and persuasively argued treatise or policy paper could be, because it throws us back on our own resources. Thinking about it, possibly in some desperation, we might come up with new and surprising ideas not just about the novel but, potentially, also about our possible future on this continent. For instance, I spoke earlier of the ordering energies and aspirations of EuroAmerican culture. In a strange way the most attractive of those energies—if not necessarily the aspirations—are to be found in the construction camp on the Colorado River. It is a disorderly and licentious place, certainly to be seen as such from the viewpoint of Oyster Bay—still another dialectic!—but of course it would have to be in order to bring together so diverse a body of Americans at the time the novel occurs. Whites, Natives, Latinos, and at least one African American intermix without much apparent regard to racial division, applying their combined energies to a great project. The project itself may be lamentable, but there is something to be said for its greatness and energy as well as its counter-historical hopefulness. (Hopefulness because the lack of racial antagonism in the construction camp seems a wish-fulfilling fantasy, given the era; nor do the workers, including sex workers like Salt, seem particularly exploited.) For all that the Colorado River project may seem the Oyster Bay gardens writ large, there is something profoundly different here. Could those energies, so inclusive of so many peoples and cultures and histories, so free from the stultifying dominion over American life of Oyster Bay and its ilk (remember, Theodore Roosevelt lives there), be directed to more positive ends? The novel itself makes no suggestion along these lines, but don't you find it interesting?

Notes

1   [Ed.: Note in this book, Becca Gercken's parallel but distinct reading of Indigo as Silko's "strongest" character in terms of cultural identity.]

2   Curiously, for a text so centrally focused on the experience of women, the most psychologically developed characters in it are men, Edward and Big Candy. Miranda (2007, pp. 136–140) traces in some detail the particular shape of Edward's character—his lack of warmth, his concern with money, his love of orchids and his wish to revive the Riverside citrus groves—back to his difficult and damaging relationships with his father and mother. This makes him a good deal more interesting than he would be considered only as an embodiment of the capitalist and imperialist urge to exploit whatever in the natural and the Indigenous might be commodified and turned to cash. Big Candy may not be quite as complicated as Edward (nor so important as a bad example), but his particular pursuit of money is clearly grounded in his entirely understandable wish to be an independent and self-defining black man in a racist society. "A man could do nothing for himself without money," thinks Candy when he is robbed, "here a man, white or colored, was nothing without money" (p. 389). And when having already lost Salt

and his son he loses his money, too, and then in pursuit of it nearly his life, we learn more of how he's been shaped by his upbringing and ancestry; he finds the strength to survive and carry on in his Afro-Indian heritage.

3   If I didn't feel bound to honor Silko's use of the term "dialectics," I might better have used "dialogics" (see Moore, 1994, who posits a crucial difference between the two terms). I should specify, in any case, that "dialectics" in my usage does not necessarily, and certainly in this case doesn't, lead to some ultimate, concluding synthesis; dialectics can remain dynamic and open, and, in the case of *Garden in the Dunes*, the most important of them certainly do.

4   Silko doesn't mention *Portrait of a Lady* directly in her "appreciation," but does cite Donatella Izzo's *Portraying the Lady: Technologies of Gender in the Short Stories of Henry James* (2001, Lincoln: U of Nebraska Press). *The American* seems particularly to fit her reference to the "good many wealthy American men" that James sends to Europe, "where their money was preyed upon" (Silko, 2012, p. 212). James apparently thought too little of "Adina" and "The Last of the Valerii" to include them in the New York edition of his works.

5   James's dualism is "relatively simple" only in comparison to Silko. When it comes to Americans he is certainly not simplistic in seeing how they differ according to gender, sophistication, wealth, or geographical origin. It matters to him whether Americans are male or female, cultured or vulgar, wealthy or not, Easterners or Westerners. But, it hardly needs saying, American Indians have no real place in his imagination. If anything, their absence is marked by the one ominous and few joking references to them that Silko locates in her "appreciation" (2012, p. 206).

6   It should be noted, however, that the novel's depiction of Mormons participating in the Ghost Dance has no historical basis. It was the opinion of many whites in 1890 that the Mormons were somehow, subversively, behind the sweep of the dance across the West. Though, given their theology, Mormons were interested in what the phenomenon might mean, they played no part in it; see Smoak.

7   Here I take issue with Deborah A. Miranda and Annette Van Dyke, who see nothing problematic in Hattie's self-exile, and also with James Barilla, who makes Hattie's return to Europe rather problematic indeed for what has to be the largest group of Silko's readers. For Van Dyke, Hattie is "a spiritual model" for "EuroAmerican readers," her story "a journey to claim an identity and a home" (2007, p. 177). In showing her development and incorporation of "a white, European indigeneity," according to

Miranda, Silko is "showing European-Americans a possible place and belief system available to them" (p. 143). Barilla is less encouraging: "those who are outside their proper territory" cannot "become native to new places," so "the appropriate place" for EuroAmericans in "Silko's vision" is "the originary homeland of Europe." If EuroAmericans want to feel better about themselves and their place in the world, they "can assuage their feelings of anomie with a return to their European homeland" (pp. 171–172). This does not square with Silko's own expressed views on what happens to "the strangers who come to this continent": "The longer they live here, the more they are being changed"; the Americas are "all inclusive": "You come here, you'll never be the same again. You'll be taken in and churned around, and what comes out is American," even if originally "European … or … Chinese … It's changed by being on this very soil, on this continent" (Arnold, 2000, pp. 180, 187). More in keeping with Silko, David Moore suggests that by offering "white audiences … a spiritual past in pre-Christian Europe," *Gardens in the Dunes* somehow indicates for them "a future in America," though he says no more than that (2007, p. 96). What if any future can or should there be for EuroAmericans wanting to stay in America, decently and honorably, shouldering not shirking (as I'm afraid Hattie does) their social, political, and ecological responsibilities?

8 When it comes to deeply Indigenous matters, Silko says, "even the terminology in English, the way of talking about it, is a secondhand kind of thing" (Arnold, 2000, p. 178).

9 The EuroWestern gardens, as Silko points out, are a "way of looking at colonialism, because everywhere the colonials went, the plants came back from there." Readers' feelings about them can vary widely along the range indicated by Hattie, Indigo, and Edward, but "if the reader's completely put off and hates [them], that's fine, because you could" (Arnold, 2000, p. 181).

10 Says Joy Porter, "the idea of a happy Sand Lizard prostitute is, of course, possible, but it does fly in the face of much scholarship devoted to unseating historical myths that stretch back to Columbus" (p. 65). What Silko is doing here, and how she gets away with it, is worth thinking about. It's not just that Salt, a teenage prostitute and bootlegger, comes uncomfortably close to the worst stereotypes of Native women, but that Indigo, a child, is the novel's chief provider of an Indigenous perspective on EuroAmerican and European culture and so in effect its chief exemplar of Native culture. This can evoke another stereotype very much to the disadvantage of colonized peoples, but somehow it doesn't, any more than Salt's way of getting a living outside the old gardens does. [Ed.:

In this regard, note Moore's introductory discussion of Indigenous respect for children as a context for reading Indigo's textual role.]

11   Speaking of Edward's vulnerability, Silko points out that she "purposely made no terrible, terrible villains" (Arnold, 2000, p. 184).

12   From Silko's point of view, inaction is not a viable option:

> there's finite land, there's finite food … There's no way around the fact that you have to share, that in the long run to have peace, for the well-being of everybody, for the health of the planet, for the health of the species, you have to share and take care of one another. And if you don't, you get what's coming, what the *Almanac of the Dead* says is coming if you don't. (Arnold, 2000, p. 185)

Delena, though busy for the moment in Mexico, is waiting in the wings. Here, too, we have yet another dialectic.

References

Arnold, E. L. (2000), "Listening to the Spirits: An Interview with Leslie Marmon Silko," in Ellen L. Arnold (ed.), *Conversations with Leslie Marmon Silko*. Jackson: University of Mississippi Press.

Beverley, R. (2013), *The History and Present State of Virginia*, Susan Scott Parish (ed.). Chapel Hill: University of North Carolina Press.

Cirlot, J. E. (1971), *A Dictionary of Symbols*, trans. Jack Sage, 2nd edition. London and Henley: Routledge and Kegan Paul.

James, H. (1986), *The Art of Criticism: Henry James on the Theory and the Practice of Fiction*, W. Veeder and S. M. Griffin (eds), Chicago: University of Chicago Press.

James, H. (1999), *Complete Stories*. Vol 1 (1864–1874), Vol 2 (1874–1884), Vol 3 (1884–1891). New York: Library of America.

Magoulick, M. (2007), "Landscapes of Miracles and Matriarchy in *Gardens in the Dunes*," in Coltelli, L. (ed.), *Reading Leslie Marmon Silko: Critical Perspectives through Gardens in the Dunes*. Pisa: Edizioni Plus, Pisa University Press, pp. 21–36.

Miranda, D. A. (2007), "A Gynostemic Revolution: Some Thoughts about Orchids, *Gardens in the Dunes*, and Indigenous Feminism at Work," in Coltelli, L. (ed.), *Reading Leslie Marmon Silko: Critical Perspectives through Gardens in the Dunes*. Pisa: Edizioni Plus, Pisa University Press, pp. 133–148.

Moore, D. L. (1994), "Decolonializing Criticism: Reading Dialectics and Dialogics in Native American Literatures." *Studies in American Indian Literatures* (Series 2) 6, 7–35.

Moore, D. L. (2007), "Ghost Dancing through History in Silko's *Garden in the Dunes and Almanac of the Dead*," in Coltelli, L. (ed.), *Reading Leslie Marmon Silko: Critical Perspectives through Gardens in the Dunes*. Pisa: Edizioni Plus, Pisa University Press, pp. 91–118.

Morisco, G. (2010), "Contrasting Gardens and Worlds: America and Europe in the Long Journey of Indigo, A Young Native American Girl," in A. Lamarra and E. Federici (eds), *Nations, Traditions and Cross-Cultural Identities: Women's Writing in English in a European Context*. Oxford: Peter Lang, pp.137–148.

Oltean, R. (2010), "From Grand Tour to a Space of Detour: Henry's James's Europe." *The Henry James Review*, 31, 46–63.

Perkins, O. (1999), "An Interview with Leslie Marmon Silko." *High Plains Literary Review*, 14:2–3, 81–124.

Porter, J. (2007), "History in *Garden in the Dunes*," in Coltelli, L. (ed.), *Reading Leslie Marmon Silko: Critical Perspectives through Gardens in the Dunes*. Pisa: Edizioni Plus, Pisa University Press, pp.57–72.

Silko, L. M. (1977, 2006), *Ceremony*. London: Penguin Books.

Silko, L. M. (1991), *Almanac of the Dead*. New York: Simon & Schuster.

Silko, L. M. (1999), *Gardens in the Dunes*. New York: Simon & Schuster.

Silko, L. M. (2012), "Delight: An Appreciation of Henry James." *The Henry James Review*, 33, 205–215.

Smoak, G. E. (1986), "The Mormons and the Ghost Dance of 1890." *South Dakota History*, 16, 269–294.

Van Dyke, A. (2007), "Walking in Balance: The European-based Spiritual Journey in Leslie Marmon Silko's *Garden in the Dunes*," in Coltelli, L. (ed.), *Reading Leslie Marmon Silko: Critical Perspectives through Gardens in the Dunes*. Pisa: Edizioni Plus, Pisa University Press, pp. 177–184.

9

"Sand Lizard Warned Her Children to Share": Philosophies of Gardening and Exchange in Silko's *Gardens in the Dunes*

Rebecca Tillett

The reason one can call a garden a state of the soul is that garden and soul are composed of the same essential ingredients... [i]f soul and garden did not share a common substance, how could the latter reanimate the former and fill it with new life?

(HARRISON, 2008, p. 134)

There has, in recent years, been a renewed international interest in the philosophies of gardens and gardening, and in the cultural and political histories these philosophies expose and enable. It is an interest that is both academic and popular, with philosophical studies assessing how gardens explore "the human condition" (Harrison, 2008) or analyzing the intersections of culture and politics (Richardson and Kingsbury, 2005), political analyses that connect the "theft" of lands held in common and the rise of capitalism to the emergence of the ideologies of technological progress and land "improvement"

(Linebaugh, 2014), and popular histories of gardening that survey the complex and problematic links between botany, collecting and empire (Fara, 2004). Additionally, Andrea Wulf's recent well-received two-volume history traces the emergence of a specifically transatlantic horticultural relationship. In *The Brother Gardeners: Botany, Empire and the Birth of an Obsession* (2009), Wulf traces developments in British and American gardening that "fostered an international community where plants and ideas could be exchanged across vast distance" (2009, p. 5); while in *The Founding Gardeners: How the Revolutionary Generation Created an American Eden* (2012), she explores the political ideologies informing the experimental gardens of George Washington's Mount Vernon, John Adam's Peacefield, Thomas Jefferson's Monticello, and James Madison's Montpelier.

Wulf's study of the Founding Fathers' profound interest in horticulture demonstrates how "native" American plants were interpreted as "a reflection of a strong and vigorous nation… imbued with patriotism," how American gardens drew upon an established "British tradition of using gardens as expressions of political ideology," and how "[p]loughing, planting and vegetable gardening" were increasingly identified as "political acts, bringing freedom and independence" as "self-sufficiency became a weapon… against British economic restrictions" (2012, p. 9, p. 187, p. 2, p. 7). Importantly, the mercantile prospects of horticulture were never a separate consideration: seed and specimen exchange between America and Britain actively created a capitalist botanical market as it became understood that "moving crops from one part of the world to another could dramatically increase their value," securing the financial prospects of the new American nation while actively "reinforc[ing] the links between commercial, imperial and scientific exploration" (Fara, 2004, p. 138, p. 95). Indeed, the very term "horticulture" embodies the significant connections being made between gardens, gardening, and science, where clear links to both "progress" and environmental "control" transplanted long-established practices drawn from classical traditions and philosophies. By the early nineteenth century, gardens had "become a standard symbol of colonial conquest" (Fara, 2004, p. 140), and it subsequently became impossible to "seve[r]" a garden from its respective cultural and political "history" (Harrison, 2008, p. x).

Of real pertinence has been the related growth in international interest in traditional Indigenous gardening practices and philosophies, led—at least initially—by an increased global awareness of climate change and an awareness of a greater need for sustainability. Importantly, the demand for such studies also demonstrates an awareness of the growing need for a greater understanding of the principles—social, political, spiritual—of agricultural sustainability. Accordingly, a range of studies have emerged or been reissued in recent years that have been immediately pertinent to my reexamination here of Silko's 1999 novel *Gardens in the Dunes*, including Gregory Cajete's *Native Science: Natural Laws of Interdependence* (2000), alongside foundational studies such as Gilbert Wilson's *Buffalo Bird Woman's Garden: The Classic Account of Hidatsa American Indian Gardening Techniques* (1917), Carol Buchanan's *Brother Crow, Sister Corn: Traditional American Indian Gardening* (1997), and Michael Caduto and Joseph Bruchac's *Native American Gardening: Stories, Projects and Recipes for Families* (1996). Also highly pertinent to my own readings have been two Euro-centric studies: Peter Linebaugh's *Stop, Thief!: The Commons, Enclosures, and Resistance* (2014), and Robert Pogue Harrison's *Gardens: A Meditation on the Human Condition* (2008). As Silko pitches a variety of gardening traditions and philosophies into dialogue within her novel via the Indigenous child narrator Indigo, so my analysis here attempts to facilitate a greater dialogue between Cajete's discussion of Indigenous science, Wilson, Buchanan, and Caduto and Bruchac's commentaries on the relationships between Indigenous gardening techniques and spiritual and political philosophies, Harrison's assessment of classical European philosophies about the earth, and Linebaugh's political reading of capitalism's engagement with the natural world. All of these critical texts intersect in interesting ways with the topics that Silko raises within *Gardens in the Dunes*.

Exploring the historical contexts for the global loss of "common" lands or lands held communally under capitalism and imperialism, Linebaugh very usefully assesses the political impacts of those losses, and also the spiritual impact on what Harrrison calls the "human condition." I will return to Linebaugh in due course. First, the works of Cajete, Wilson, Buchanan, Caduto and Bruchac, and Harrison have all proved invaluable when thinking of diverse cultural interactions with gardens and the natural world, in particular in relation to Silko's novel, which itself offers a variety of cultural perspectives on the topic; and both offer very interesting critical and philosophical intersections. A comparison of these writers' work creates fascinating dialogues between Indigenous gardening practices, classical European philosophies of the garden, and emergent contemporary reconsiderations of the significance of the garden as a cultural space. Cajete's text draws the reader's attention to the ways in which "Native science is a metaphor for a wide range of tribal processes of perceiving, thinking, acting, and 'coming to know' that have evolved through human experience with the natural world. Native science is born of a lived and storied participation with the natural landscape" (2000, p. 2). This emphasis on a deeply interactive gardening experience moves beyond simplistic notions of economics, commerce, or nourishment to point to what Jeffrey Hanson identifies, in his introduction to Wilson's study, as profound "cultural relationships with nature" (1917, rep. 1987, p. xxiii). Harrison's philosophical meditation offers valuable comparable insights on the historical cultural significance of the European garden, the spiritual importance of interactions between humans and the earth, and the relationships between environmental damage and the profound damage caused to "the human condition" of individuals, communities, and nations. And, much like the gardens that Silko represents in her novel, Harrison draws interesting classical European parallels with Cajete's analysis of a "lived and storied participation" (2000, p. 2), arguing that not only would "a garden severed from history ... be superfluous," but also "[h]istory without gardens would be a wasteland," in large part because of the philosophy of "care" that gardening both requires and embodies (2008, p. x, p. 7). Cajete's examination of Pueblo gardening philosophies and practise traces similar relationships, commenting that "[t]he instinctual connection to plants enters the human experience in numerous ways" (2000, p. 127); and it is this profound connection between humans and plants that Buchanan describes as "so close [as] to be flesh of flesh" (1997, p. 6). As Hanson argues, this Indigenous "agricultural legacy" is "imbedded not only in the soil but also in the lives, minds, and hearts of those who inherited it, nourished it, and preserved it" (1917, rep. 1987, p. xii). As a result, Cajete notes that the garden is the site of a "deep understanding of 'practiced' relationship" between humans and the earth, which was inseparable from the human "responsibility to care" for the earth (2000, p. 131). Given that "care" can be defined as the effort made to do something correctly, safely, or without causing damage, as things that are done to keep someone/ thing healthy, safe, and so on, and as things that are done to keep someone/thing in good condition, care as a concept would seem especially pertinent both to Silko's writing and my own reading of it here, and also to the growing environmental concerns of the twenty-first century.

Alongside the critical examinations of the implicit and explicit links between botany, gardening, empire, and capitalist exchange, Harrison's philosophical study of how gardens relate to the human condition finds a "correlation between care and gardens" in the European classical tradition that emphasizes the importance of what is "freely given rather than... aggressively acquired" (2008, p. 7, p. 9). Cajete's emphasis both on human "participation with nature" and on the garden as a site of "collaborative enterprise" extends the dialogue to consider the ways in which the "freely given" might practically operate (2000, p. 128). Harrison's subsequent argument is for "a transformation of perception, a fundamental change in one's way of seeing the world," which interprets the garden as a specifically communal educational space: a "sit[e] of conversation, dialogue, friendship, storytelling—in short, communalization" (2008, p. 7, p. 9, p. 30, p. 45). This, for Harrison, is simultaneously a transformation of contemporary understandings and a return to classical traditions and practices. Crucially, it is obvious that an understanding of the garden as an educational space is central to Pueblo gardening practices: as Cajete suggests, Pueblo gardens and gardening practices emphasize the significance of the "experiential" process of gardening as an educational process (2000, p. 128). Significantly, Cajete's exploration of the garden as a communal space extends limited interpretations of the "educational" into the sharing of food growing practices, the communal production of surplus goods for trade, and the use of the garden space for spiritual, ceremonial, and ritual purposes (2000, pp. 128–129).

In spite of the profit-driven "industries" of horticulture and botany, Cajete, Buchanan, and Harrison all argue that the garden continues to "pla[y] a crucial pedagogical role" for humanity (Harrison, 2008, p. 111, p. 75). Harrison's assertion is that the classical Epicurean garden was not only a site of teaching, but also

a place from which and in which reality itself could be reconceived, its possibilities reimagined. Or better, it was a place where the human and social virtues that were trampled on by the so-called real world could reflourish under carefully husbanded circumstances. (2008, p. 81)

As Cajete comments, the garden is a place for the "sharing" of all things (2000, p. 129), and in particular a place that facilitates knowledge exchange. It is a place where, Buchanan notes, the "next generation" can be educated in "the ways of the tribe" because gardening as "an activity...formed the basis of [Indigenous] culture, art, social and religious life" (1997, p. 54, p. 8). This renewed critical dialogue engages with contemporary meanings of gardens and gardening in ways that *Gardens in the Dunes* productively revisits.

Class, empire, and capitalism in the garden

Silko's various textual gardens are purposefully located within complex and problematic EuroAmerican histories of class, empire, and capitalism, and of cultural and horticultural pedagogy and practice. As Harrison argues, developments in horticulture can be read within a European (and later American) political history, where the social hierarchies that emerged from feudalism were actively and irrevocably shaped by both capitalism and empire. Europe's and America's very richest social groups used gardens to display their wealth and social status, and to firmly trace how their possession of the natural world echoed their "possession" of imperial territories and peoples. Harrison notes that, in stark contrast to Epicurean ideals, the new formal gardens such as those at Versailles harnessed the scientific and technological developments championed by the Enlightenment to enable extant social "vices" to "assum[e] exquisitely cultivated forms," through a visual demonstration of "an absolutist presumption of power" that was tied explicitly to established European social structures and hierarchies (2008, p. 111, p. 112). These were, ironically, the very "Old World" social structures identified as corrupt and corrupting by America's Founding Fathers, and those that they determined to eliminate in the new nation.

Accordingly, *Gardens'* deceptively gentle tour of a variety of gardens at the close of the nineteenth century acts to expose "how very political gardens are"; how central horticulture was (and still is) to the imperial (and neo-imperial) enterprise; how, in the "New World," "the plant collectors followed the Conquistadors" (Silko, in Arnold, 1998, p. 3). As a result, the novel not only demonstrates the links between imperialism, capitalism, and horticulture, but also explores how a range of cultural worldviews and social hierarchies are expressed through gardens, cultivation, and ideologies of "improvement." Silko carefully demonstrates various forms of horticultural exchange, and traces the metamorphosis of "trade" into "commerce" within the capitalist system. From the seeds collected and traded by the Sand Lizards and a variety of local gardeners and food producers, Silko extends her scope to explore the emergence of an international horticultural industry that transformed plants into valuable commodities: rubber, citron, orchids. As *Gardens* suggests, this transformation in turn laid the foundations for the emergence of the immensely powerful multinational corporate agribusinesses of the twenty-first century, which are currently extending horticulture's links with science via controversial experimentations with chemical pesticides and the genetic modification of food; and with international politics, via the exertion of unheralded political influence over elected national governments. Taking Silko's recognition of the politics of gardens and gardening as its starting point, we may situate her novel and its culturally divergent gardens within a wider history of American and European gardens and increasingly political and economic philosophies of gardening. Moreover, we may explore how what is often viewed as a seemingly innocuous "domestic" leisure activity actively traces and exposes vital human relationships to the "natural" world; and how the anonymity of industrial internationalization transforms local forms of horticultural exchange into "for-profit" trade that has profound effects on individuals, communities, and nations; and on our understandings of and relationships with the "natural" world.

It is via gardens and developments in gardening that *Gardens* examines the epistemological foundations of the later twentieth-century/late capitalist societies that are depicted in Silko's earlier novel *Almanac of the Dead* (1991). As David L. Moore comments, for readers familiar with Silko's work, it soon becomes clear that

"*Gardens*' orchids grow out of *Almanac*'s blood-soaked soil" (2007, p. 92). If, as Silko has noted, "*Almanac* talks about how capitalism destroys a people, a continent" then *Gardens* "is about what capitalism makes people do to one another" (Arnold, 1998, p. 21). *Gardens* is, as a result, profoundly human, interrogating the ways in which our very humanity is predicated upon our relationships with the natural world. As Melissa Levine comments,

> gardens are what unite Silko's diverse cast of characters, suggesting that what makes us human is our impact on our environment. Humans change, mold, manipulate, use and abuse the natural world more than any other species; our differences are defined by our approach to this relationship—whether we make an attempt to lessen our impact or allow it to rage unfettered.

Demonstrating the impact of powerful cultural ideologies upon our attitudes toward the land, *Gardens* explores how such ideologies directly influence, and even determine, the ways that the humans of the text also relate to one another.

The term "garden" is itself linguistically and historically embedded within human relationships, and suggestive of complex and problematic human hierarchies. As Martin Hoyles writes:

> The word garden comes from the Old English *geard*, meaning a fence or enclosure, and from *garth*, meaning a yard or a piece of enclosed ground. Enclosure is essential to gardening, and this raises fundamental questions, such as who is doing the enclosing, who owns the lands, and who is being kept out. (2005, p. 29)

Gardens are, therefore, often an "expression of power and oppression in the world" (Hoyles, 2005, p. 33), and this is especially true of European and American gardens, which emerged from the profound sociopolitical and ideological changes that accompanied the consolidation of elite power via the converging interests of class, capital, and empire. Within such dominant western cultural epistemologies, the concept of private property ownership emerged as central to the social power hierarchies that themselves depended (as they continue to depend) upon the eradication of the very notion of lands held communally or in common. And this sociopolitical understanding is crucial to the ideologies that Silko's novel explores.

As Linebaugh's recent study on the theft of common land argues, the term "commons" does not refer solely to the land or to the people, instead it embodies the undeniable "relationship" between the two (2014, p. 18). A central feature of the transformation of exchange in this crucially important period of horticultural historical development was the "exchange" of land use, benefits, and ultimately ownership, from the hands of the many to the hands of the few. As Linebaugh powerfully argues, this exchange was actually a profoundly far-reaching act of "theft," which not only stole the majority of the earth's natural resources for the benefit of a small minority, but also violently fractured human relationships with the natural world within the majority of Western cultures (2014). *Gardens'* profoundly human focus explores the far-reaching ramifications of this violent fracturing, and the possibility of repairing that fracture via a range of garden spaces that Linebaugh defines as spaces of "reciprocity" or "commonality" (2014, p. 19).

The pedagogical garden and knowledge exchange

Silko's exploration of sociopolitical human and natural histories, and of the variety of human-natural relationships that can and have been established, is demonstrated by the fictional gardens that populate the text. The means of creation and the defined end purpose of Silko's varied gardens act in concert to explore the nature of the relationships between their human owners or caretakers and the earth. Distributed along a wide spectrum of relationships that stretch from absolute fracture to sustainable reciprocal interaction, Silko's textual gardens trace long cultural histories, assessing changes in understandings—cultural, political, economic, scientific—of the pedagogical nature of gardens, and the impact of those changes on the human condition. The pedagogical lessons of Silko's various textual gardens include gardening's extensive and varied political and cultural histories. Importantly, the knowledge exchange that these textual gardens facilitate includes an exchange with Silko's reader, who is required to trace and acknowledge the political histories not only of human relationships with the earth but, more widely, of the relationships of capitalism and empire to the environment. A crucial part of that knowledge exchange is a holistic understanding of the dangers of short-term thinking with regard to the earth; and of the ramifications of building relationships either upon absolute fracture, or upon sustainability and reciprocity.

Right at the start of *Gardens*, we are told that "Sand Lizard warned her children to share" and are alerted to the dangers of "being greedy" (1999, p. 17). In its original context—notably, the context in which Silko uses it—the term "share" denotes an exchange that is "equal" or "in common" between individuals, groups, and life forms. This understanding of commonality is foundational to Silko's text, and is instantly recognizable in Cajete's description of the Pueblo garden as "a collaborative enterprise involving not only the individual farmer but the entire community and the land itself" (2000, p. 128). Sharing thus includes working together productively, both as communities and with the land. Our deeper understanding of *Gardens'* message of sharing is facilitated by the Indigenous child narrator Indigo, whose innocent responses enable Silko to actively defamiliarize everyday EuroAmerican experiences and cultural attitudes that routinely deny and negate commonality and exchange. As a result, Indigo's inability to comprehend what she sees as dangerously inexplicable human behavior, and her genuine horror at witnessing the appalling ways that humans treat one another and the earth, in turn forces us to question our contemporary human behaviors and cultural epistemologies that bear a striking resemblance to those we are shown. Above all, it forces us to question our understanding of the notion of "exchange," which seems under late capitalism to be slipping away from its original meaning of "reciprocal giving and receiving" and instead assuming connotations of "trade," of "buying and selling commodities," and—most significantly—of personal or corporate "profit" or profiteering. It is no accident that corporate capitalism has transformed (even inverted) the original meaning of the term "share," re-defining it as a vehicle for "for-profit ownership." In this context, *Gardens* traces human understandings of exchange of all kinds through the ways in which the characters interact with, and relate to, the earth. Reading Silko's gardens pedagogically, what becomes significant is the *form* of the knowledge exchange between humans and the earth. This form can be traced through the different human relationships forged with the earth, between "products" that are "aggressively acquired" and those that are "freely given"

(Harrison, 2008, p. 9); and it can also be traced via the differences in human relationships to those lands exclusively appropriated and to those shared and held in common (Linebaugh, 2014, p. 19).

Aggressive acquisition and exclusive appropriation

Thus, *Gardens* exposes the correlations between land ownership and land use that are often actively obscured by political, social, and corporate elites. In Edward Palmer and his sister, Susan Palmer James, the aggressively acquired and exclusively appropriated converge, and what becomes clear are the ways in which aggressive acquisition and exclusive appropriation have a profound effect on Edward and Susan's understandings of and relationships to the earth. Much like the destroyers within Silko's first novel *Ceremony*, both Edward and Susan are so detached from the earth that "they see no life," and "the world is a dead thing for them" (1977, p. 135). More problematically, "they see only objects" (1977, p. 135), and the environmental and human damage that subsequently ensues can be traced in the promotion—most obviously evident in Silko's earlier novel *Almanac*—of an exploitative, manipulative, and ultimately oppressive relationship that privileges elite humans at the expense of the earth. Significantly, these exploitative and oppressive attitudes are directly linked to historical sociopolitical relationships, and Silko draws attention to how the exclusivity and exclusion evident in the gardens of California and Long Island are themselves dependent upon wealth and social status, and/or upon industry, science and technology. In short, *Gardens* exposes how sociopolitical and corporate elites maintain their status through their relationships to the earth.

Appropriately, therefore, Susan and Edward respectively represent two distinct American historical and political moments: the settlement of New York State and the creation of an Eastern sociopolitical elite; and the settlement of California and the birth of corporate agribusiness via the scientific horticultural creation of an "orange empire" (Sackman, 2005). And, while Susan's example is domestic, in the sense both that her garden relates to a single family and that it exists within the national borders of the United

States, Edward's corporate, imperial, and scientific horticultural expeditions by contrast operate on a scale that is global. In this way, Silko shows how domestic and international policies are interlinked—in the example of the Palmers, literally *related*—and how local individual and communal relationships with the earth feed into global environmental policies and their impacts.

As a resident of the socially exclusive Oyster Bay area of Long Island, Susan Palmer James' attachment to her garden is almost wholly domestic and individual: it seems solely dictated by the personal or familial social and political prestige that her garden display can bring. In this context, clear historical connections can be drawn to the rigid hierarchy of the gardens of Versailles, and to the ways in which early British and American landscape design acted as a showcase for wealth and privilege. Susan's garden is, therefore, an exclusive and appropriated space where she can display personal social and political power. Importantly, this power is demonstrated through the ways in which Susan's gardens are designed, redesigned, planted, and transplanted. Rather than taking the time to allow her elaborate and costly Italianate gardens to achieve full maturity, Susan's radical garden redesign is dictated by her desire to create "an English landscape garden" for her charitable Renaissance-inspired "Masque of the Blue Garden" ("the premier event of the summer season"), which acts as a forum for a public display of her wealth and status (1999, p. 188, p. 80). Susan's relationship with the earth is therefore limited by the growing power of an emergent disposable consumer culture that demands immediate results. Indeed, it could be argued that Susan's sole relationship with her garden appears to be limited to the physical relationship she has with her gardener who is, notably, of a much lower social status. Susan's fetishization of "novelty and fashion" is, as Barbara K Robins suggests, further evidence of "the destroyer's vision" within "Silko's lexicon" (2007, p. 50). In this context, not only is the local or domestic linked to historical developments in capitalism that created a popular consumer culture, but the local is also linked to the kinds of disposable "solutions" that capitalism continues to posit globally for the environmental problems it causes.

In this case, Susan's garden redesign demands immediate results: although the workmen produce "newly created hills" and transplant "large azaleas and mature dogwoods," the appearance of the hills is still too "new" (1999, p. 184). As a remedy, Susan "locate[s] two great copper beeches at an old farm" and "relocates" them in a very public display of "conspicuous consumption" (Arnold, 1999, p. 20). Susan's local solution thus draws from the kinds of short-term solutions that capitalism offers, exposing clear links with global environmental problems and a range of enabling environmental practices that "see no life" in the "objects" they exploit. Consequently, Silko's description of the beech trees' relocation is worth citing in full:

> The route of the two giant beech trees on their wagons took them through downtown Oyster Bay and necessitated workmen to temporarily take down electrical and telephone lines to allow the huge trees to pass... Indigo was shocked by the sight: wrapped in canvas and big chains on the flat wagon was a great tree lying helpless, its leaves shocked limp, followed by its companion; the stain of damp earth like dark blood seeped through the canvas. As the procession inched past, Indigo heard low creaks and groans—not sounds from the wagons but from the trees. (1999, p. 185)

Here the undeniable relatedness of human and tree is made clear, marked by the blood-like stains that seep from the wounded life form, and the groans that it emits. And further parallels are drawn between the hierarchical treatment and disempowerment of the natural world (the tree that lies in "chains") and the identical treatment of fellow humans within capitalist sociopolitical hierarchies. Alongside its depiction of conspicuous consumption, Susan's garden therefore also shows the ways in which "capitalism consumes the world," both natural and human, "without giving back" (Arnold, 1999, p. 103).

The consumptive drive that refuses to "give back" is perhaps most evident in the character of Susan's brother, Edward and his accumulative interventions into global and imperial horticultural markets. The first clue to our understanding of Edward is his pet monkey Linnaeus, named to signify the long-accepted Europe and American scientific method for categorizing and ordering the natural world. While Carl Linnaeus (1707–1778) was responsible, as Patricia Fara argues, for imposing a scientific system that was "clearly driven by" and thus inseparable from "his political agenda," and for "naturalis[ing]" the "prejudices of Enlightenment

Christian moralists," he was also responsible for an "intertwin[ing]" of scientific research "with commercial development and imperial exploitation" that created "an interdependent relationship between science and the state that endures today" (2004, pp. 37–38, p. 21, p. 17, p. 18). Importantly, Edward is also depicted as fully cognizant of the established connections between science and commerce, and of his seemingly paradoxical role as a scientific entrepreneur. Edward's father could "easily" have "renewed" the declining family fortunes through the "sale of [the] sweet oranges" he cultivated in the family citrus groves, but "did not want the bother" of trading (1999, p. 92). He is therefore shown to be the antithesis of the corporate businessmen who created California's "orange empire": the "horticultural wizard[s]" who proved via scientific methods of grafting and hybridization not only that California's orange producers were "the Edison[s] of the plant world," but also that American citrus production could become a profitable capitalist industry (Sackman, 2005, p. 5).

In direct contrast to his father, who Edward seems to identify as both a wastrel and one who has wasted valuable scientific and financial opportunities, Edward understands himself to be both scientist and capitalist: he is a "distinguished botanist" who nonetheless illegally accumulates rare "specimens" for "private collectors" (1999, p. 80, p. 131). Emphasizing his scientific credentials—"to Edward, the garden *was* a research laboratory" (1999, p. 75)—Silko nonetheless makes clear the inextricability of either science or capitalism from empire: Edward's stated desire is explicitly imperial, "to discover a new plant species that would bear his name" (1999, p. 80). Edward's role as both collector and profiteer therefore not only links him to specific imperial histories, but also connects those imperial histories directly to horticultural developments, and to subsequent capitalist and corporate developments in agribusiness. What *Gardens* makes clear are the local and global impacts of Edward's actions: he is employed not only by the American Bureau of Plant Industry to undertake clandestine and often illegal expeditions to source and obtain financially viable botanical specimens such as orchids, rubber, and citron, but also by foreign governments to mask their attempts to intervene in various global horticultural industries. Thus, Edward's ill-fated orchid collecting trip to Brazil, which leaves him seriously wounded, also acts to enable the presence of Mr. Vicks, a British collector on "a special mission for Her Majesty's Government," who aims to illegally obtain "disease resistant specimens" (1999, p. 131). While Mr. Vicks' mission is presented as a desire to overcome an incurable parasite infection within British colonial rubber plantations, it has the simultaneous economic benefit of also breaking Brazil's "world monopoly" of the rubber market (1999, p. 131).

Edward's ever-decreasing wealth drives his increasingly desperate attempts to secure his financial future via a range of misjudged or illegal ventures: the collection of rare orchids in Brazil; the attempted theft of citron cuttings in Corsica; the investment in the site of a supposedly valuable meteor. Edward's forms of exchange are exposed as acts of aggressive acquisition, and the costs to the natural world are made clear. In Brazil, a badly wounded Edward is abandoned by his "colleagues" who subsequently devastate the rain forest with fire because their "investors wanted no unpleasant surprises from rivals to drive down the price" (1999, p. 144). Again, there is an added "bonus" in that this destructive act also eradicates any alternative markets and ensures a British monopoly, both commercial and political. In this sense, Edward's expeditions serve to expose the ways in which the convergent interests of horticulture, science, and capitalism produces a profit-driven worldview that fails, often willfully, to recognize the need for sustainable relationships or the interrelatedness of all life. Through Edward, Silko demonstrates how our humanity is predicated upon our relationships with the earth, how this influences our treatment of other human beings, and how both have a direct impact upon our own well-being.

Accordingly, Edward's acts of aggressive acquisition are accompanied by his own rapidly declining health. In Brazil, he suffers a badly broken leg, which never heals properly and, which, tellingly, causes him increased pain whenever he enters into additional capitalist ventures that further disrupt his relationship with the earth. In the American southwest, Edward's meteor site is shown to be a sacred Indian site where "the 'baby,' or meteor iron, wrapped in layers of feather blanket, wore a tiny necklace and matching bracelet of tiny beads" and where "[f]uneral offerings of food and a toy whistle were carefully arranged in the stone cavity with the meteor iron" (1999, p. 415). Hattie's subsequent dream is of a "live baby…in the stone cavity," whose "excavat[ion]" by Edward and his colleague with a "large steel pick and heavy shovel" caused "blood [to] spur[t] everywhere and a tiny severed leg" (1999, pp. 415–416). While the severed leg here evokes the violent fracturing of human relationships with the earth represented by Edward's various expeditions, crucially it also points to the personal costs to Edward himself, exposing not only the relatedness of human and earth, but also the profound and devastating human costs of such acts of aggressive acquisition and exclusive appropriation. Edward's death is, therefore, shown to be a direct result of his own attitudes. His careless and thoughtless behavior toward the earth is echoed by his equally careless and thoughtless lack of self-care, if not active self-harm. It is Edward's own greed that eventually kills him.

Freely given and held in common

The incontrovertible links between a lack of self-care or willful self-harm and greed are made concrete via Sand Lizard's warning that humans must "share" (1999, p. 17). *Gardens'* recurring focus is, therefore, on the requirement that we share and resist the temptation to be greedy. This, the text demonstrates, is the fundamental basis not only of reciprocal and sustainable human relationships with the earth—the ability and desire to develop a philosophy of "care"—but also of constructive and favorable human interactions. In this context, the Sand Lizard gardens in the dunes can be interpreted as an example of that which is both freely given and held in common. Sand Lizard philosophies are traced through the dune gardens, which, in contrast to Edward's mercantile horticultural understandings, privilege a philosophy of human care that returns us to the original, reciprocal meanings of "sharing" and "exchange" evident in the critical considerations of Cajete, Wilson, Buchanan, Caduto and Bruchac, and Harrison.

As it soon becomes apparent, one of the reasons that Sand Lizard warns her children to share the produce of the gardens is because an equal distribution of the gardens' "wealth" is the only way to ensure the continuance of life of all kinds (1999, p. 17). Importantly, this sharing is also spiritual, a recognition that the physical world is linked to, and inseparable from, the worlds beyond the physical:

> The first ripe fruit of each harvest belongs to the spirits of our beloved ancestors, who come to us as rain; the second ripe fruit

should go to the birds and wild animals, in gratitude for their restraint in sparing the seeds and sprouts earlier in the season. Give the third ripe fruit to the bees, ants, mantises, and others who cared for the plants. A few choice pumpkins, squash, and bean plants were simply left in the sand beneath the mother plants to shrivel dry and return to the earth... Old Sand Lizard insisted her garden was reseeded in that way because human beings are undependable; they might forget to plant at the right time or they might not be alive next year. (1999, p. 17)

What is immediately evident is the wider community of gardeners here—ancestors, birds, animals, insects, and the earth itself—all of whose contributions to a successful harvest are recognized via their entitlement to share in the "proceeds." Most significantly, the contribution of this wider community to the continuance of human life is recognized: Sand Lizard not only specifies the fragility and impermanence of human life—its "undependab[ility]"— but also expresses Indigenous understandings of the complex interdependencies between human and non-human life that are endangered by the short-term thinking, aggressive acquisition, and exclusive appropriation characteristic of capitalism. As Sand Lizard makes clear through an emphasis on the equal value of all life forms, any threat to the natural environment of the gardens in the dunes is also a threat to human life.

It is through *Gardens'* explorations of Indigo's Indigenous philosophies of gardening that the pedagogic role of the garden is foregrounded. What are especially instructive are the comparisons Silko encourages us to make between Indigo's and Edward's respective understandings of and relationships with the earth. In direct contrast to Edward's "research laboratory" garden where the sole scientist conducts his experimentations upon the "objects" of his study, Indigo is taught by Grandma Fleet that the gardens in the dunes are a collective responsibility that require an understanding of sharing: "[e]ach person had plants to care for" and "the harvest was shared by everyone" (1999, p. 75, p. 18). Perhaps most significant is the striking difference between the ways in which seeds and cuttings are exchanged or traded in the novel. Here, fundamental and problematic differences between the "freely given" and the "aggressively acquired" can be traced in the differences between exchanging seeds and taking cuttings: as James Barilla argues, while "[s]eeds are symbols of biological sovereignty and wildness; cuttings represent the transformation of plant into commodity"(2007, p. 168). Thus, Edward's mercantile profit-driven pursuit of highly valuable plant "specimens" via costly international expeditions funded by national governments is contrasted with Indigo's continuation of Sand Lizard customs regarding the collection of discarded seeds, the exchanging of seeds with others, and the care taken to ensure that enough seeds are left so that plants can reseed themselves. Silko's exploration of Sand Lizard traditions in this context demonstrates Cajete's statement that Native science acts to explore the storied origins "of the how and why of the things of nature and the nature of things" (2000, p. 13), even while Edward's scientific experimentation claims to have sole access to such "truths." Whereas Edward strives to write his own story onto the land and its plant life, Indigo instead understands the garden as a space of communal exchange and sharing.

The pedagogic nature of the gardens in Silko's text is dependent upon an understanding of giving freely, holding in common, and sharing. Such an understanding could be argued to be the basic educational and cultural building blocks taught to small children in the majority of human cultures, which, as a result, appear to be rooted in basic common sense. But it is striking that our ability or desire to share as adults is profoundly affected by the ongoing and increasingly powerful convergence of the interests of capitalism, class, and empire, which advocate and actively practice "cultures of greed." The majority of cultures of European origin are at a distinct disadvantage since those lands traditionally held in common, which promoted and ensured the continuation of philosophies of sharing and community, have been the subject of aggressive acquisition by an elite minority. With the loss of commonly held and tended land, there has been both a loss of understandings of the importance of sharing and community, and a growth in individualistic pursuit of lands that can be exclusively appropriated. The result, as we can see in the early twenty-first century, is vast inequalities of wealth and misery on a global scale. As Silko has carefully demonstrated via the example of Edward, greed ultimately kills and we must resist its temptations. The need to consider the potential of the garden as a pedagogic space is clearly urgent.

What *Gardens* makes evident is that the garden is a space for exchange of all kinds, including knowledge exchange, should the gardener be willing to enter into a reciprocal relationship with the earth. The twenty-first century is already plagued by controversies surrounding innovative developments in human "relationships" with the earth, including the profound damage caused by the extraction methods of both fracking and tar sands oil, and the riskiness of oil transportation via above-ground pipelines covering vast geographic distances. Based almost entirely on a relationship of greed, these examples are conspicuous due primarily to their adherence to the short-term lack of self-care associated with the operations of late capitalism. However, if we choose to accept Harrison's argument that the garden is a space in which our realities can be "reimagined," and where "human and social virtues" that have been "trampled on by the...real world" can be encouraged to "reflourish under carefully husbanded circumstances" (2008, p. 81), then we might find the right conditions to recultivate our understandings of sharing and community. Under such conditions, we might even be encouraged to achieve the kind of "biological synergism" with the earth that Cajete points to as the cornerstone of the Indigenous "practiced relationship" (2000, p. 131). And, in order to do so, we might consider not only Linebaugh's interpretation of commonly held land as a space of "reciprocity" and "commonality," but also his suggestion that the "universality of expropriation" of common lands in the West by a social elite via the operations of capitalism, and the profound effects this has had on cultures of European origin, demands "reparations for what has been lost and taken" (2014, p. 256). This would demand that we embrace the central tenets, practices, and philosophies of Indigenous gardening traditions, such as agricultural techniques that are "environmentally sound and socially acceptable" (Buchanan, 1997, p. 111). It would, crucially, also demand that we recognize that the relationship between culture and agriculture is one of interdependence, that agricultural diversity is bound to cultural diversity, and therefore that we act to actively preserve the kinds of cultural diversity that are often threatened by the globalizing processes of capitalism. As Gary Paul Nabhan argues, "the preservation of traditional agroecosystems must occur in conjunction with the maintenance of the culture of the local people. The conservation and management of agrobiodiversity is not possible without the preservation of cultural diversity" (1989, rep. 2002, p. x).

If *Gardens* is indeed, as Silko herself claims, about "what capitalism makes people do to one another" via a drive to "consum[e] ... the world without giving back" (Arnold, 1998, p. 21; Arnold, 1999, p. 103), then the critical studies I have highlighted throughout my argument here offer us some pertinent guidance. Significantly, Harrison's philosophical and recuperative reading argues that "gardening is a form of education" where the "disproportion between giving and taking [that] is first and foremost a principle of life" can be reassessed outside of an individualist and capitalist frame (2008, p. 32). It is, in this context, a "transformation of perception, [and] a fundamental change in one's way of seeing the world," to the extent that gardening itself acts as "an opening of worlds" (2008, p. 30). The result, Harrison argues, is an awareness of exchange, sharing and reciprocity as a biological principle: "life exists where giving exceeds taking" (2008, p. 32, p. 33). The process is, for Buchanan, "more than the survival of the body. It is the survival of the spirit also," where an emphasis on sustainability, what Buchanan terms "acceptance gardening," "acts to accept what nature provides and uses human means to ensure a future of plenty" (1997, p. 7; p. 10). As Caduto and Bruchac argue, Indigenous gardening practice is "a cooperative activity" predicated upon the central understanding that "in order to receive something from the garden, we must give something back" (1996, p. 64).

References

Arnold, E. (1998), "Listening to the Spirits: An Interview with Leslie Marmon Silko." *Studies in American Indian Literatures*, 10:3, 1–33.

Arnold, E. (1999), "Gardens in the Dunes." *Studies in American Indian Literatures*, 11:2, 101–104.

Barilla, J. (2007), "Biological Invasion Discourse and Leslie Marmon Silko's *Gardens in the Dunes*," in Coltelli, L. (ed.), *Reading Leslie Marmon Silko: Critical Perspectives through Gardens in the Dunes*. Pisa: Pisa University Press, pp. 165–176.

Buchanan, C. (1997), *Brother Crow, Sister Corn: Traditional American Indian Gardening*. Berkeley, CA: Ten Speed Press.

Caduto, M. J. and J. Bruchac (1996), *Native American Gardening: Stories, Projects and Recipes for Families*. Golden, CO: Fulcrum Publishing.

Cajete, G. (2000), *Native Science: Natural Laws of Interdependence*. Santa Fe: Clear Light Press.

Fara, P. (2004), *Sex, Botany and Empire: The Story of Carl Linnaeus and Joseph Banks*. London: Icon Books.

Hanson, J. R. (1987), "Introduction," in Wilson, G. L. (ed.), *Buffalo Bird Woman's Garden: The Classic Account of Hidatsa American Indian Gardening Techniques*. Minneapolis: Minnesota Historical Society, pp. xi–xxiii.

Harrison, R. P. (2008), *Gardens: An Essay on the Human Condition*. Chicago: University of Chicago Press.

Hoyles, M. (2005), "The Garden and the Division of Labour," in Richardson, T., and N. Kingsbury (eds), *Vista: the Culture and Politics of Gardens*. London: Frances Lincoln, pp. 21–38.

Levine, M.(1999), 'You Are What You Grow: An American Indian Girl Finds Seeds of Identity in Gardens Across Cultures.' *San Francisco Chronicle*. http://www.sfgate.com/books/article/You-Are-What-You-Grow-An-American-Indian-girl-2934558.php.

Linebaugh, P. (2014), *Stop Thief! The Commons, Enclosures, and Resistance*. Oakland, CA: PM Press.

Moore, D. L. (2007), "Ghost Dancing through History in Silko's *Gardens in the Dunes* and *Almanac of the Dead*," in Coltelli, L. (ed.), *Reading Leslie Marmon Silko: Critical Perspectives through Gardens in the Dunes*. Pisa: Pisa University Press, pp. 91–118.

Nabhan, G. P. (1989, rep. 2002), *Enduring Seeds: Native American Agriculture and Wild Plant Conservation*. Tucson, AZ: University of Arizona Press.

Richardson, T. and N. Kingsbury (2005), *Vista: the Culture and Politics of Gardens*. London: Frances Lincoln.

Robins, B. K. (2007), "Tips for Nurturing the Home Garden," in Coltelli, L. (ed.), *Reading Leslie Marmon Silko: Critical Perspectives through Gardens in the Dunes*. Pisa: Pisa University Press, pp. 37–56.

Sackman, D. C. (2005), *Orange Empire: California and the Fruits of Eden*. Berkeley: University of California Press.

Silko, L. M. (1977), *Ceremony*. New York: Penguin, 1986.

Silko, L. M. (1999), *Gardens in the Dunes*. New York: Simon and Schuster.

Wilson, G. L. (1917, rep. 1987), *Buffalo Bird Woman's Garden: The Classic Account of Hidatsa American Indian Gardening Techniques*. Minneapolis: Minnesota Historical Society.

FURTHER READING

Arnold, E. L. (ed.) (2000), *Conversations with Leslie Marmon Silko*. Jackson: University Press of Mississippi.

Barnett, L. K. and Thorson, J. L. (eds) (2001), *Leslie Marmon Silko: A Collection of Critical Essays*. Albuquerque: University of New Mexico Press.

Blaisdell, B. (ed.) (2014), *Great Short Stories by Contemporary Native American Writers*. New York: Dover.

Chavkin, A. (ed.) (2002), *Leslie Marmon Silko's Ceremony: A Casebook*. New York: Oxford.

Coltelli, L. (ed.) (2008), *Reading Leslie Marmon Silko: Critical Perspectives through Gardens in the Dunes (Essays and Studies)*. Pisa University Press.

Fitz, B. E. (2005), *Silko: Writing Storyteller and Medicine Woman*. Norman: University of Oklahoma Press.

Graulich, M. (ed.) (1993), *"Yellow Woman": Leslie Marmon Silko*. New Brunswick, NJ: Rutgers University Press.

Jaskoski, H. (1998), *Studies in Short Fiction Series: Leslie Marmon Silko*. New York: Twayne Publishers.

Low, D. (ed.) (2004), Special Issue: Teaching Leslie Marmon Silko's 'Ceremony', *American Indian Culture and Research Journal*, 28 (1).

Nelson, R. M. (2008), *Leslie Marmon Silko's Ceremony: The Recovery of Tradition*. New York: Peter Lang.

Rainwater, C. (ed.) (forthcoming), *All of Us Remembering: New Perspectives on Leslie Marmon Silko's Storyteller*, Albuquerque: University of New Mexico Press.

Silko, L. M. (1974, 1993), *Laguna Woman*. Tucson: Flood Plain Press.

Silko, L. M. (1977, 2006), *Ceremony*, 30th Anniversary Edition. New York: Penguin.

Silko, L. M. (1981, 2012), *Storyteller*. New York: Penguin.

Silko, L. M. (1985, 2009), *The Delicacy and Strength of Lace: Letters between Leslie Marmon Silko and James Wright*. Anne Wright and Joy Harjo (eds). Minneapolis, MN: Graywolf Press.

Silko, L. M. (1991), *Almanac of the Dead*. New York: Penguin.

Silko, L. M. (1994), *Sacred Water: Narratives and Pictures*. Tucson: Flood Plain Press.

Silko, L. M. (1996), *Yellow Woman and a Beauty of the Spirit*. New York: Simon and Schuster.

Silko, L. M. (1999), *Gardens in the Dunes: A Novel*. New York: Simon and Schuster.

Silko, L. M. (2011), *The Turquoise Ledge: A Memoir*. New York: Penguin.

Silko, L. M. (2013), *Oceanstory*. Odyssey Editions (Kindle): Amazon Digital Services.

Snodgrass, M. E. (2011), *Leslie Marmon Silko: A Literary Companion*. Jefferson, NC: McFarland.

Tillett, R. (ed.) (2014), *Howling for Justice: New Perspectives on Leslie Marmon Silko's Almanac of the Dead*. Tucson: University of Arizona Press.

NOTES ON CONTRIBUTORS

Carolyn Dekker is Assistant Professor of English at Finlandia University. She received her PhD from the University of Michigan in 2014. She recently edited Jean Toomer's *A Drama of the Southwest: The Critical Edition of a Forgotten Play* (2016), and her work has been published in *MELUS Multi-Ethnic Literature of the United States*.

Lincoln Faller is retired Professor of English Language & Literature at the University of Michigan. His areas of expertise include literature of the American Southwest; Native American literature; seventeenth- and eighteenth-century English literature; Defoe; mythology of crime; and rise of the novel. In addition to many articles and chapters, his books include *Turned to Account: The Forms and Functions of Criminal Biography in Late Seventeenth and Early Eighteenth-Century England* (1987) and *Novel Criminals: Defoe, Crime, and a New Kind of Writing* (1993).

Mascha N. Gemein is Assistant Professor of Practice in the Office of Instruction and Assessment at the University of Arizona. Her postdoctoral work in American Indian Studies focused on ontological facets of environmental justice discourse and complemented her dissertation, "Multispecies Thinking from Alexander von Humboldt to Leslie Marmon Silko: Intercultural Communication Toward Cosmopolitics" (2013).

Becca Gercken is Associate Professor of English at the University of Minnesota—Morris, with specialties in American Indian Literature and Multicultural Literature. She teaches also in African and Black American Studies. Her articles have appeared in *Studies in American Indian Literatures*; *The American Indian Quarterly*; *American Indian Culture and Research Journal*; and *African American Review*, among other publications.

Penelope M. Kelsey is Professor of English and Ethnic Studies at the University of Colorado at Boulder. In addition to her articles, her books include *Tribal Theory in Native American Literature: Dakota and Haudenosaunee Writing and Worldviews* (2009) and *Reading the Wampum: Essays on Hodinöhsö:ni' Visual Code and Epistemological Recovery* (2014), in addition to an edited collection, *Maurice Kenny: Celebrations of a Mohawk Writer* (2011).

Deborah L. Madsen is Professor of American Studies at the University of Geneva. Most recently, she is editor of *The Routledge Companion to Native American Literature* (2015). Among her more than a dozen books, her other works include *Feminist Theory and Practice* (2000); *Understanding Contemporary Chicana Literature* (2001); *Beyond the Borders: American Literature and Post-Colonial Theory* (2003); *Understanding Gerald Vizenor* (2009); *Native Authenticity: Transnational Perspectives on Native American Literary Studies* (2010); *Louise Erdrich: Tracks, The Last Report on the Miracles at Little No Horse, The Plague of Doves* (Bloomsbury Studies in Contemporary North American Fiction) (2011).

David L. Moore is Professor of English at the University of Montana, specializing in American Studies, Native American literatures, Peace Studies, Baha'i Studies, ecocriticism, and theory. In addition to numerous journal articles, his publications include an edited volume of *American Indian Quarterly* and the book *That Dream Shall Have a Name: Native Americans Rewriting America* (2013).

Beth H. Piatote is Associate Professor and Coordinator of Native American Studies in the Department of Ethnic Studies at the University of California—Berkeley. She specializes in Native American literature, history, law, and culture; American literature and cultural studies; Ni:mi:pu: (Nez Perce) language and literature. In addition to numerous articles in journals including *American Indian Quarterly*, *Studies in American Literature*, *Kenyon Review*, and *Paradoxa*, plus chapters in collections, she is the author of the book *Domestic Subjects: Gender, Citizenship, and Law in Native American Literature* (2013).

Rebecca Tillett is Senior Lecturer in American Studies at the University of East Anglia, UK. Her recent book publications include *Howling for Justice: New Perspectives on Leslie Marmon Silko's Almanac of the Dead* (2014), and *Indigenous Bodies* (2013). She is a founding member of the Native Studies Research Network, UK.

Kimberly Gail Wieser is Assistant Professor of English and Affiliated Faculty in Native American Studies and in Environmental Studies at the University of Oklahoma. She is coauthor of *Reasoning Together: The Native Critics Collective* (2008) and the author of *Back to the Blanket: Recovered Rhetorics and American Indian Studies*, forthcoming from Oxford University Press.

INDEX

Note: The letter "n" following locators refers to notes.

Ingram Content Group UK Ltd.
Milton Keynes UK
UKHW022143060423
419740UK00011B/249